CW00386124

■ Pouring into a Boston glass.

■ Sealing the shaker.

■ Shaking a Boston shaker.

■ Breaking the seal between glass and can.

■ Using a Hawthorne strainer.

A standard shaker consists of three parts and hence is sometimes referred to as a three-piece shaker. The three pieces are 1) a flat-bottomed, conical base or 'can', 2) a top with a built-in strainer and 3) a cap.

I strongly recommend this style of shaker for the amateur or inexperienced bartender due to its ease of use. Be sure to purchase a shaker with a capacity of at least one pint as this will allow you to mix two short drinks at once. Large shakers also mix more effectively.

To use:
1/ Pour all ingredients into the base of the shaker. Fill it two-thirds full with ice.
2/ Place the top and cap firmly on the base.
3/ With one hand on the top and the other on the bottom, shake vigorously. The cap should always be on the top when shaking and should point away from guests.
4/ After shaking briskly for a count of around 20 seconds, lift off the cap, hold the shaker by its base with one finger securing the top and pour the drink through the built-in strainer.

metal to make a watertight seal with the glass. Avoid those which rely on a rubber ring to seal. I now only use Alessi Boston tins as I find these seal without a thump and open with the lightest tap (even though the glass is too delicate and the designer bit on the base tends to fall off the tin).

However good your Boston shaker, these devices demand an element of skill and a practice period is usually required for a new user to become proficient.

To use:
1/ Combine ingredients with plenty of ice in the glass part of the shaker (Boston glass). (I've noticed that US bartenders often assemble their drink in the steel tin rather than the glass part of the Boston. They also drive on the wrong side of the road – nuff said.)

2/ Place the metal half over the top of the glass half and lightly tap the top with the heel of your hand to create a seal. Closing the shaker too tightly will make it difficult to open.

3/ With one hand on the top and the other on the bottom, shake vigorously. The glass part should always be on the top when shaking and should point away from guests. (An ex-girlfriend of mine still has a dent in her forehead from a flying Boston glass in a bar.)

4/ After shaking for a count of around 20 seconds, hold the metal part of the shaker with one hand by the base. With your other hand, tap the metal close to where you estimate the glass rim sits inside the tin. This will break the seal between the glass and the metal, allowing you to lift off the glass. If you fail to break the seal on your first attempt, turn the shaker one quarter turn and repeat the process.

5/ Place a coil rimmed strainer (also known as a Hawthorne strainer) over the top of the metal half and strain the mixture into the glass. (Please don't attempt to mimic those flash bartenders who, after shaking, open their Bostons just enough to pour through the gap, thus excluding ice cubes without using a strainer. This method may look great and save washing a strainer but it lets unacceptable amounts of small ice fragments into the finished drink, particularly if the drink is to be served 'up'.)

FINE STRAIN

'Standard shakers' have a built in strainer and Boston shakers are used with a coil rimmed (Hawthorne) strainer as explained previously. But most cocktails which are served without ice benefit from an additional finer strain to remove small fragments of fruit and/or flecks of ice. A fine sieve, like a tea strainer, held between the shaker and the glass is perfect for this task. Some bartenders refer to this as 'double straining'.

STIR

If a cocktail recipe calls for you to 'stir with ice and strain', stir the drink in a mixing glass using a bar spoon with a twisted stem. If a lipped mixing glass is not available, the glass half of a Boston shaker will suffice, or the base of a standard shaker, if you must.

Place ice and ingredients into the mixing glass. Slide the back of the spoon down the inside of the mixing glass and twirl gently between thumb and finger. The spoon will rotate inside the mixing glass, gently stirring the drink. Strain the drink into a glass using a coil rimmed (Hawthorne) strainer, or the top of a standard shaker if you are using a standard shaker.

Some bartenders (and I'm one) prefer to use the flat end of a bar spoon to stir a drink. Simply place the flat end on top of the ice in the mixing glass and start to stir, working the spoon down the drink as you go.

BLEND

When a cocktail recipe calls for you to 'blend with ice', place ingredients and ice into a blender and blend until a smooth, even consistency is achieved. Ideally you should use crushed ice, as this lessens wear on the blender's blades. You should place liquid ingredients in the blender first, adding ice and/or ice cream last. If you have a variable speed blender, always start slow and build up.

BUILD

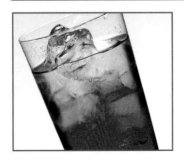

The term 'build drink' refers to making a cocktail by combining the ingredients in the glass in which the cocktail will be served. For simplicity, recipes for 'built' drinks in this guide include the instruction "pour ingredients into glass and stir" or similar.

LAYER

As the name would suggest, layered drinks include layers of different ingredients, often with contrasting colours. The effect is achieved by carefully pouring each ingredient into the glass so that it floats on its predecessor.

The success of this technique is dependent on the density (specific gravity) of the liquids used. As a rule of thumb, the less alcohol and the more sugar an ingredient contains, the heavier it is. The heaviest ingredients should be poured first and the lightest last. Syrups are non-alcoholic and contain a lot of sugar so are usually the heaviest ingredient. Liqueurs, which are high in sugar and lower in alcohol than spirits, are generally the next heaviest ingredient. The exception to this rule is cream or cream liqueurs, which can float, especially when whipped.

One brand of a particular liqueur may be heavier or lighter than another. The relative temperatures of ingredients may also affect their ability to float or sink. Hence a degree of experimentation is inevitable when creating layered drinks.

Layering can be achieved in one of two ways. The first involves pouring down the twisting handle of a bar spoon, keeping the flat, disc-shaped end of the spoon over the surface of the previous layer so that the liquid disperses over the surface of the drink. Alternatively you can hold the bowl end of a bar spoon (or a large teaspoon) in contact with the side of the glass and over the surface of the drink, and pour over it.

MUDDLE

Muddling means pummelling fruits, herbs and spices with a muddler (a blunt tool similar to a pestle) so as to crush and release juices and oils. (You can also use a rolling pin.) As when using a pestle and mortar, push down on the muddler with a twisting action.

Only attempt to muddle in the base of a shaker or a suitably sturdy glass. Never attempt to muddle hard, unripe fruits in a glass as the pressure required could break the glass and cause injury. I've witnessed a bartender slash his hand open on a broken glass while muddling and can't over-emphasize how careful you should be.

FLOAT

This refers to floating the final ingredient on top of a cocktail by slowly pouring it over a spoon. See 'Layering' for the two ways in which to do this.

FROSTING

Some use this term to describe the frosted effect on glasses stored in a freezer or refrigerator. 'Frosting' can also describe coating the rim of a glass with salt or sugar. In this guide I use the phrases 'rim glass' for coating the rim of a glass with salt or sugar (see 'Salt / Sugar Rim') and 'chill glass' for freezing glasses.

MEASURING

The balancing of each ingredient within a cocktail is key to making a great drink. Therefore the accuracy with which ingredients are measured is critical to the finished cocktail.

SHOT

Please follow the alcohol content guidelines included in this guide and choose a sensibly sized measure equal to 25ml or one US fluid ounce (29.6ml) at most.

In this guide I've expressed the measurements of ingredients in 'shots'. Ideally a shot is a 25ml measure (UK) or a 1oz measure (US). Alternatively, use a clean medicine measure or even 'half an egg cup' to measure a 'shot'. I recommend using a straight-sided jigger or other measure to enable accurate judgement of fractions of a shot. Accurately judging a quarter or half measure on sloping sided measures is near impossible.

Whatever the measure you use as a shot, be sure to use the same measure for all the ingredients so that the proportions of one ingredient to the other remain as the recipe intended. Also, unless you're using a graduated measure, fill to the rim for one whole shot.

SPOON

The measure 'spoon' refers to a bar spoon, which is slightly larger than a standard teaspoon. If you are using a 1oz thimble measure an eighth of a shot is roughly equal to a bar spoon.

FREEPOURING

This term refers to pouring measures of drink without using a physical measure. In well trained, experienced hands, fairly accurate pouring is achievable by counting time and estimating the amount of liquid flowing through a bottle's spout while pouring. In the wrong hands this is a terribly inaccurate method and I strongly recommend the use of a thimble or other physical measure.

During my tenure as editor of CLASS, a UK drinks industry magazine, I devised a pour table which measured the accuracy of free-pouring by weighing the liquid poured. At countless bartender exhibitions and events this device illustrated that few professional bartenders can free-pour within twenty percent accuracy, particularly when pouring fractions of a shot.

ICE

A plentiful supply of fresh ice is essential to making good cocktails. Fortunately most supermarkets and liquor stores now sell bags of ice (avoid the hollow, tubular kind and the thin wafers of ice). Alternatively, if you're making your own in ice cube trays, use bottled or filtered water to avoid the taste of chlorine often apparent in municipal water supplies. I have a Hoshizaki commercial ice making machine which produces large solid cubes, and thoroughly recommend it.

Your ice should be dry, almost sticky to the touch. Never use 'wet' ice that has started to thaw.

When serving a drink over ice, always fill the glass with ice, rather than just adding a few cubes. The greater quantity of ice makes the drink much colder, the ice lasts longer and so melting ice does not dilute the drink. Unfortunately, many drinkers perceive this as a way of reducing the quantity of liquid in a glass so that bars can make more profit. Customers who ask for some ice to be removed and their drink to be topped up are merely showing their ignorance.

Never use ice in a cocktail shaker twice, even if it's to mix the same drink as last time. You should always throw away ice after straining the drink and use fresh ice to fill the glass if so required. Unless otherwise stated, all references to ice in this guide mean cubed ice.

If crushed ice is required for a particular recipe, the recipe will state 'crushed ice'. This is available commercially. Alternatively you can crush cubed ice in an ice-crusher or simply bash a bag of it with a rolling pin.

If a glass is broken near your ice stocks, melt the ice with warm water, clean the container and re-stock with fresh ice. If this occurs in a busy bar and you are not immediately able to clean the ice well, mark the contaminated well with a liberal coating of grenadine syrup and draw ice from another station.

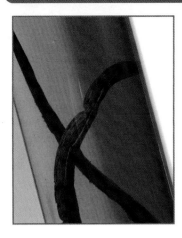

Some recipes call for an infused spirit. An example of this is vanilla infused rum, which is made by putting three split vanilla pods in a bottle of rum and leaving for a fortnight. Warming the bottle and turning it frequently can speed up this process.

Other herbs, spices and even fruits can be infused in a similar manner in vodka, gin, rum, whiskey and Tequila. Whatever spirit you decide to use, pick a brand that has an alcohol content of 40% alc./vol. or more.

Be aware that when the level of spirit in a bottle drops below the level of the flavouring, the alcohol loses its preservative effect and the flavouring can go off. Also be careful not to load the spirit with too much flavour or leave it to infuse for too long. I recommend sampling the infusion every couple of days to ensure the taste is not becoming overpowering.

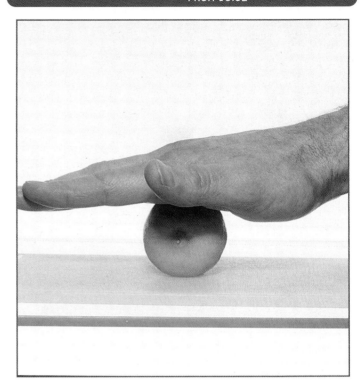

The dilution of a cocktail is key to achieving the right balance. It varies according to how fresh your ice is, how hard you shake your drink and how much ice you use.

Even if a recipe doesn't call for a splash of water, don't be scared to add a dash if you feel it needs it. As with making ice, use bottled or filtered water. Always keep a bottle of still water in your refrigerator next to the bottle of sugar syrup.

Don't consume eggs if:

1. You are uncertain about their freshness. **2.** There is a crack or flaw in the shell. **3.** They don't wobble when rolled across a flat surface. (Only consume wobbly eggs.) **4.** The egg white is watery instead of gel-like. **5.** The egg yolk is not convex and firm. **6.** The egg yolk bursts easily. **7.** They smell foul.

Raw eggs can be hazardous to health so you may decide it is safer to use commercially produced pasteurised egg white, particularly if you are pregnant (but then you probably shouldn't be drinking cocktails anyway). Sadly I don't think it's possible to taste many cocktails at their best without the use of fresh, unpasteurised egg. I believe the small chance of Salmonella poisoning is a risk worth taking. Let's be honest, I've suffered more upset stomachs from drinking too much alcohol than I have through bad eggs. That said it's worth taking steps to reduce the risk and I therefore recommend you use small, organic, free range eggs. Always store eggs in a refrigerator and use well before the sell-by date.

In an ideal world fruit would always come from a tree and not a bottle or carton, so (with the exception of cranberry juice) the best way to obtain your juices is to squeeze, press or use a juice extractor on fresh fruit. If you buy packaged juice don't use products made from concentrate. Look for terms such as 'freshly squeezed', 'pressed' and 'not from concentrate' on the label and look in supermarket chill cabinets, not on the ambient shelf.

Poorer quality, heavily pasteurised juices tend to be sweeter and less flavoursome than fresh or 'not from concentrate' packaged juices. This can ruin a drink formulated to be made with fresh juices.

Before cutting fruit such as limes or lemons to juice, roll the fruit over the surface of your cutting board whilst applying pressure with the palm of your hand. Surprisingly, this will enable you to squeeze more juice from each fruit. Also try to avoid storing limes and lemons in the refrigerator as cold fruits yield less juice.

When using a spinning juicer, be careful not to grind the pith of citrus fruit as this can make the juice bitter. Fruits such as pears and pineapples are best juiced in a centrifugal juice extractor. The juice of soft berries can usually be released by simply muddling in the base of your shaker or glass.

Keep juices refrigerated and be aware of 'sell-by' and 'use-by' dates. Always shake a juice container before use – effervescence is a sign of off juice which should be discarded.

PURÉES

Fruit purées are made from fresh fruit which have been chopped up and liquidised. Bars tend to use commercially available frozen purées which often have added sugar. If using such a product you may have to adjust the balance of your drink to allow for the extra sweetness. Some fruits, such as mangos, are best used in this way and in such cases recipes in this guide may state 'sweetened purée'. When making your own sweetened purée add roughly five percent sugar syrup to your puréed fruit.

SUGAR SYRUP

Many cocktails benefit from sweetening but granulated sugar does not dissolve easily in cold drinks. Hence pre-dissolved sugar syrup (also known as 'simple syrup') is used.

Commercially made 'gomme sirop' (gum syrup) is sugar syrup with the addition of gum arabic, the crystallised sap of the acacia tree. Some brands of gomme sirop also include orange blossom or other flavourings. In taste, sirop de gomme is very clearly distinguishable from sugar syrup. Many bartenders don't like using gomme syrup but prefer to use simple or sugar syrup. Others prefer gomme as it adds mouth-feel and smoothness to some drinks.

You can buy sugar syrup commercially or mix it yourself as follows: gradually pour and stir two cups of granulated sugar into a saucepan containing one cup of hot water and simmer until the sugar is dissolved. (I use cane sugar.)

Note that the longer you boil the water and sugar, the stronger the syrup will be and that if you boil it for too long your syrup will be too strong and liable to crystallise. You may want to add a splash of extra water to counter this.

Allow the syrup to cool and pour into an empty bottle. Ideally, you should fine strain your syrup into the bottle to remove any undissolved crystals which could otherwise encourage crystallisation. If kept in a refrigerator this mixture will last for a couple of months.

A wide range of flavoured sugar syrups are commercially available. Orgeat (almond), grenadine, passion fruit and vanilla are among the most popular.

HALF AND HALF

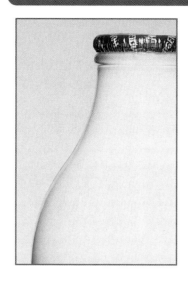

This is a blend of 50% milk and 50% cream pre-mixed by some bartenders for use in cocktails. In this guide I've listed these ingredients separately.

CREAM OF COCONUT

This is a non-alcoholic, sticky blend of coconut juice, sugar, emulsifier, cellulose, thickeners, citric acid and salt. Fortunately it tastes better than it sounds and is an essential ingredient of a good Piña Colada. One 15oz/425ml can will make approximately 25 drinks. Once it has been opened the contents should be transferred to a suitable container and stored in a refrigerator. This may thicken the product, so gentle warming may be required prior to use. Coconut milk is very different and cannot be substituted.

SOUR MIX

Sour mix is a term for a blend of lemon juice or lime juice mixed with sugar syrup. Commercial pre-mixed sour mix is available in a dried crystal or powdered form, often with the addition of pasteurised egg white. Margarita mix is a similar pre-mix, but with the addition of orange flavours.

Many bartenders rightly frown on the use of such pre-mixes. I strongly advocate the use of freshly squeezed juice and sugar syrup.

GRENADINE

This sweet, red pomegranate flavoured sugar syrup has little or no alcoholic content. It is usually made from red berries such as cherries, strawberries and raspberries, with added flavour from vanilla essence.

GARNISH

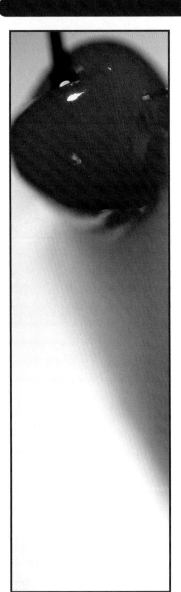

Garnishes are used to decorate cocktails and are often anchored to the rim of the glass. Strictly speaking, garnishes should be edible so please forget about paper parasols. Fruit should be unblemished and washed prior to use.

Cut citrus fruits have a maximum shelf life of 24 hours when refrigerated. Cherries and olives should be stored refrigerated and left in their own juices. Olives should be washed before use to prevent an oily appearance to the drink.

Anything from banana chunks, strawberries or redcurrants to coffee beans, confectionery, basil leaves and slices of fresh ginger can be used as a garnish. The correct garnish will often enhance the aroma and flavour as well as the look of a drink.

The term 'split' refers to the cut in a piece of fruit used to fix it to the rim of a glass. A 'wheel' is a circular slice of citrus fruit. For wedges see under Lemon / Lime Wedges.

Garnishes such as olives, cherries or pickled onions are sometimes served on cocktail sticks. A 'sail' is a whole slice of citrus fruit served on a cocktail stick mast, often accompanied by a cherry.

Celery sticks may be placed in drinks as a stirring rod. Cinnamon sticks are often served in hot drinks and toddies.

To sprinkle chocolate on the surface of a drink you can either shave chocolate using a vegetable peeler or crumble a Cadbury's Flake bar. 'Dust with chocolate' refers to the use of chocolate or cocoa powder.

Citrus peels are often used as a garnish (see 'Flamed Zest'). A 'Horse's Neck' is the entire peel of either an orange, a lemon or a lime, cut in a continuous spiral and placed so as to overhang the rim of the glass. A 'twist' is a narrow sliver of fruit zest twisted over the drink to release the oils in the skin and then dropped in. Thin, narrow lengths of citrus peel may also be tied in a knot.

Mint sprigs are often used to garnish cups and juleps.

DUST

You 'dust' a drink by sprinkling ground nutmeg, chocolate powder etc. on top of it. When dusting with nutmeg it is always best to grate fresh nutmeg over the drink, although the powdered product may be used if fresh is not available.

ZEST TWIST

This is the flavouring of a drink by releasing the aromatic oils from a strip of citrus zest. Using a knife or peeler, cut a half inch (12mm) thick length of zest from an unwaxed, cleaned fruit so as to leave just a little of the white pith. Hold each end (coloured side down) over the glass by the thumb and forefinger of each hand. Turn one end clockwise and the other anticlockwise so as to twist the peel and force some of its oils over the surface of the drink. Deposit any flavoursome oils left on the surface of the peel by wiping the coloured side around the rim of the glass. Finally drop the peel onto the surface of the drink. Some prefer to dispose of the spent twist rather than drop it into the drink. What a waste.

FLAMED ZEST TWIST

This is a dramatic garnish which involves burning the aromatic oils emitted from citrus fruit zest over the surface of a drink. Lemons and limes are sometimes treated in this way but oranges are most popular. Firm, thick-skinned navel oranges, like Washington Navels, are best.

First cut as wide a strip of zest as is possible - wider than you would for the usual twist (above). Hold the cut zest, peel side down, between the thumb and forefinger about four inches above the drink and gently warm the zest with a lighter flame. Then pinch the peel by its edges so that its oils squirt through the flame towards the surface of the drink. There should be a flash as the oils ignite. (Be careful not to hold the flame too close to the drink as this will leave a smoky film on the glass.) Finally, wipe the zest round the rim of the glass.

FLAME

The term ignite, flame or flambé means that the drink should be set alight. Please exercise extreme care when setting fire to drinks. Be particularly careful not to knock over a lit drink and never attempt to carry a drink which is still alight. Before drinking cover the glass so as to suffocate the flame and be aware that the rim may be hot.

ORDER TO FOLLOW

When making a cocktail, you should work in the order below.

1. Select glass and chill or heat if required
2. Prepare garnish if required
3. Add ingredients
4. Add ice (add last to minimise melt) if required
5. Mix (and strain or pour) or build if required
6. Add garnish if required
7. Consume or serve to another

LEMON / LIME WEDGES

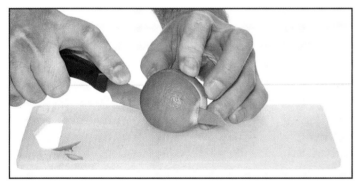

Wedges of lemons and limes are often required to squeeze into drinks or to use on the rim as a garnish. A wedge is an eighth segment of the fruit. Cut the 'knobs' from the top and bottom of the fruit. Slice the fruit in half lengthwise, then cut each half into four equal wedges lengthwise. A 'split' wedge of fruit refers to an incision in the fruit which allows it to be anchored on the glass rim.

SALT / SUGAR RIM

Some recipes call for the rim of the glass to be coated with salt, sugar or other ingredients such as desiccated coconut or chocolate. When using salt, moisten the rim of the glass by whipping a cut wedge of lime around the outside edge of the rim, then dip the outside edge into a saucer of salt. For sugar, chocolate etc., use an orange slice instead of a lime wedge or run the outside edge of the glass over a sponge or paper towel you have moistened with a suitable liqueur.

Whatever you are using to rim the glass should only end up on the outside. If some of your garnish should become stuck to the inside edge of the glass and threaten to contaminate the cocktail, remove it using a fresh fruit wedge or paper towel.

Iodised table salt is too salty to use on the rim of a glass, so sea salt should be used instead. Both salt and sugar can be made finer by blending in a clean, dry blender.

It is good practice to salt or sugar only two-thirds of the rim of a glass. This allows the drinker the option of avoiding the salt or sugar. If you are preparing for a party it is acceptable to rim your glasses several hours before they are required. The lime juice or liqueur will dry and crystals will form a kind of hard crust around the rim of the glass. The glasses can then be placed in a refrigerator to chill ready for use.

A professional piece of equipment with the unfortunate title of a 'rimmer' has three sections, one with a sponge for water or lime juice, one containing sugar and another containing salt. Beware, as this encourages dipping the glass onto a moist sponge and then into the garnish, and so contaminating the inside of the glass.

Cocktails are something of a luxury. You don't just ping a cap and pour. They take time and skill to mix so deserve a half decent glass. Before you start, check your glassware is clean and free from chips and marks such as lipstick. Always handle glasses by the base or the stem to avoid leaving finger marks on the glass. Never put your fingers inside a glass.

Ideally glassware should be chilled in a freezer prior to use. This is particularly important for Martini and flute glasses, in which drinks are usually served without ice. It takes about half an hour to sufficiently chill a glass in the freezer.

Alternatively, you can chill a glass by filling it with ice (ideally crushed, not cubed) and then topping it up with water. Leave the glass to cool while you prepare the drink, then discard the ice and water once you are ready to pour.

This method is may be quicker than chilling in the freezer but it's not nearly so effective.

Conversely, to warm a glass ready for a hot cocktail, place a bar spoon in the glass and fill it with hot water. Then discard the water and pour in the drink. Only then should you remove the spoon, which is there to help disperse the shock of the heat.

There are thousands of differently shaped glasses, but if you own those mentioned on these pages you have a glass to suit practically every drink and occasion. If you haven't, a set of Collins, Martinis, Old-fashioneds and possibly flutes if you fancy Champagne cocktails will allow you to serve the majority of drinks in this guide. Then you can just use the Old-fashioned instead of a Rocks and a Martini in place of a Coupette.

GLASSWARE

MARTINI

Those in the old guard of bartending insist on calling this a 'cocktail glass'. It may be! But to most of us a 'V' shaped glass is a Martini glass. Anything bigger than a 7oz is ridiculous, as a true Martini warms up too much in the time it takes to drink such a large one. Chill before use.

Capacity to brim: 7oz / 20cl

SLING

This elegant glass has recently become fashionable again – partly due to the popularity of long drinks such as the Russian Spring Punch.

Capacity to brim: 11oz / 32cl

SHOT

Shot glasses come in all shapes and sizes. You'll need small ones if you're sensible and big ones if you're not!

Capacity to brim: 2oz / 6cl

FLUTE

Flutes are perfect for serving Champagne cocktails as their tall, slim design helps maintain the wine's fizz. Chill before use.

Capacity to brim: 6oz / 17cl

TODDY

Frequently referred to as a 'liqueur coffee glass', which is indeed its main use, this glass was popularised by the Irish Coffee. Toddy glasses have a handle on the side, allowing you to comfortably hold hot drinks.
Capacity to brim: 8.5oz / 25cl

GOBLET

Not often used for cocktails, but worth having, if for no other reason than to enjoy your wine. An 11oz glass is just big enough to be luxurious but not so big as to overwhelm a dinner party bottle poured amongst six.
Capacity to brim: 11oz / 32cl

HURRICANE

Sometimes referred to as a 'poco grande' or 'Piña Colada glass'. This big-bowled glass is commonly used for frozen drinks. It screams out for a pineapple wedge, cherry and possibly a paper parasol as well. Very Del Boy.
Capacity to brim: 15oz / 43cl

COLLINS

In this guide I refer to tall glasses as 'Collins'. A hi-ball is slightly squatter than a Collins but has the same capacity. A 12oz Collins glass is perfect for tall cocktails and will also hold the contents of a standard 330ml bottle of beer.
Capacity to brim: 12oz / 34cl

OLD-FASHIONED

Another glass whose name refers to the best-known drink served in it. Cocktails aside, this is a great glass from which to enjoy spirits such as whiskey. Choose a luxuriously large glass with a thick, heavy base.
Capacity to brim: 11oz / 32cl

BOSTON

A tall, heavy conical glass with a thick rim designed to be combined with a Boston tin to form a shaker. It can also be used as a mixing glass for stirred drinks.
Capacity to brim: 17oz / 48cl

ROCKS

Like an Old-fashioned with a thick rim, this is usually made from toughened glass - perfect for drinks that require muddling in the glass. A hardy glass if there is such a thing.
Capacity to brim: 9oz / 27cl

MARGARITA

Also known as a 'Coupette', this is commonly referred to as a 'Margarita glass' as it is used to serve the hugely popular cocktail of the same name. Its rim cries out for salt.
Capacity to brim: 8oz / 24cl

SNIFTER / BRANDY BALLOON

Sometimes referred to as a snifter glass, the bigger the bowl, the more luxurious it appears. Use to enjoy cocktails and deluxe aged spirits such as Cognac.
Capacity to brim: 12oz / 35cl

ABSOLUT® VODKA

In 1879, Lars Olsson Smith introduced a vodka called 'Absolut rent brännvin,' which translates as 'Absolutely pure vodka'. After Lars Olsson's death the brand enjoyed little success under the ownership of the Swedish state liquor monopoly. Then in 1979, the brand's centenary, the bottle was redesigned in the style of an old Swedish medicine bottle. The name 'Absolute Pure Vodka' was shortened to Absolut (the original Swedish spelling). The slogan 'Country of Sweden' was added, as was the silver medallion with an image of Lars Olsson Smith. These changes made it a major hit.

Absolut is produced in the small southern Swedish town of Åhus using winter wheat from the Skåne region of southern Sweden. Unlike many other vodkas, Absolut does not require or undergo any charcoal filtration or any other form of chemical filtration.

Lightly peppery hints with light bready and malty notes, a slight hint of dried fruit and a caramelised sweetness. Absolut is probably more identified with cocktails than any other vodka brand. 40% alc./vol. (80°proof)

Web: www.absolutvodka.com **Producer:** Swedish Wine & Spirits Corporation, Stockholm, Sweden.
UK distributor: Maxxium UK Ltd, Stirling, Scotland.
Tel: 01786 430 500 **Email:** enquiries@maxxium.com

ALMOND MARTINI NEW

Glass: Martini
Garnish: Float flaked almonds
Method: Shake all ingredients with ice and fine strain into chilled glass.

2	shot(s)	Absolut vodka
1/2	shot(s)	Freshly squeezed lemon juice
1/2	shot(s)	Almond (orgeat) syrup
1	shot(s)	Pressed apple juice
2 dashes		Fee Brothers peach bitters (optional)

Origin: Created in 2004 by Matt Pomeroy at Baltic, London, England.
Comment: Almond inspired with hints of apple and lemon juice.

APPLE MARTINI #1 (SIMPLE VERSION) UPDATED

Glass: Martini
Garnish: Cherry in base of glass
Method: Shake all ingredients with ice and fine strain into chilled glass.

2 1/2	shot(s)	Absolut vodka
2	shot(s)	Pressed apple juice
1/4	shot(s)	Sugar (gomme) syrup

Variant: Sour Apple Martini
Origin: Formula by yours truly in 2004.
Comment: This is subtitled the simple version for good reason but, if freshly pressed juice is used, it's as good if not better than other Apple Martini recipes.

APRICOT COSMO NEW

Glass: Martini
Garnish: Apricot slice
Method: Stir apricot preserve with vodka so as to dissolve preserve. Add other ingredients, shake with ice and fine strain into chilled glass.

2	shot(s)	Absolut vodka
1	spoon	Apricot preserve (St. Dalfour)
1	shot(s)	Cranberry juice
1/4	shot(s)	Passion fruit syrup
1/2	shot(s)	Freshly squeezed lime juice
2	dashes	Fee Brothers orange bitters

Origin: Created in 2004 at Aura Kitchen & Bar, London, England.
Comment: The apricot preserve adds a flavoursome tang to the contemporary classic.

BALALAIKA UPDATED

Glass: Martini
Garnish: Orange zest twist
Method: Shake all ingredients with ice and fine strain into chilled glass.

1 1/2	shot(s)	Absolut vodka
1 1/2	shot(s)	Cointreau / triple sec
1 1/2	shot(s)	Freshly squeezed lemon juice

Comment: Richly flavoured with orange and lemon.

BALLET RUSSE UPDATED

●●●●○○

Glass: Martini
Garnish: Lime wedge on rim
Method: Shake all ingredients with ice and fine strain into chilled glass.

2	shot(s)	Absolut vodka
³/₄	shot(s)	Sisca crème de cassis
1	shot(s)	Freshly squeezed lime juice
¹/₄	shot(s)	Sugar (gomme) syrup

Comment: Intense sweet blackcurrant balanced by lime sourness.

CAIPIROVSKA / CAIPIROSCA

●●●●●

Glass: Rocks
Method: Muddle lime in base of glass. Add other ingredients and fill glass with crushed ice. Churn drink with barspoon and serve with short straws.

³/₄	fresh	Lime cut into wedges
2	shot(s)	Absolut vodka
³/₄	shot(s)	Sugar (gomme) syrup

Comment: Lacks the character of a cachaça based Caipirinha.

BITTER SWEET SYMPHONY NEW

●●●●○○

Glass: Martini
Garnish: Dried apricot on cocktail stick
Method: Shake all ingredients with ice and fine strain into chilled glass.

¹/₂	shot(s)	Absolut vodka
1	shot(s)	Cointreau / triple sec
1	shot(s)	Bols apricot brandy liqueur
¹/₂	shot(s)	Freshly squeezed lime juice
1¹/₂	shot(s)	Freshly squeezed grapefruit juice

Origin: Adapted from a drink created in 2003 by Wayne Collins for Maxxium UK.
Comment: This roller coaster ride of bitter and sweet mainly features apricot and grapefruit.

CAPE CODDER

●●●●●○

Glass: Old-fashioned
Garnish: Redcurrants
Method: Shake all ingredients with ice and strain into ice-filled glass.

2	shot(s)	Absolut vodka
3	shot(s)	Cranberry juice
¹/₄	shot(s)	Freshly squeezed lime juice

Variation: Without lime juice this is a Cape Cod. Lengthened with soda this becomes the Cape Cod Cooler.
Comment: A dry and refreshing but not particularly interesting.

BLACK 'N' BLUE CAIPIROVSKA

●●●●●○

Glass: Rocks
Method: Muddle berries in base of glass. Add other ingredients. Fill glass with crushed ice and churn (stir). Serve with two short straws.

6	fresh	Blackberries
10	fresh	Blueberries
2	shot(s)	Absolut vodka
¹/₂	shot(s)	Freshly squeezed lime juice
¹/₂	shot(s)	Sugar (gomme) syrup

Comment: A great fruity twist on the regular Caipirovska.

COBBLED RASPBERRY MARTINI NEW

●●●●●◐

Glass: Martini
Garnish: Raspberries on stick
Method: Muddle raspberries in base of shaker. Add other ingredients, shake with ice and fine strain into chilled glass.

12	fresh	Raspberries
2	shot(s)	Absolut vodka
1	shot(s)	Shiraz Red wine
¹/₂	shot(s)	Sugar (gomme) syrup

Origin: Created by yours truly in 2004.
Comment: The addition of a splash of wine to a simple raspberry Martini adds another level of complexity.

BLOODY MARY (MODERN RECIPE)

●●●●●◐

Glass: Collins
Garnish: Salt & pepper rim plus celery stick
Method: Shake all ingredients with ice and strain into ice-filled glass.

2	shot(s)	Absolut vodka
5	shot(s)	Fresh tomato juice
¹/₂	shot(s)	Freshly squeezed lemon juice
8	drops	Tabasco sauce
4	dashes	Worcestershire sauce
¹/₂	spoon	Horseradish sauce
¹/₂	shot(s)	Tawny Port
2	pinch	Celery salt
2	pinch	Black pepper

Variant: Peppered Mary
Comment: A fiery Mary with the heat fuelled by horseradish. If you like to fight a hangover with spice, this is for you.

COSMOPOLITAN # 2 (POPULAR VERSION) UPDATED

●●●●○

Glass: Martini
Garnish: Flamed orange zest twist
Method: Shake all ingredients with ice and fine strain into chilled glass.

2	shot(s)	Absolut vodka
³/₄	shot(s)	Cointreau / triple sec
1¹/₄	shot(s)	Cranberry juice
¹/₄	shot(s)	Freshly squeezed lime juice

Comment: A simple version of this modern day classic, but good all the same.

CUCUMBER SAKE-TINI NEW

●●●●○

Glass: Martini
Garnish: Three cucumber slices
Method: Muddle cucumber in base of shaker. Add other ingredients, shake with ice and fine strain into chilled glass.

1½ inch		Peeled diced cucumber
1½	shot(s)	Absolut vodka
1½	shot(s)	Sake
¼	shot(s)	Sugar (gomme) syrup

Origin: Created in 2004 by Lisa Ball, London, England.
Comment: Subtle and dry. Cucumber and sake are made for each other.

DETROIT MARTINI UPDATED

●●●●○

Glass: Martini
Garnish: Mint sprig
Method: Lightly bruise mint in base of shaker with muddler. Add other ingredients, shake with ice and fine strain into chilled glass.

7	fresh	Mint leaves
2½	shot(s)	Absolut vodka
½	shot(s)	Sugar (gomme) syrup
¾	shot(s)	Chilled mineral water

Origin: Dick Bradsell created this drink, which is based on the Cowboy Martini.
Comment: You can also add a touch of lime juice.

DOUBLE GRAPE MARTINI NEW

●●●●◖

Glass: Martini
Garnish: Grapes on stick
Method: Muddle grapes in base of shaker. Add other ingredients, shake with ice and fine strain into chilled glass.

12	fresh	Seedless white grapes
2	shot(s)	Absolut vodka
¾	shot(s)	Sauvignon Blanc / unoaked Chardonnay wine
½	shot(s)	Sugar (gomme) syrup

Origin: Created by yours truly in 2004.
Comment: The wine adds complexity to a simple Grape Martini.

DOWA NEW

●●●●○

Glass: Old-fashioned
Method: Stir honey and vodka in shaker tin so as to dissolve honey. Add lime wedges and muddle. Add crushed ice and shake lightly before pouring into glass. Serve with straws.

2½	shot(s)	Absolut vodka
4	spoons	Runny honey
¾	fresh	Lime cut into wedges

Origin: This cocktail is particularly popular in upscale hotel bars in Kenya where it is enjoyed by the safari set.
Comment: Very similar to the Caipirovska in its use of vodka, lime and crushed ice: the honey makes the difference.

ESPRESSO MARTINI

●●●●●

Glass: Martini
Garnish: Float 3 coffee beans
Method: Shake all ingredients with ice and strain into glass.

2	shot(s)	Absolut vodka
2	shot(s)	Espresso coffee (cold)
½	shot(s)	Kahlúa coffee liqueur
¼	shot(s)	Sugar (gomme) syrup

Origin: A straight-up version of Dick Bradsell's Pharmaceutical Stimulant.
Comment: Forget the vodka Red Bull, this is the connoisseur's way of combining caffeine and vodka.

FRENCH MARTINI # 1

●●●●○

Glass: Martini
Method: Shake all ingredients with ice and fine strain into chilled glass.

2	shot(s)	Absolut vodka
2½	shot(s)	Pressed pineapple juice
½	shot(s)	Chambord black raspberry liqueur

Comment: Black raspberries and pineapple laced with vodka. Simple, delicious and very fruity.

GINGER MARTINI NEW

●●●●○

Glass: Martini
Garnish: Brandy snap biscuit
Method: Muddle ginger in base of shaker. Add other ingredients, shake with ice and fine strain into chilled glass.

2	slices	Fresh root ginger (thumbnail sized)
2	shot(s)	Absolut vodka
¾	shot(s)	Stone's green ginger wine
¾	shot(s)	Pressed apple juice
½	shot(s)	Freshly squeezed lime juice
¼	shot(s)	Sugar (gomme) syrup

Origin: Discovered in 2003 at Hurricane Bar and Grill, Edinburgh, England.
Comment: This Martini may be served chilled but its flavour is distinctly warming.

GRAPE MARTINI NEW

●●●●○

Glass: Martini
Garnish: Grapes on stick
Method: Muddle grapes in base of shaker. Add other ingredients, shake with ice and fine strain into chilled glass.

12	fresh	Seedless white grapes
2	shot(s)	Absolut vodka
½	shot(s)	Sugar (gomme) syrup

Origin: Formula by yours truly in 2004.
Comment: Simple but remarkably tasty.

GRAPPLE MARTINI NEW ●●●●○

Glass: Martini
Garnish: Grapes on stick
Method: Muddle grapes in base of shaker. Add other ingredients, shake with ice and fine strain into chilled glass.

7	fresh	Seedless white grapes
2	shot(s)	Absolut vodka
3/4	shot(s)	Sauvignon Blanc / unoaked Chardonnay wine
1	shot(s)	Pressed apple juice
1/4	shot(s)	Sugar (gomme) syrup

Origin: Adapted from a recipe created in 2003 by Chris Setchell at Las Iguanas, UK.
Comment: A rounded, fruity Martini-style drink.

HARD LEMONADE NEW ●●●●○

Glass: Collins
Garnish: Lemon wheel in glass
Method: Shake first three ingredients with ice and strain into ice-filled glass. Top up with soda and serve with straws.

2	shot(s)	Absolut vodka
2	shot(s)	Freshly squeezed lemon juice
1	shot(s)	Sugar (gomme) syrup
Top up with		Soda water (club soda)

Variant: Ray's Hard Lemonade
Origin: Discovered in 2004 at Spring Street Natural Restaurant, New York City, USA.
Comment: Refreshing lemonade with a kick. Great for a hot afternoon.

HOT TUB MARTINI NEW ●●●●○

Glass: Martini
Garnish: Pineapple wedge on rim
Method: Shake first three ingredients with ice and fine strain into chilled glass. Top up with Prosecco.

1 1/2	shot(s)	Absolut vodka
1/4	shot(s)	Chambord black raspberry liqueur
1	shot(s)	Pressed pineapple juice
Top up with		Prosecco sparkling wine

Origin: Adapted from a drink discovered in 2004 at Teatro, Boston, USA.
Comment: Basically a French Martini with bubbles.

ICE 'T' KNEE NEW ●●●●◐

Glass: Martini
Garnish: Lemon zest twist
Method: Stir all ingredients with ice and strain into chilled glass.

2	shot(s)	Absolut vodka
1 1/2	shot(s)	Jasmine tea (cold)
3/4	shot(s)	Icewine

Origin: Created by yours truly in 2004.
Comment: Honeyed palate topped off with tannin and jasmine.

KIWI BELLINI NEW ●●●●○

Glass: Flute
Garnish: Kiwi slice on rim
Method: Cut kiwi fruit in half, scoop out flesh into base of shaker and muddle. Add other ingredients, shake with ice and fine strain into chilled glass.

1	fresh	Kiwi fruit
1 1/4	shot(s)	Absolut vodka
1/4	shot(s)	Freshly squeezed lemon juice
1/4	shot(s)	Sugar (gomme) syrup
Top up with		Prosecco

Origin: Adapted from a drink discovered at Zuma, London, England in 2004.
Comment: Lemon fresh kiwi, fortified with vodka and charged with Prosecco.

KIWI COLLINS NEW ●●●●○

Glass: Collins
Garnish: Kiwi slice
Method: Cut kiwi fruit in half, scoop out flesh into base of shaker and muddle. Add vodka, lemon juice and sugar, shake with ice and strain into ice-filled glass. Top up with soda water.

1	fresh	Kiwi fruit
2	shot(s)	Absolut vodka
1 1/2	shot(s)	Freshly squeezed lemon juice
1/2	shot(s)	Sugar (gomme) syrup
Top up with		Soda water (club soda)

Origin: Formula by yours truly.
Comment: A fruity adaptation of a Vodka Collins.

KIWI MARTINI (SIMPLE) NEW ●●●●○

Glass: Martini
Garnish: Kiwi slice on rim
Method: Cut kiwi fruit in half, scoop out flesh into base of shaker and muddle. Add other ingredients, shake with ice and fine strain into chilled glass.

1	fresh	Kiwi fruit
2	shot(s)	Absolut vodka
1/2	shot(s)	Sugar (gomme) syrup

Origin: Formula by yours truly in 2004.
Comment: You may need to adjust the sugar depending on the ripeness of your fruit.

LCB MARTINI NEW ●●●●○

Glass: Martini
Garnish: Lemon zest twist
Method: Shake all ingredients with ice and fine strain into chilled glass.

2	shot(s)	Absolut vodka
3/4	shot(s)	Sauvignon Blanc / unoaked Chardonnay wine
2	shot(s)	Freshly squeezed pink grapefruit juice
1/4	shot(s)	Sugar (gomme) syrup

Origin: Created by yours truly in 2004 and named after Lisa Clare Ball.
Comment: A sweet and sour, citrus fresh Martini.

MADRAS

Glass: Collins
Garnish: Orange wheel in glass
Method: Shake all ingredients with ice and strain into ice-filled glass.

2	shot(s)	Absolut vodka
3	shot(s)	Cranberry juice
2	shot(s)	Freshly squeezed orange juice

Comment: A Seabreeze but with orange juice in place of grapefruit juice, making it slightly sweeter.

MELON MARTINI (FRESH) UPDATED

Glass: Martini
Garnish: Melon wedge on rim
Method: Cut melon into 8 segments and deseed. Cut cubes of flesh from skin of one segment and muddle in base of shaker. Add other ingredients, shake with ice and fine strain into chilled glass.

1/8	fresh	Cantaloupe / Galia melon
2	shot(s)	Absolut vodka
1/4	shot(s)	Sugar (gomme) syrup

Variant: Substitute Midori melon liqueur for sugar syrup.
Comment: Probably the most popular of all the fresh fruit martinis.

MOMO SPECIAL

Glass: Collins
Garnish: Mint sprig
Method: Muddle mint with vodka in base of shaker. Add lime juice and sugar, shake with ice and strain into ice-filled glass. Top up with soda and stir.

2	shot(s)	Absolut vodka
12	fresh	Mint leaves
1/2	shot(s)	Freshly squeezed lime juice
1/2	shot(s)	Sugar (gomme) syrup
Top up with		Soda water (club soda)

Origin: Created in 1998 by Simon Mainoo at Momo, London, England.
Comment: Light green in colour and minty in flavour. The flavour is much enriched by macerating the mint in the vodka some hours before making.

ORCHARD BREEZE

Glass: Collins
Garnish: Apple slice on rim
Method: Shake all ingredients with ice and strain into ice-filled glass.

2	shot(s)	Absolut vodka
2 1/2	shot(s)	Pressed apple juice
1 1/2	shot(s)	Sauvignon Blanc wine
3/4	shot(s)	Elderflower cordial
1/4	shot(s)	Freshly squeezed lime juice

Origin: Created in 2002 by Wayne Collins for Maxxium UK.
Comment: Refreshing, summery combination of white wine, apple, lime and elderflower laced with vodka.

ORIENTAL GRAPE MARTINI NEW

Glass: Martini
Garnish: Grapes on stick
Method: Muddle grapes in base of shaker. Add other ingredients, shake with ice and fine strain into chilled glass.

12	fresh	Seedless white grapes
1 1/2	shot(s)	Absolut vodka
1 1/2	shot(s)	Sake
1/4	shot(s)	Sugar (gomme) syrup

Variant: Double Grape Martini, Grape Martini, Grapple
Origin: Created by yours truly in 2004.
Comment: Sake adds some oriental intrigue to what would otherwise be a plain old Grape Martini.

PASSION FRUIT MARTINI #1 NEW

Glass: Martini
Garnish: Star fruit or physalis (Cape gooseberry)
Method: Cut passion fruit in half and scoop out flesh into shaker. Add other ingredients, shake with ice and fine strain into chilled glass.

1	fresh	Passion fruit
2	shot(s)	Absolut vodka
1/2	shot(s)	Sugar (gomme) syrup

Origin: Formula by yours truly in 2004.
Comment: A simple but tasty cocktail that wonderfully harnesses the flavour of passion fruit.

PEAR & ELDERFLOWER MARTINI

Glass: Martini
Garnish: Pear slice on rim
Method: Shake all ingredients with ice and fine strain into chilled glass.

2	shot(s)	Absolut vodka
2	shot(s)	Freshly extracted pear juice
1/2	shot(s)	Elderflower cordial

Origin: Created in 2001 by Angelo Vieira at St. Martins, London, England.
Comment: Pear and elderflower are a match made in St Martins Lane.

PINEAPPLE & CARDAMOM MARTINI

Glass: Martini
Garnish: Pineapple leaf on rim
Method: Break away outer shells of cardamom pods and muddle inner seeds in base of shaker. Add other ingredients, shake with ice and fine strain into chilled glass.

4	pods	Green cardamom
2	shot(s)	Absolut vodka
2	shot(s)	Pressed pineapple juice
1/4	shot(s)	Sugar (gomme) syrup

Origin: Created in 2002 by Henry Besant at Lonsdale House, London, England.
Comment: This is about as good as it gets: a spectacular pairing of fruit and spice.

PINEAPPLE & GINGER MARTINI UPDATED

Glass: Martini
Garnish: Pineapple wedge on rim
Method: Muddle ginger in base of shaker. Add other ingredients, shake with ice and fine strain into chilled glass.

2	slices	Fresh root ginger (thumbnail sized)
2	shot(s)	Absolut vodka
2	shot(s)	Pressed pineapple juice
1/8	shot(s)	Sugar (gomme) syrup

Comment: Smooth rich pineapple flavour with hints of vodka and ginger.

PLUM MARTINI NEW

Glass: Martini
Garnish: Plum quarter on rim (unpeeled)
Method: Cut plum into quarters, remove stone and peel. Muddle plum pieces in base of shaker. Add other ingredients, shake well with ice and fine strain into chilled glass.

1	fresh	Plum (stoned and peeled)
2	shot(s)	Absolut vodka
3/4	shot(s)	Cinzano Extra Dry vermouth
1/2	shot(s)	Sugar (gomme) syrup

Origin: Formula by yours truly in 2004.
Variant: Substitute vanilla sugar syrup for plain syrup.
Comment: Fortified plum juice in a Martini glass.

POMPANSKI MARTINI

Glass: Martini
Garnish: Orange peel twist
Method: Shake all ingredients with ice and strain into glass.

1 3/4	shot(s)	Absolut vodka
1/2	shot(s)	Cointreau / triple sec
1 1/2	shot(s)	Freshly squeezed grapefruit juice
1/4	shot(s)	Sugar (gomme) syrup
1	spoon	Cinzano Extra Dry vermouth

Comment: Dry and zesty with the sharp freshness of grapefruit and a hint of orange.

PORT & MELON MARTINI NEW

Glass: Martini
Garnish: Melon wedge on rim
Method: Cut melon into eight segments and deseed. Cut cubes of flesh from skin of one segment and muddle in base of shaker. Add other ingredients, shake with ice and fine strain into chilled glass.

1/8	fresh	Cantaloupe / Galia melon
1 1/2	shot(s)	Absolut vodka
1 1/2	shot(s)	Dry white Port (e.g. Dow's Fine White)
1	pinch	Ground ginger

Origin: Created by yours truly in 2004.
Comment: The classic seventies starter served as a Martini.

RASPBERRY MARTINI #3 (SIMPLE) NEW

Glass: Martini
Garnish: Raspberries on stick
Method: Muddle raspberries in base of shaker. Add other ingredients, shake with ice and fine strain into chilled glass.

12	fresh	Raspberries
2	shot(s)	Absolut vodka
1/2	shot(s)	Sugar (gomme) syrup

Comment: The simplest of raspberry Martinis but still a great tasting drink.

RASPBERRY MULE

Glass: Collins
Garnish: Lime wedge
Method: Muddle raspberries in base of a shaker. Add other ingredients apart from ginger beer, shake with ice and strain into ice-filled glass. Top up with ginger beer and stir.

12	fresh	Raspberries
2	shot(s)	Absolut vodka
1	shot(s)	Freshly squeezed lime juice
1/2	shot(s)	Sugar (gomme) syrup
Top up with		Ginger beer

Comment: The fruity alternative to a Moscow Mule.

RAY'S HARD LEMONADE NEW

Glass: Collins
Garnish: Mint sprig
Method: Lightly bruise mint in base of shaker with muddler. Add vodka, lemon juice and sugar, shake with ice and fine strain into ice-filled glass. Top up with soda and serve with straws.

7	fresh	Mint leaves
2	shot(s)	Absolut vodka
1	shot(s)	Freshly squeezed lemon juice
2	shot(s)	Freshly squeezed lime juice
1	shot(s)	Sugar (gomme) syrup
Top up with		Soda water (club soda)

Variant: Hard Lemonade
Origin: Discovered in 2004 at Spring Street Natural Restaurant, New York City, USA.
Comment: Alcoholic lemonade with mint or a vodka variation on the Mojito. However you describe it, it works.

RUSSIAN SPRING PUNCH UPDATED

Glass: Sling
Garnish: Lemon slice & berries
Method: Shake first four ingredients with ice and strain into glass filled with crushed ice. Top up with Champagne, stir and serve with straws.

1	shot(s)	Absolut vodka
1/4	shot(s)	Sisca crème de cassis
1	shot(s)	Freshly squeezed lemon juice
1/4	shot(s)	Sugar (gomme) syrup
Top up with		Champagne

Origin: My version of a drink created by Dick Bradsell, London, England.
Comment: Well balanced, complex and refreshing – one of the best drinks to emerge during the 1990s.

SAKINI

Glass: Martini
Garnish: Olives on stick
Method: Stir ingredients with ice and strain in to chilled glass.

1	shot(s)	Sake
2¹/₂	shot(s)	Absolut vodka

Comment: Very dry with the sake giving an almost wine-like delicacy.

SALTY DOG

Glass: Martini
Garnish: Salt rim
Method: Shake all ingredients with ice and fine strain in chilled glass.

2	shot(s)	Absolut vodka
2¹/₄	shot(s)	Freshly squeezed grapefruit juice
¹/₈	shot(s)	Luxardo Maraschino liqueur (optional)

Origin: Circa 1960s, creator unknown.
Comment: Also great with gin.

SEABREEZE (SIMPLE)

Glass: Collins
Method: Shake all ingredients with ice and strain into ice-filled glass.

2	shot(s)	Absolut vodka
4	shot(s)	Cranberry juice
2	shot(s)	Freshly squeezed grapefruit juice

Origin: Thought to have originated in New York City and popularised during the mid 90s by Absolut.
Comment: Few bartenders shake this simple drink, instead simply pouring ingredients into the glass.

SHOWBIZ UPDATED

Glass: Martini
Garnish: Blackcurrants
Method: Shake all ingredients with ice and fine strain into chilled glass.

1³/₄	shot(s)	Absolut vodka
1	shot(s)	Sisca crème de cassis
1³/₄	shot(s)	Freshly squeezed grapefruit juice

Comment: Sweet cassis soured with grapefruit and fortified with vodka.

SOUR APPLE MARTINI #1 (POPULAR US VERSION) NEW

Glass: Martini
Garnish: Cherry in glass
Method: Shake all ingredients with ice and fine strain into chilled glass.

2	shot(s)	Absolut vodka
1¹/₂	shot(s)	Sourz Sour Apple liqueur
¹/₄	shot(s)	Rose's lime cordial

Variant: Toffee Apple Martini, Apple & Melon Martini and other Apple Martinis.
Comment: A hugely popular drink across North America. Some bars add some sour mix in place of Rose's, others add a dash of fresh lime and sugar.

STRAWBERRY MARTINI NEW

Glass: Martini
Garnish: Strawberry on rim
Method: Muddle strawberries in base of shaker. Add other ingredients, shake with ice and fine strain into chilled glass.

5	fresh	Hulled strawberries
2¹/₂	shot(s)	Absolut vodka
¹/₂	shot(s)	Sugar (gomme) syrup
2	pinch	Black pepper

Origin: Created by yours truly in 2004.
Comment: Rich strawberries fortified with vodka and a hint of pepper spice.

STRAWBERRY 'N' BALSAMIC MARTINI UPDATED

Glass: Martini
Garnish: Strawberry on rim
Method: Muddle strawberries in base of shaker. Add other ingredients, shake with ice and fine strain into chilled glass.

5	fresh	Hulled strawberries
2¹/₂	shot(s)	Absolut vodka
¹/₈	shot(s)	Balsamic vinegar
¹/₂	shot(s)	Sugar (gomme) syrup

Origin: My version of a drink that became popular in London in 2002 and I believe originated in Che.
Comment: The balsamic adds a little extra interest to the fortified strawberries.

SUNSTROKE UPDATED

Glass: Martini
Garnish: Orange zest twist (round)
Method: Shake all ingredients with ice and fine strain into chilled glass.

1	shot(s)	Absolut vodka
1	shot(s)	Cointreau / triple sec
2³/₄	shot(s)	Freshly squeezed pink grapefruit juice

Comment: Fresh, fruity and balanced. One to sip in the shade.

TAWNY-TINI NEW

Glass: Martini
Garnish: Orange zest twist
Method: Shake all ingredients with ice and fine strain into chilled glass.

2	shot(s)	Absolut vodka
2	shot(s)	Warre's Otima Tawny Port
¹/₄	shot(s)	Maple syrup

Comment: Dry yet rich. Port combines wonderfully with the maple syrup and is further fortified by the grainy vodka.

TURKISH COFFEE MARTINI

Glass: Martini
Garnish: Float three coffee beans
Method: Break away outer shells of cardamom pods and muddle seeds in base of shaker. Add other ingredients, shake with ice and fine strain into glass.

10	pods	Green cardamom
2	shot(s)	Absolut vodka
2	shot(s)	Espresso coffee (cold)
1/2	shot(s)	Sugar (gomme) syrup

Origin: I created this drink in 2003.
Comment: Coffee is often made with cardamom in Arab countries. This drink harnesses the aromatic, eucalyptus, citrus flavour of cardamom coffee and adds a little vodka zing.

TWINKLE

Glass: Martini
Garnish: Lemon zest twist
Method: Shake first two ingredients with ice and fine strain into chilled glass. Top up with Prosecco (or Champagne).

3	shot(s)	Absolut vodka
3/4	shot(s)	Elderflower cordial
Top up with		Prosecco (or Piper-Heidsieck brut Champagne)

Origin: Created in 2002 by Tony Conigliaro at Lonsdale House, London, England.
Comment: It's hard to believe this floral, dry, golden tipple contains three whole shots of vodka.

VODKA COLLINS

Glass: Collins
Method: Shake first three ingredients with ice and strain into ice-filled glass. Top up with soda.

2	shot(s)	Absolut vodka
1	shot(s)	Freshly squeezed lemon juice
1/2	shot(s)	Sugar (gomme) syrup
Top up with		Soda water (club soda)

AKA: Joe Collins
Comment: Tom Collins with vodka.

VODKA SOUR

Glass: Snifter
Garnish: Lemon wheel & maraschino cherry on stick
Method: Shake all ingredients with ice and strain into ice-filled glass.

2	shot(s)	Absolut vodka
1	shot(s)	Freshly squeezed lemon juice
1/2	shot(s)	Sugar (gomme) syrup
4	dashes	Angostura aromatic bitters
1/2	fresh	Egg white

Comment: A great drink balancing sweet and sour.

VODKATINI

Glass: Martini
Garnish: Lemon zest twist / olives
Method: Stir vermouth with ice in a mixing glass and strain to discard excess vermouth, leaving only a coating on the ice. Pour vodka into mixing glass containing coated ice, stir and strain.

| 1/2 | shot(s) | Cinzano Extra Dry vermouth |
| 2 1/2 | shot(s) | Absolut vodka |

Variant: Various flavours may be steeped in the vodka such as cardamom, fennel, ginger, lavender, mint and star anise.
Comment: Great with infused vodka.

WASABI MARTINI NEW

Glass: Martini
Garnish: Float strips of yaki nori seaweed.
Method: Squeeze a pea-sized quantity of wasabi paste onto a barspoon and stir into vodka until dissolved. Add other ingredients, shake with ice and fine strain into chilled glass.

2	shot(s)	Absolut vodka
1	pea	Wasabi paste
3/4	shot(s)	Freshly squeezed lemon juice
1/2	shot(s)	Sugar (gomme) syrup

Origin: Created in 2004 by Philippe Guidi at Morton's, London, England.
Comment: Wonderfully balanced with spicy heat and a zesty finish.

WATERMELON MARTINI

Glass: Martini
Garnish: Watermelon wedge on rim
Method: Muddle watermelon in base of shaker. Add other ingredients, shake with ice and fine strain into chilled glass.

1 1/2	cupfuls	Diced ripe watermelon
2	shot(s)	Absolut vodka
1/2	shot(s)	Sugar (gomme) syrup

Comment: So fruity, you can almost convince yourself this is a health drink! Simple yet beautiful.

WHITE RUSSIAN UPDATED

Glass: Old-fashioned
Garnish: Dust with grated nutmeg
Method: Shake all ingredients with ice and strain into ice-filled glass.

1 1/2	shot(s)	Absolut vodka
1/2	shot(s)	Kahlúa coffee liqueur
3/4	shot(s)	Double (heavy) cream
3/4	shot(s)	Milk

Variant: Shake and strain vodka and coffee liqueur, then float cream.
Comment: A Black Russian smoothed with cream.

ABSOLUT CITRON® VODKA

Absolut had long established itself as the original premium fashionable vodka when Absolut Citron was launched. It was an immediate hit, particularly in New York City where it was widely used in the popular Cosmopolitan cocktail. Absolut Citron is of course made using Absolut vodka, every drop of which originates from one source - Åhus, Sweden. Absolut is distilled not once, twice or ten times, but continuously. This is flavoured with extracts of mandarin, orange, lemon, lime and grapefruit.

Absolut Citron has a clean taste of freshly squeezed lemon juice with hints of lemon zest and lemon meringue. Underlying this is the wheatiness of pure grain vodka and a taste reminiscent of Schweppes Bitter Lemon. 40% alc./vol. (80°proof)

Web: www.absolut.com **Producer:** Swedish Wine & Spirits Corporation, Stockholm, Sweden.
UK distributor: Maxxium UK Ltd, Stirling. **Tel:** 01786 430 500.
Email: enquiries@maxxium.com

BASIL BEAUTY

Glass: Martini
Garnish: Pineapple wedge on rim
Method: Lightly muddle basil in base of shaker. Cut passion fruit in half and scoop contents into shaker. Add other ingredients, shake with ice and fine strain into chilled glass.

4	fresh	Basil leaves
1	whole	Passion fruit
2	shot(s)	Absolut Citron vodka
2	shot(s)	Pressed pineapple juice
¼	shot(s)	Freshly squeezed lime juice
½	shot(s)	Coconut syrup

Origin: Created in 2003 by Wayne Collins for Maxxium UK.
Comment: Pineapple, passion fruit, hints of lime, basil and coconut all laced with citrus vodka.

COLLECTION MARTINI

Glass: Martini
Garnish: Lime wedge
Method: Vigorously shake all ingredients with ice and strain into glass.

¾	shot(s)	Absolut vodka
¾	shot(s)	Absolut Citron vodka
¾	shot(s)	Bénédictine D.O.M liqueur
¾	shot(s)	Bols blackberry liqueur (crème de mûre)
½	shot(s)	Freshly squeezed lime juice

Origin: Originally created by Matthew Randall whilst at The Collection, London, England.
Comment: Honey, spice and vodka enhanced by blackberries. Very alcoholic edge.

COSMOPOLITAN #1

Glass: Martini
Garnish: Flamed orange zest twist
Method: Shake all ingredients with ice and fine strain into chilled glass.

1½	shot(s)	Absolut Citron vodka
1	shot(s)	Cointreau / triple sec
1¼	shot(s)	Cranberry juice
¼	shot(s)	Freshly squeezed lime juice
3	dashes	Fee Brothers orange bitters
½	spoon	Rose's lime cordial

AKA: Stealth Martini
Origin: The Cosmopolitan appeared sometime in the 1980s - exactly where or who first created it is unknown.

LEMON MARTINI

Glass: Martini
Garnish: Orange twist dropped into drink
Method: Shake ingredients with ice and strain into glass.

1½	shot(s)	Absolut Citron vodka
1	shot(s)	Freshly squeezed lemon juice
¼	shot(s)	Sugar (gomme) syrup
¼	shot(s)	Cointreau / triple sec
½	spoon	Fee Brothers orange bitters

Origin: Created by Dick Bradsell at Fred's, London, England, in the late 80s.
Comment: Orange undertones add citrus depth to the lemon explosion.

LEMONGRAD

Glass: Collins
Garnish: Lemon wedge squeezed over drink
Method: Pour all ingredients into ice-filled glass and lightly stir.

2	shot(s)	Absolut Citron vodka
1	shot(s)	Belvoir elderflower cordial
1/2	shot(s)	Freshly squeezed lemon juice
Top up with		Tonic water

Origin: Created in 2002 by Alex Kammerling, London, England.
Comment: A great summer afternoon drink. Fresh lemon with elderflower and quinine.

LENINADE

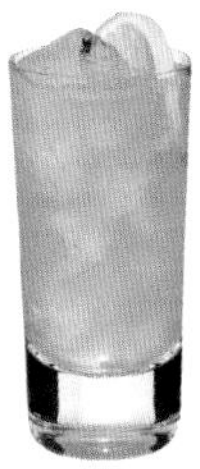

Glass: Collins
Garnish: Orange wheel dropped into drink
Method: Shake first four ingredients with ice and strain into ice-filled glass. Top up with soda water.

1½	shot(s)	Absolut Citron vodka
1	shot(s)	Freshly squeezed lemon juice
¼	shot(s)	Sugar (gomme) syrup
¼	shot(s)	Cointreau / triple sec
Top up with		Soda water

Origin: Created by Dick Bradsell at Fred's, London, England, in the late 80s.
Comment: Orange undertones add citrus depth to the lemon explosion.

MANGO MARTINI NEW

Glass: Martini
Garnish: Dried mango on stick
Method: Shake all ingredients with ice and fine strain into chilled glass.

| 2 | shot(s) | Sweetened mango purée |
| 2½ | shot(s) | Absolut Citron vodka |

Origin: Formula by yours truly in 2004.
Comment: This drink doesn't work nearly so well with plain vodka – if citrus vodka is not available, try using gin.

ROYAL COSMOPOLITAN NEW

Glass: Martini
Garnish: Flamed orange zest twist
Method: Shake first four ingredients with ice and fine strain into chilled glass. Top up with Champagne.

1	shot(s)	Absolut Citron vodka
1/2	shot(s)	Cointreau / triple sec
1	shot(s)	Cranberry juice
¼	shot(s)	Freshly squeezed lime juice
Top up with		Piper-Heidsieck Brut Champagne

Origin: Created in 2003 by Wayne Collins for Maxxium UK.
Comment: The classic Cosmopolitan with a layer of fizz on top adding a biscuity complexity. Sex And The City meets Ab Fab.

RUBY MARTINI

Glass: Martini
Garnish: Lemon wedge on rim
Method: Shake all ingredients with ice and fine strain into chilled glass.

1½	shot(s)	Absolut Citron vodka
1	shot(s)	Cointreau / triple sec
2	shot(s)	Squeezed pink grapefruit juice
¼	shot(s)	Sugar (gomme) syrup

Origin: Several appearances in episodes of the hit US TV series, Sex And The City, helped this drink become fashionable in 2002, particularly in New York City. It is thought to have originated at the Wave restaurant in Chicago's W Hotel.
Comment: A sour, citrus-led derivation of the Cosmopolitan.

SATURN MARTINI UPDATED

Glass: Martini
Garnish: Grapes on stick
Method: Muddle grapes in base of shaker. Add other ingredients, shake with ice and fine strain into chilled glass.

7	fresh	Seedless white grapes
1½	shot(s)	Absolut Citron vodka
2	shot(s)	Runny honey
1½	shot(s)	Unoaked Chardonnay / Sauvignon Blanc

Origin: Created in 2001 by Tony Conigliaro at Isola, Knightsbridge, London, England.
Comment: Delicate, beautifully balanced and subtly flavoured.

WHITE COSMO NEW

Glass: Martini
Garnish: Orange zest twist
Method: Shake all ingredients with ice and fine strain into chilled glass.

2	shot(s)	Absolut Citron vodka
¾	shot(s)	Cointreau / triple sec
1¼	shot(s)	White cranberry & grape juice
¼	shot(s)	Freshly squeezed lime juice

AKA: Cosmo Blanco
Origin: Emerged during 2002 in New York City.
Comment: Just what it says on the tin.

ZAKUSKI MARTINI

Glass: Martini
Garnish: Cucumber peel
Method: Muddle cucumber in base of shaker. Add other ingredients, shake with ice and fine strain into glass.

1	inch	Peeled cucumber (chopped)
2	shot(s)	Absolut Citron vodka
1/2	shot(s)	Freshly squeezed lemon juice
1/3	shot(s)	Sugar (gomme) syrup
1/2	shot(s)	Cointreau / triple sec

Origin: Created in 2002 by Alex Kammerling, London, England.
Comment: Appropriately named after the Russian snack.

ABSOLUT KURANT® VODKA

Absolut Kurant comes in the familiar Absolut bottle which artists from Warhol onwards have made iconic. Only the purple livery distinguishes it from the rest of the range. It is of course based on Swedish Absolut vodka and is flavoured with natural extracts of black-currant. Blackcurrant, a distant cousin of the grape, is a fragrant dark berry which grows on shrubs that grow up to six feet high.

Absolut Kurant has a distinct character of blackcurrant. A hint of tartness and sweetness is added to the wheaty vodka. 40% alc./vol. (80°proof)

Web: www.absolut.com
Producer: Swedish Wine & Spirits Corporation, Stockholm, Sweden.
UK distributor: Maxxium UK Ltd, Stirling.
Tel: 01786 430 500.
Email: enquiries@maxxium.com

BERRY NICE NEW

Glass: Collins
Garnish: Blackberries
Method: Muddle blackberries in base of shaker. Add next three ingredients, shake with ice and strain into ice-filled glass. Top up with ginger beer.

9	fresh	Blackberries
2	shot(s)	Absolut Kurant vodka
1/4	shot(s)	Chambord black raspberry liqueur
1/2	shot(s)	Freshly squeezed lemon juice
Top up with		Jamaican ginger beer

Origin: Adapted from a drink created in 2001 in the UK's The Living Room chain of bars.
Comment: Rich blackberry flavour with a strong ginger finish.

CRIMSON TIDE NEW

Glass: Old-fashioned
Garnish: Raspberries
Method: Muddle raspberries in base of shaker. Add other ingredients, shake with ice and strain into glass filled with crushed ice.

7	fresh	Raspberries
1 1/4	shot(s)	Absolut Kurant vodka
1	shot(s)	Frangelico hazelnut liqueur
1/2	shot(s)	Chambord black raspberry liqueur
1/4	shot(s)	Freshly squeezed lime juice

Comment: A medium-sweet tidal wave of flavours.

DOUBLE VISION UPDATED

Glass: Martini
Garnish: Blackcurrants on stick
Method: Shake all ingredients with ice and fine strain into chilled glass.

1	shot(s)	Absolut Citron vodka
1	shot(s)	Absolut Kurant vodka
1	shot(s)	Pressed apple juice
1	shot(s)	Freshly squeezed lime juice
1/2	shot(s)	Sugar (gomme) syrup
4	dashes	Angostura aromatic bitters

Comment: Citrus fresh with strong hints of apple and red berries.

FRUIT & NUT CHOCOLATE MARTINI

Glass: Martini
Garnish: Crumbled Cadbury's Flake bar
Method: Shake all ingredients with ice and fine strain into chilled glass.

1	shot(s)	Absolut Kurant vodka
1/2	shot(s)	Frangelico hazelnut liqueur
1/2	shot(s)	Bols white crème de cacao
1/2	shot(s)	Chambord black raspberry liqueur
1/2	shot(s)	Baileys Irish Cream liqueur
3/4	shot(s)	Double (heavy) cream
3/4	shot(s)	Milk

Comment: Naughty but nice – one for confec-tionery lovers.

KURANT AFFAIR

Glass: Collins
Method: Shake all ingredients with ice and strain into ice-filled glass.

1½	shot(s)	Absolut Kurant vodka
1½	shot(s)	Absolut Citron vodka
5	shot(s)	Freshly pressed apple juice

Comment: Berry vodka and apple juice mask the citrus vodka's flavour in this tall, refreshing summery drink.

METROPOLITAN

Glass: Martini
Garnish: Flamed orange twist
Method: Shake all ingredients with ice and fine strain into chilled glass.

2	shot(s)	Absolut Kurant vodka
½	shot(s)	Cointreau / triple sec
1	shot(s)	Cranberry juice
½	shot(s)	Freshly squeezed lime juice
½	shot(s)	Rose's lime cordial

Origin: Created in 1993 by Chuck Coggins at Marion's Continental Restaurant & Lounge, New York City.
Comment: A Cosmo with more than a hint of blackcurrant.

NUTS & BERRIES NEW

Glass: Martini
Garnish: Float raspberry and almond flake
Method: Stir all ingredients with ice and strain into chilled glass.

1	shot(s)	Wyborowa almond vodka
1	shot(s)	Absolut Kurant vodka
¼	shot(s)	Frangelico hazelnut liqueur
¼	shot(s)	Chambord black raspberry liqueur
1	shot(s)	7-Up

Origin: Created by yours truly in 2004.
Comment: The inclusion of a carbonate (7-Up) may annoy some classical bartenders but it adds flavour, sweetness and dilution.

PALE RIDER

Glass: Collins
Method: Shake ingredients with ice and strain into ice-filled glass.

2	shot(s)	Absolut Kurant vodka
½	shot(s)	Teichenné peach schnapps liqueur
2	shot(s)	Cranberry juice
1	shot(s)	Pressed pineapple juice
1	shot(s)	Freshly squeezed lime juice
¾	shot(s)	Sugar (gomme) syrup

Origin: Created in 1997 by Wayne Collins at Navajo Joe, London, England.
Comment: A rollercoaster of flavours with a sweet fruity finish.

SKI BREEZE

Glass: Collins
Method: Pour ingredients into ice-filled glass and stir.

2	shot(s)	Absolut Kurant vodka
3	shot(s)	Pressed apple juice
3	shot(s)	Ginger ale

Comment: Simple, understated and delicious.

SWEET LOUISE

Glass: Martini
Garnish: Blackberry
Method: Shake ingredients with ice and strain into glass.

1	shot(s)	Chambord black raspberry liqueur
1	shot(s)	Absolut Kurant vodka
1	shot(s)	Disaronno Originale amaretto
1	shot(s)	Passion fruit juice
¼	shot(s)	Grenadine syrup
¾	shot(s)	Freshly squeezed lime juice.

Origin: Monte's Club, London.
Comment: Lots of contrasting flavours work very well together.

TRIFLE MARTINI

Glass: Martini
Garnish: Hundreds & thousands
Method: Shake ingredients with ice and strain into glass.

2	shot(s)	Absolut Kurant vodka
½	shot(s)	Chambord black raspberry liqueur
2	shot(s)	Drambuie Cream liqueur

Origin: Created by Ian Baldwin at GE Club, London, England.
Comment: A cocktail that tastes like its namesake.

VENUS MARTINI

Glass: Martini
Garnish: Raspberry in drink
Method: Muddle raspberries in base of shaker. Add other ingredients, shake with ice and fine strain into a chilled glass.

7	fresh	Raspberries
2	shot(s)	Plymouth gin
1	shot(s)	Cointreau / triple sec
¼	shot(s)	Sugar (gomme) syrup
4	dashes	Peychaud's aromatic bitters (optional)

Comment: Raspberry with hints of bitter orange and gin – surprisingly dry.

ABSOLUT MANDRIN® VODKA

Absolut Mandrin is easily recognisable due to its clever punt, painted orange to mimic the fruit. Amazingly the first 100,000 bottles produced had to be hand painted. If you have one unopened, keep it – they are collector's pieces.

First launched in the US in July 2000, Absolut Mandrin is flavoured with mandarin and orange extracts. In keeping with all Absolut vodkas only natural ingredients are used.

Lightly sharp with hints of mandarin, orange squash, rich orange liqueur and a smidgen of aniseed. Perfumed orange squash finish. 40% alc./vol. (80°proof)

Web: www.absolut.com
Producer: Swedish Wine & Spirits Corporation, Stockholm, Sweden.
UK distributor: Maxxium UK Ltd, Stirling. **Tel:** 01786 430 500.
Email: enquiries@maxxium.com

BLUE MONDAY

Glass: Martini
Garnish: Orange zest twist
Method: Shake all ingredients with ice and fine strain into chilled glass.

1	shot(s)	Absolut Mandrin vodka
¼	shot(s)	Bols Blue Curaçao
2	shot(s)	Freshly squeezed lemon juice
1	shot(s)	Sugar (gomme) syrup

Origin: Created in 2003 by yours truly.
Comment: A citrus fresh Martini.

BUG JUICE

Glass: Collins
Garnish: Orange wheel in drink
Method: Shake all ingredients with ice and fine strain into chilled glass.

2	shot(s)	Absolut Mandrin vodka
1	shot(s)	Passoã passion fruit liqueur
3½	shot(s)	Pressed pineapple juice

Origin: Created in 2003 by yours truly.
Comment: Fortunately this drink is named after its orange colour rather than its orange, passion and pineapple taste.

CHILL-OUT MARTINI

Glass: Martini
Garnish: Pineapple wedge on rim
Method: Shake all ingredients with ice and fine strain into chilled glass.

1½	shot(s)	Absolut Mandrin vodka
1½	shot(s)	Malibu coconut rum
1½	shot(s)	Baileys Irish Cream liqueur
1½	shot(s)	Freshly squeezed orange juice

Comment: Smooth, creamy sweet orange and surprisingly strong.

CREAMSICLE

Glass: Martini
Garnish: Orange zest twist
Method: Shake all ingredients with ice and fine strain into chilled glass.

1½	shot(s)	Absolut Mandrin vodka
1	shot(s)	Grand Marnier liqueur
¾	shot(s)	Double cream
¾	shot(s)	Milk
¼	shot(s)	Sugar (gomme) syrup

Origin: Adapted from a cocktail discovered in 1999 at Lot 61, New York City.
Comment: A milky orange number with surprisingly pleasant taste.

EDEN NEW

Glass: Collins
Garnish: Orange zest string
Method: Shake first three ingredients with ice and strain into ice-filled glass. Top up with tonic water.

2	shot(s)	Absolut Mandrin vodka
¹/₂	shot(s)	Elderflower cordial
1¹/₂	shot(s)	Pressed apple juice
Top up with		Tonic water

Origin: Created in 2003 by Sylvain Solignac at Circus Bar, London, England.
Comment: Orange zest predominates in this long refreshing drink.

M.G.F. NEW

Glass: Martini
Garnish: Orange zest twist
Method: Shake all ingredients with ice and fine strain into chilled glass.

1	shot(s)	Absolut Mandrin vodka
1	shot(s)	Absolut Citron vodka
1	shot(s)	Pressed pink grapefruit juice
1	shot(s)	Freshly squeezed lemon juice
¹/₂	shot(s)	Sugar (gomme) syrup

Origin: Discovered in 2003 at Claridge's Bar, London, England.
Comment: One for lovers of short, sharp drinks.

ORANGE MOJITO

Glass: Collins
Garnish: Mint sprig
Method: Lightly muddle mint in base of glass. Add other ingredients and half fill glass with crushed ice. Churn (stir) with bar spoon. Fill with crushed ice and churn some more. Top up with soda, stir and serve with straws.

8	fresh	Mint leaves
1¹/₂	shot(s)	Absolut Mandrin vodka
¹/₂	shot(s)	Mandarine Napoléon liqueur
¹/₂	shot(s)	Havana Club light rum
1	shot(s)	Freshly squeezed lime juice
¹/₂	shot(s)	Sugar (gomme) syrup
Top up with		Soda water (club soda)

Origin: Created in 2001 by Jamie MacDonald while working in Sydney, Australia.
Comment: Mint and orange combine to make a wonderfully fresh drink.

ORANJINIHA

Glass: Collins
Garnish: Orange slice in glass
Method: Shake all ingredients with ice and strain into a glass filled with crushed ice.

2	shots	Absolut Mandrin vodka
3	shot(s)	Freshly squeezed orange juice
1	shot(s)	Freshly squeezed lemon juice
1	shot(s)	Sugar (gomme) syrup

Origin: Created in 2002 by Alex Kammerling, London, England.
Comment: This tall, richly flavoured orange drink makes a simple Screwdriver taste very sad.

QUADRUPLE ORANGE MARTINI

Glass: Martini
Garnish: Orange zest twist
Method: Shake all ingredients with ice and strain into glass.

¹/₂	shot(s)	Absolut Mandrin vodka
1	shot(s)	Grand Marnier liqueur
2	shot(s)	Freshly squeezed orange juice
¹/₄	shot(s)	Campari
¹/₂	fresh	Egg white

Origin: In 1998 I created a Triple Orange Martini using plain vodka. I renamed it with the advent of orange flavoured vodka, which peps up the orange notes.
Comment: Bags of orange flavour, toned down by Campari and softened by egg white.

SATSUMA MARTINI

Glass: Martini
Garnish: Orange zest twist
Method: Shake all ingredients with ice and fine strain into chilled glass.

1¹/₂	shot(s)	Absolut Mandrin vodka
³/₄	shot(s)	Grand Marnier liqueur
2	shot(s)	Pressed apple juice
¹/₂	spoon	Fee Brothers Orange bitters

Origin: Discovered in 2002 at the Fifth Floor Bar, London, England.
Comment: Tastes like its namesake – hard to believe the dominant ingredient is apple.

SOUTH CHINA BREEZE

Glass: Collins
Garnish: Half orange wheel
Method: Shake all ingredients with ice and strain into ice-filled glass.

2	shot(s)	Absolut Mandrin vodka
3	shot(s)	Freshly squeezed grapefruit juice
1¹/₂	shot(s)	Lychee syrup from tinned fruit
4	dashes	Angostura aromatic bitters

Comment: Orange and grapefruit with an oriental influence by way of lychee.

URBAN OASIS

Glass: Martini
Garnish: Orange zest twist
Method: Shake all ingredients with ice and fine strain into chilled glass.

1¹/₂	shot(s)	Absolut Mandrin vodka
¹/₂	shot(s)	Absolut Kurant vodka
¹/₄	shot(s)	Chambord black raspberry liqueur
2	shot(s)	Pressed pineapple juice

Origin: Discovered in 2003 at Paramount Hotel, New York City.
Comment: Alcoholic orange sherbet – how bad is that?

ABSOLUT RASPBERRI®

Perhaps more than any other drinks brand, Absolut is famous for its packaging. The red and grey Raspberri bottle does not disappoint. According to its makers, "The strong, true shade of red refers to the passionate intensity and ripeness of the raspberry taste," while "The grey underlines its sophisticated, grown-up appeal: as it is made from pure raspberries and does not contain any added sweeteners."

This raspberry-flavoured line extension of the original premium vodka lives up to its distinguished older siblings and looks good on the back bar.

Absolut Raspberri has a clean, intensely rich flavour of ripe raspberries, so strong that its perfumed aroma jumps out of the bottle when you open it.

Web: www.absolut.com
Producer: Swedish Wine & Spirits Corporation, Stockholm, Sweden.
UK distributor: Maxxium UK Ltd, Stirling. Tel: 01786 430 500.
Email: enquiries@maxxium.com

AMARO DOLCE

Glass: Rocks
Method: Muddle lime in glass to release the juices and oils in the skin of the lime. Pour rest of ingredients into glass, add crushed ice and stir. Serve with a straw.

1	whole	Lime cut into eighths
1	shot(s)	Absolut Raspberri Vodka
1	shot(s)	Campari
1	shot(s)	Freshly squeezed lime juice
3/4	shot(s)	Sugar (gomme) syrup

Origin: Created in 2002 by Alex Kammerling, London, England.
Comment: Not to everyone's taste, this Caipirinha-like drink features that distinctive bitter Campari edge.

BLUE RASPBERRY MARTINI

Glass: Martini
Garnish: Raspberries
Method: Shake all ingredients with ice and fine strain into chilled glass.

2	shot(s)	Absolut Raspberri vodka
1/2	shot(s)	Bols Blue curaçao
3/4	shot(s)	Freshly squeezed lime juice
1/2	shot(s)	Sugar (gomme) syrup
3/4	shot(s)	Chilled water

Origin: Discovered in 2002 at The Sky Bar, Sunset Boulevard, Los Angeles, USA, where sour mix is used instead of fresh lime juice and sugar.
Comment: As turquoise-blue drinks go this one is surprisingly adult and tasty.

CASCADE MARTINI

Glass: Martini
Garnish: Raspberries on stick
Method: Shake all ingredients with ice and fine strain into chilled glass.

8	fresh	Raspberries
1 1/2	shot(s)	Absolut Raspberri vodka
2 1/2	shot(s)	Cranberry juice
1/2	shot(s)	Freshly squeezed lemon juice
1/4	shot(s)	Chambord black raspberry liqueur
1/4	shot(s)	Vanilla syrup

Comment: Rich raspberry with hints of citrus and vanilla.

ESQUIRE MARTINI UPDATED

Glass: Martini
Garnish: Blackberry
Method: Stir all ingredients with ice and strain into glass

1 1/2	shot(s)	Absolut vodka
3/4	shot(s)	Absolut Raspberri vodka
3/4	shot(s)	Parfait Amour

Origin: Created by Dick Bradsell for Esquire Magazine.
Comment: One for hardened Martini drinkers.

FRENCH MARTINI #2

Glass: Martini
Garnish: Three raspberries
Method: Shake all ingredients with ice and fine strain into chilled glass.

2 1/2	shot(s)	Absolut Raspberri vodka
2	shot(s)	Pressed pineapple juice
1/4	shot(s)	Chambord black raspberry liqueur

Comment: This yellow rather than pink French Martini is drier than the more common version also listed in this guide.

KOI YELLOW

Glass: Martini
Garnish: Float rose petal
Method: Shake all ingredients with ice and fine strain into chilled glass.

2	shot(s)	Absolut Raspberri vodka
1/2	shot(s)	Cointreau / triple sec
1	shot(s)	Freshly squeezed lemon juice
1/2	shot(s)	Sugar (gomme) syrup

Origin: The signature drink at Koi Restaurant, Los Angeles, USA.
Comment: Sherbet / raspberry Martini with a sweet and citrus sour finish.

RASPBERRY MOCHA'TINI

Glass: Martini
Garnish: Three raspberries on stick
Method: Shake all ingredients with ice and fine strain into chilled glass.

1	shot(s)	Espresso coffee (cold)
1 1/2	shot(s)	Absolut Raspberri vodka
3/4	shot(s)	Bols Brown crème de cacao
3/4	shot(s)	Bols Raspberry (framboise) liqueur

Origin: Discovered in 2002 at Lot 61, New York City.
Comment: Sweet chocolate and raspberry tempered by dry coffee and vodka.

RASPBERRY SAKE'TINI

Glass: Martini
Garnish: Three fresh raspberries.
Method: Shake all ingredients with ice and fine strain into chilled glass.

1 1/2	shot(s)	Sake
1 1/2	shot(s)	Absolut Raspberri vodka
1/2	shot(s)	Sisca Crème de cassis
2	shot(s)	Pressed pineapple juice

Comment: Fruity with wafts of sake – not dissimilar to a French Martini in flavour.

THE RED ARMY

Glass: Rocks
Garnish: Two raspberries
Method: Muddle raspberries in base of shaker. Add other ingredients, shake with ice and strain into a glass filled with crushed ice.

12	fresh	Raspberries
2	shot(s)	Absolut Raspberri vodka
1	shot(s)	Freshly squeezed lime juice
3/4	shot(s)	Sugar (gomme) syrup
1/2	shot(s)	Cointreau / triple sec
1/2	shot(s)	Bols Raspberry (framboise) liqueur

Origin: Created in 2002 by Alex Kammerling, London, England.
Comment: Very, very fruity.

STRASBERI SLING

Glass: Sling
Garnish: Mint sprig
Method: Shake all the ingredients with ice and strain into a glass.

1 1/2	shot(s)	Absolut Raspberri vodka
1	shot(s)	Pimm's no.1
1/2	shot(s)	Sugar (gomme) syrup
1	shot(s)	Freshly squeezed lime juice
4	shot(s)	Pressed apple juice

Origin: Created in 2002 by Alex Kammerling, London, England.
Comment: Raspberry and apple combine beautifully in this refreshing drink with its clean citrus tang.

TARTINI

Glass: Martini
Garnish: Raspberry
Method: Muddle raspberries in base of shaker. Add other ingredients, shake with ice and strain into ice-filled glass.

12	fresh	Raspberries
2	shot(s)	Absolut Raspberri vodka
1/2	shot(s)	Chambord black raspberry liqueur
1 1/2	shot(s)	Cranberry juice

Origin: Adapted from a cocktail I found at Soho Grand, New York City.
Comment: Rich raspberry flavour, well balanced with bite.

VERDI MARTINI

Glass: Martini
Garnish: Pineapple wedge on rim
Method: Shake all ingredients with ice and fine strain into chilled glass.

1 3/4	shot(s)	Absolut Raspberri vodka
1/2	shot(s)	Midori melon liqueur
1/2	shot(s)	Teichenné peach schnapps liqueur
1	shot(s)	Pressed pineapple juice
1	shot(s)	Pressed apple juice
1/4	shot(s)	Freshly squeezed lime juice

Origin: Adapted from a drink discovered in 2002 at the Fifth Floor Bar, London, England.
Comment: A melange of fruits combine in a gluggable short drink.

ABSOLUT VANILIA®

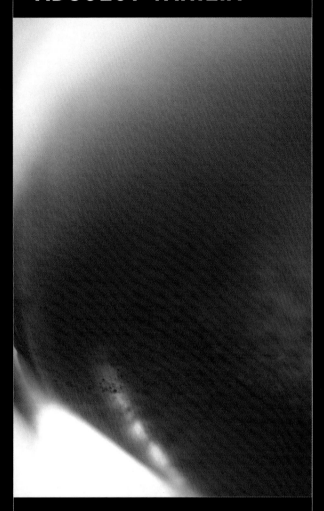

Absolut Vanilia was launched in the USA, Absolut's main market, early in 2003.

The Swedes have something of a reputation for design and Absolut's subtle variations on their iconic bottle seem to get better with every release. With its silver-white almost space-like bottle, Absolut Vanilia does not disappoint and presents a striking image on any back bar.

Absolut Vanilia is flavoured with vanilla from Madagascar and is much less sweet and more complex than other vanilla vodkas, with no added sugar. Pleasing peppery vodka notes precede hints of butterscotch, white and dark chocolate. Absolut Vanilia adds a wonderful vanilla, almost confectionery flavour to cocktails.

Web: www.absolut.com **Producer:** Swedish Wine & Spirits Corporation, Stockholm, Sweden.
UK distributor: Maxxium UK Ltd, Stirling. **Tel:** 01786 430 500.
Email: enquiries@maxxium.com

EASTER MARTINI

Glass: Martini
Garnish: Crumbled Flake bar
Method: Break away outer shells of cardamom pods and muddle inner seeds in base of shaker. Add other ingredients, shake with ice and fine strain into chilled glass.

4	pods	Green cardamom
2	shot(s)	Absolut Vanilia vodka
1	shot(s)	Bols white crème de cacao
¼	shot(s)	Sugar (gomme) syrup
½	shot(s)	Chilled water
½	fresh	Egg white

Origin: Created in 2003 by Simon King at MJU Bar, Millennium Hotel, London, England.
Comment: A standard Chocolate Martini with extra interest thanks to the clever use of vanilla and cardamom.

HUNK MARTINI

Glass: Martini
Garnish: Cherry in drink
Method: Shake all ingredients with ice and fine strain into chilled glass.

2	shot(s)	Absolut Vanilia vodka
1¾	shot(s)	Pressed pineapple juice
½	shot(s)	Freshly squeezed lime juice
¼	shot(s)	Sugar (gomme) syrup

Origin: The drink Carrie and co discovered in the summer of 2003. In this series the Sex And The City stars dropped Cosmopolitans in favour of Hunks – no change there then!
Comment: Pineapple and vanilla combine wonderfully.

PURR-FECT MARTINI

Glass: Martini
Garnish: Orange zest twist
Method: Stir all ingredients with ice and strain into chilled glass.

2	shot(s)	Absolut Vanilia vodka
1	shot(s)	Cinzano Extra dry vermouth
1	shot(s)	Cinzano Rosso (sweet) vermouth
4	dashes	Angostura aromatic bitters

Origin: I created this drink in 2003.
Comment: Aromatic and complex, spiced vanilla and orange.

RUSSIAN BRIDE

Glass: Martini
Garnish: Dust with chocolate powder
Method: Shake all ingredients with ice and fine strain into chilled glass.

2	shot(s)	Absolut Vanilia vodka
¾	shot(s)	Kahlúa coffee liqueur
¼	shot(s)	Bols White crème de cacao
½	shot(s)	Double (heavy) cream
½	shot(s)	Milk

Origin: Created in 2002 by Miranda Dickson Revolution Vodka Bar chain.
Comment: A little on the sweet side for some but vanilla, coffee and chocolate smoothed with cream is a tasty combination.

SNOW FALL MARTINI

Glass: Martini
Garnish: Vanilla pod
Method: Muddle vanilla pod in base of shaker. Add other ingredients, shake with ice and fine strain into chilled glass.

1/2	pod	Vanilla
2	shot(s)	Absolut Vanilia vodka
1 1/4	shot(s)	Double (heavy) cream
1 1/4	shot(s)	Milk
1/4	shot(s)	Sugar (gomme) syrup

Origin: Discovered in 2002 at Lot 61, New York.
Comment: A very light alcoholic version of a vanilla milkshake.

THRILLER FROM VANILLA UPDATED

Glass: Martini
Garnish: Half vanilla pod
Method: Muddle vanilla in base of shaker. Add other ingredients, shake with ice and fine strain into chilled glass.

1/4	pod	Vanilla
3/4	shot(s)	Absolut Vanilia vodka
3/4	shot(s)	Plymouth gin
1/2	shot(s)	Cointreau / triple sec
2	shot(s)	Freshly squeezed orange juice

Origin: Discovered in 2003 at Oporto, Leeds, England. The "Thriller in Manila" was the name given to the 1975 heavyweight fight between Muhammad Ali and Smokin' Joe Frazier.
Comment: Orange and creamy vanilla fortified with a hint of gin.

TRIANGULAR MARTINI

Glass: Martini
Garnish: Toblerone chocolate on rim
Method: Stir honey with vodka in base of shaker so as to dissolve honey. Add other ingredients, shake with ice and fine strain into chilled glass.

2	spoons	Runny honey
1 1/2	shot(s)	Absolut Vanilia vodka
1/2	shot(s)	Disaronno Originale amaretto
1 1/4	shot(s)	Bols brown crème de cacao
3/4	shot(s)	Double (heavy) cream
1/2	fresh	Egg white

Origin: Created by yours truly in 2003.
Comment: Nibble at the garnish as you sip honeyed, chocolate and almond flavoured liquid candy.

TURKISH DELIGHT

Glass: Martini
Garnish: Turkish Delight on rim
Method: Stir honey and vodka in base of shaker so as to dissolve honey. Add other ingredients' shake with ice and fine strain into chilled glass.

2	spoons	Runny honey
1	shot(s)	Absolut vodka
1	shot(s)	Absolut Vanilia vodka
1/2	shot(s)	Bols White crème de cacao
1/8	shot(s)	Rosewater
3/4	shot(s)	Chilled water
1/2	fresh	Egg white

Origin: Created by yours truly in 2003.
Comment: Rosewater, honey, chocolate and vanilla provide a distinctly Turkish Delight flavour - fortified with vodka.

VACATION UPDATED

Glass: Martini
Garnish: Pineapple wedge or orange slice on rim
Method: This drink can be finished with your choice of three different coloured and flavoured liqueurs. Shake first five ingredients with ice and fine strain into chilled glass. Then pour your choice of final ingredient into the centre of the drink. It should sink.

2	shot(s)	Absolut Vanilia vodka
1/2	shot(s)	Malibu coconut rum liqueur
1/2	shot(s)	Freshly squeezed lime juice
1	shot(s)	Pressed pineapple juice
1/4	fresh	Egg white
1/4	shot(s)	Chambord (red) or Midori (green) or Bols Blue curaçao (blue)

Origin: My adaptation (in 2003) of the signature drink at the Merc Bar, New York City, USA.
Comment: A great looking, fairly sweet cocktail with hints of vanilla, coconut and pineapple.

VANILIA SENSATION

Glass: Martini
Garnish: Float apple slice
Method: Shake all ingredients with ice and fine strain into chilled glass.

2	shot(s)	Absolut Vanilia vodka
1	shot(s)	Sourz Sour Apple liqueur
1/2	shot(s)	Cinzano Extra Dry vermouth

Origin: A drink created in 2003 and promoted by Absolut.
Comment: A pleasing vanilla twist on an apple Martini.

VANILLA'TINI

Glass: Martini
Garnish: Half vanilla pod
Method: Stir all ingredients with ice and strain into chilled glass.

2 1/2	shot(s)	Absolut Vanilia vodka
1/2	shot(s)	Frangelico hazelnut liqueur
1 1/2	shot(s)	Chilled 7-Up / lemonade

Origin: Discovered in 2003 at Paramount Hotel, New York City.
Comment: Vanilla, hazelnut and a hint of creamy citrus in an interesting medium dry Martini.

VANITINI

Glass: Martini
Garnish: Pineapple wedge on rim
Method: Shake all ingredients with ice and fine strain into chilled glass.

2	shot(s)	Absolut Vanilia vodka
2	shot(s)	Sauvignon Blanc wine
3/4	shot(s)	Sourz Pineapple liqueur
1/4	shot(s)	Bols Blackberry liqueur

Origin: Created in 2003 by yours truly.
Comment: Vanilla and pineapple are dried by the acidity of the wine, and sweetened and flavoured by blackberry liqueur.

ANGOSTURA AROMATIC BITTERS®

These famous bitters were first made in 1824 by the German Surgeon-General of a military hospital in the town of Angostura, Venezuela, to help treat stomach disorders and indigestion. In 1875, due to unrest in Venezuela, production was moved to Trinidad. It was here that the laid-back Caribbean attitude affected Angostura's packaging. One day a new batch of labels was ordered and a simple mistake led to them being too big for the bottles. The error was spotted in time but everyone thought somebody else would deal with the problem. No one did, so they simply stuck the labels on the bottles intending to fix the next batch. No one quite got round to it and the oversized label became a trademark of the brand.

One of the smallest bottles on any bar, but packed with flavour. Turkish coffee, jasmine, dried mint, fruit poached with cloves and cinnamon, cherry with orange and lemon zest – a dash of Angostura adds that little something to bring cocktails to life. 44.7% alc./vol. (89.4°proof)

Web. www.in-the-spirit.co.uth**Producer:** Angostura Ltd, Laventille, Port of Spain, Trinidad, W. Indies.
UK distributor: Paragon Vintners, Regent Gate, 21 Dartmouth Street, London, SW1H 9BP. **Tel:** 020 7887 1800

CHAMPAGNE COCKTAIL

Glass: Flute
Garnish: Orange peel twist
Method: Rub sugar cube with orange peel, then place in base of glass and soak with Angostura. Cover soaked cube with Cognac, then top up with Champagne.

1	cube	Brown sugar
3	dashes	Angostura aromatic bitters
1	shot(s)	Rémy Martin Cognac
Top up with		Piper-Heidsieck Brut Champagne

Origin: Said to have originated from a winning recipe by John Dougherty named Business Brace at the 1899 New York Cocktail competition.
Comment: A classic cocktail that gets sweeter as you reach the dissolving cube at the bottom.

CLUB COCKTAIL UPDATED

Glass: Martini
Garnish: Stemmed maraschino cherry in drink
Method: Stir all ingredients with ice and fine strain into chilled glass.

2	shot(s)	Mount Gay Eclipse golden rum
1/2	shot(s)	Cinzano Rosso (sweet) vermouth
1/2	shot(s)	Cinzano Extra Dry vermouth
1/2	shot(s)	Maraschino syrup
4	dashes	Angostura aromatic bitters
3/4	shot(s)	Chilled mineral water

Origin: David Embury once wrote, "There are as many Club Cocktails as there are clubs." I based this one on a drink created by Michael Butt in 2002 at Milk & Honey, London, England.
Comment: An aromatic, spirited, classical cocktail.

LEMON LIME & BITTERS

Glass: Collins
Garnish: Lime wedge
Method: Squeeze lime wedges and drop into glass. Add Angostura bitters and fill glass with ice. Top up with lemonade and stir. Serve with straws.

4	fresh	Lime wedges
5	dashes	Angostura aromatic bitters
Top up with		Lemonade / 7-Up

AKA: LLB
Origin: First made and very popular in Australia.
Comment: If you're unlucky enough to be the driver, this refreshing long drink is a good almost no alcohol option.

MANHATTAN PERFECT

Glass: Martini
Garnish: Twist of orange & cherry on stick
Method: Stir all ingredients with ice and strain into chilled glass.

2 1/2	shot(s)	Buffalo Trace Bourbon
1/2	shot(s)	Cinzano Rosso (sweet) vermouth
1/2	shot(s)	Cinzano Extra Dry vermouth
4	dashes	Angostura aromatic bitters

Variant: Manhattan Dry and see under Manhattan Sweet.
Comment: The Manhattan version most popularly served – medium dry.

MOSCOW MULE

Glass: Collins
Garnish: Mint sprig & lime squeeze
Method: Shake first four ingredients with ice and strain into ice-filled glass. Top up with ginger beer and stir.

2	shot(s)	Absolut vodka
1	shot(s)	Freshly squeezed lime juice
1/2	shot(s)	Sugar (gomme) syrup
3	dashes	Angostura aromatic bitters
Top up with		Ginger beer

Comment: A long, vodka based drink with spice provided by ginger beer and Angostura.

OLD FASHIONED UPDATED ●●●●○

Glass: Old-fashioned
Garnish: Orange (or lemon) twist
Method: Stir one shot of Bourbon with two ice cubes in a glass. Add sugar syrup and Angostura and two more ice cubes. Stir some more and add another two ice cubes and another shot of Bourbon. Stir lots more so as to melt ice and add more ice. The melting and stirring in of ice cubes is essential to the dilution and taste of the drink.

2 1/2	shot(s)	Buffalo Trace Bourbon
1/2	shot(s)	Sugar (gomme) syrup
3	dashes	Angostura aromatic bitters

Variation: In the USA orange segments and even a maraschino cherry may sometimes be muddled in this drink.
Variant: Brubaker Old-fashioned, Call Me Old Fashioned.
Origin: Like the Martini, the glass this cocktail is served in has taken the name of the drink.
Comment: The Old Fashioned tames Bourbon, making it smooth and remarkably easy to drink.

PINK GIN NEW ●●●●○

Glass: Martini
Garnish: Lemon zest twist
Method: Stir all ingredients with ice and strain into chilled glass.

2	shot(s)	Plymouth gin (from freezer)
2	shot(s)	Chilled mineral water
1	dash	Angostura aromatic bitters

Comment: Normally I'd advocate liberal use of Angostura bitters but this refined and subtle drink benefits from frugality.

PINK GIN & TONIC UPDATED ●●●●○

Glass: Collins
Garnish: Lime slice
Method: Pour gin and Angostura into ice-filled glass, then top up with tonic water and stir.

2	shot(s)	Plymouth gin
4	dashes	Angostura aromatic bitters
Top up with		Tonic water

Comment: Basically a G&T with an extra pep of flavour from Angostura, this has a wider appeal than the original Pink Gin.

PISCO SOUR ●●●●●

Glass: Old-fashioned
Method: Shake first four ingredients with ice and strain into glass. Apply three dashes of bitters to the frothy head of the drink.

2 1/2	shot(s)	ABA Pisco
1	shot(s)	Freshly squeezed lime juice
1	shot(s)	Sugar (gomme) syrup
1/2	fresh	Egg white
3	dashes	Angostura aromatic bitters

Origin: The national drink of both Chile and Peru.
Comment: Traditionally this drink is blended with crushed ice, but I prefer it served straight-up in an old-fashioned glass – only be sure to drink it quickly while it's cold. A sublime drink which shows off the complexity of Pisco.

PLANTERS PUNCH

Glass: Collins
Garnish: Slice of orange and mint sprig in glass.
Method: Shake all ingredients with cubed ice and strain into ice-filled glass.

1 1/2	shot(s)	Myers's Planters' Punch rum
1/2	shot(s)	Freshly squeezed lime juice
1	shot(s)	Sugar (gomme) syrup
2	shot(s)	Chilled mineral water
4	dash(es)	Angostura aromatic bitters

Origin: Invented in the late 19th century by the founder of Myers's rum, Fred L. Myers.
Comment: A drink which harnesses the rich flavours of Myers's rum.

RUM PUNCH ●●●●●

Glass: Collins
Garnish: Lime wheel and cherry
Method: Shake all ingredients with cubed ice and strain into glass filled with crushed ice.

3/4	shot(s)	Freshly squeezed lime juice (sour)
1 1/2	shot(s)	Sugar (gomme) syrup (sweet)
2 1/4	shot(s)	Wray & Nephew overproof rum (strong)
3	shot(s)	Chilled mineral water (weak)
4	dashes	Angostura aromatic bitters

Comment: The classic proportions of this drink (followed above) are 'one of sour, two of sweet, three of strong and four of weak' – referring to lime juice, sugar syrup, rum and water respectively.

WHISKEY SOUR UPDATED ●●●●○

Glass: Old-fashioned
Garnish: Cherry & lemon slice sail
Method: Shake all ingredients with ice and strain into ice-filled glass

2	shot(s)	Buffalo Trace Bourbon
3/4	shot(s)	Freshly squeezed lemon juice
1	shot(s)	Sugar (gomme) syrup
1/2	fresh	Egg white
4	dashes	Angostura aromatic bitters

Comment: This recipe follows the classic sour proportions: three quarter part of the sour ingredient (lemon juice), one part of the sweet ingredient (sugar syrup) and two parts of the strong ingredient (whiskey) (3:4:8).

APPLETON ESTATE V/X® JAMAICA RUM

Appleton Estate V/X Jamaica Rum is the flagship brand of the Appleton Estate Jamaica Rum family.

This full-bodied, medium sweet rum is a perfect example of the famous estate rums for which Appleton is renowned.

An exceptional blend of several rums of varying ages with an average age of between five and ten years, Appleton Estate V/X Jamaica rum boasts a warm golden colour, a rich aroma and flavourful taste.

Smooth and mellow, Appleton Estate V/X Jamaica Rum can be enjoyed in sophisticated rum cocktails, or blended in long drinks with your favourite mixer.

40% alc./vol. (80°proof)

Web: www.rum.co.uk
Producer: J.Wray & Nephew Ltd, Kingston, Jamaica.
UK distributor: J. Wray & Nephew (UK) Ltd, 3rd Floor, 52-54 Southwark Street, London, SE1 1UN.
Tel: 020 7378 8858
Email: info@rum.co.uk

AÑEJO HIGHBALL

Glass: Collins
Garnish: Orange slice
Method: Shake first four ingredients with ice and strain into ice-filled glass. Top up with ginger beer.

1¹/₂	shot(s)	Appleton Estate V/X aged rum
¹/₂	shot(s)	Grand Marnier Liqueur
¹/₄	shot(s)	Freshly squeezed lime juice
2	dashes	Angostura aromatic bitters
Top up with		Jamaican ginger beer

Origin: Created in 2002 by the famous New York bartender, Dale DeGroff. 'Añejo', which is the Spanish for 'old', refers to the aged rum used in the recipe.
Comment: Neither sweet nor overly alcoholic - simply tasty and refreshing.

BOSSANOVA #2

Glass: Collins
Method: Shake ingredients with ice and strain into ice-filled glass.

1¹/₂	shot(s)	Appleton Estate V/X aged rum
1¹/₂	shot(s)	Galliano liqueur
1	shot(s)	Bols apricot brandy liqueur
1¹/₂	shot(s)	Pressed pineapple juice
¹/₂	shot(s)	Freshly squeezed lemon juice
¹/₂	fresh	Egg white

Comment: Frothy with a subtle anis backgound.

CASTRO

Glass: Martini
Method: Shake ingredients with ice and strain into glass.

1¹/₂	shot(s)	Appleton Estate V/X aged rum
³/₄	shot(s)	Calvados or applejack brandy
1¹/₂	shot(s)	Freshly squeezed orange juice
³/₄	shot(s)	Freshly squeezed lime juice
³/₄	shot(s)	Rose's lime cordial
1/2	shot(s)	Sugar (gomme) syrup

Comment: Named after the Cuban dictator who holds the record for the longest presidency of any country. The bearded wonder would approve of this rum based sweet and sour cocktail.

DARK DAIQUIRI

Glass: Martini
Garnish: Lime wedge on rim
Method: Shake ingredients vigorously with ice and strain into chilled glass.

1¹/₂	shot(s)	Appleton Estate V/X aged rum
¹/₂	shot(s)	Pusser's Navy rum
¹/₂	shot(s)	Freshly squeezed lime juice
¹/₂	shot(s)	Sugar (gomme) syrup
1	shot(s)	Chilled water

Comment: The fine sweet and sour balance of a great Daiquiri with hints of molasses.

DIRTY BANANA

Glass: Collins
Garnish: Banana slice on rim
Method: Blend all ingredients with crushed ice.

1½	shot(s)	Appleton Estate V/X aged rum
1	shot(s)	Kahlúa coffee liqueur
1	shot(s)	Bols crème de banane
1	half	Peeled & chopped banana
1	shot(s)	Double (heavy) cream
1	shot(s)	Milk

Origin: This cocktail is hard to avoid when holidaying in Jamaica. It's not sophisticated, but it's very tasty.
Comment: Long, creamy and filling banana drink with a 'dirty' flavour and colour courtesy of coffee liqueur.

DOWNHILL RACER UPDATED

Glass: Martini
Garnish: Pineapple wedge on rim
Method: Shake all ingredients with ice and fine strain into chilled glass.

1¾	shot(s)	Appleton Estate V/X aged rum
¾	shot(s)	Disaronno Originale amaretto
1¾	shot(s)	Pressed pineapple juice

Comment: Aged rum sweetened, softened and flavoured with pineapple and amaretto.

GOLDEN GIRL

Glass: Martini
Garnish: Grated orange zest
Method: Shake all ingredients with ice and fine strain into chilled glass.

1¼	shot(s)	Appleton Estate V/X aged rum
1	shot(s)	Pressed pineapple juice
1	shot(s)	Warre's Otima Tawny Port
¼	shot(s)	Sugar (gomme) syrup
1	fresh	Egg

Origin: Created by Dale DeGroff, New York, USA. I've slightly increased the proportions of rum and port from Dale's original recipe.
Comment: This appropriately named velvety drink is something of a refined dessert in a glass.

GRAPEFRUIT DAIQUIRI

Glass: Martini
Garnish: Cherry
Method: Shake ingredients with ice and strain into glass.

2	shot(s)	Appleton Estate V/X aged rum
1½	shot(s)	Freshly squeezed grapefruit juice
¾	shot(s)	Sugar (gomme) syrup / passion fruit syrup

Comment: The flavours of rum and grapefruit combine perfectly – clean and fresh.

HOP TOAD

Glass: Martini
Garnish: Apricot wedge on rim
Method: Shake all ingredients with ice and fine strain into a chilled glass.

1¾	shot(s)	Appleton Estate V/X aged rum
1	shot(s)	Bols apricot brandy liqueur
1	shot(s)	Freshly squeezed lime juice
½	shot(s)	Sugar (gomme) syrup

Variant: Made with brandy this is sometimes known as a Bullfrog.
Origin: First published in Tom Bullock's Ideal Bartender, circa 1917.
Comment: Alcoholic apricot jam with a lovely twang of aged rum.

MAI TAI (ORIGINAL)

Glass: Old-fashioned
Garnish: Lime wedge (pineapple) & fresh mint
Method: Shake with ice and strain into a glass filled with crushed ice.

2	shot(s)	Appleton Estate V/X aged rum
1	shot(s)	Freshly squeezed lime juice
½	shot(s)	Grand Marnier liqueur
½	shot(s)	Orgeat (almond) syrup
¼	shot(s)	Sugar (gomme) syrup

Origin: In 1934, Victor Jules Bergeron, or Trader Vic as he became known, opened his first restaurant in Oakland, San Francisco. He served Polynesian food with a mix of Chinese, French and American dishes cooked in Chinese wood-fired ovens. As well as his distinctive food, Vic also became famous for the rum based cocktails he created, particularly the Mai Tai.
Comment: Originally Trader Vic made this drink using 17-year-old rum from Jamaica. Later, when supplies of this dwindled, he started using a combination of rums to achieve the desired flavour. Sheer demand in his chain of restaurants later necessitated the introduction of a pre-mixed Mai Tai mix. This original formula is basically a zoomed up Daiquiri – and works well.

MULATA DAIQUIRI

Glass: Martini
Garnish: Lime wedge on rim
Method: Shake all ingredients with ice and fine strain into chilled glass.

2	shot(s)	Appleton Estate V/X aged rum
½	shot(s)	Bols brown crème de cacao
½	shot(s)	Freshly squeezed lime juice
¼	shot(s)	Sugar (gomme) syrup

Comment: A classic Daiquiri with aged rum and a hint of chocolate.

VOODOO

Glass: Collins
Garnish: Cinnamon sprinkled over a flame
Method: Shake and strain into an ice filled glass.

2	shot(s)	Appleton Estate V/X aged rum
1	shot(s)	Cinzano Rosso vermouth
4	shot(s)	Pressed apple juice
1	shot(s)	Freshly squeezed lime juice
1	shot(s)	Sugar (gomme) syrup

Origin: Created in 2002 by Alex Kammerling, London, England.
Comment: The rich flavour of the aged rum marries well with apple and lime juice.

BOLS® APRICOT BRANDY LIQUEUR

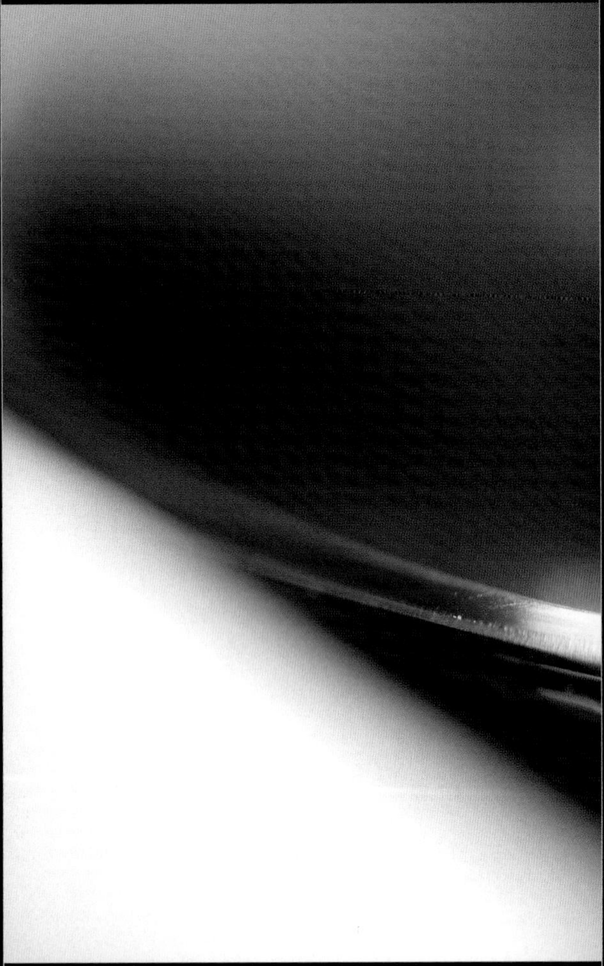

Apricot Brandy is sometimes also known as 'apry'. It is a liqueur produced by infusing apricots in selected Cognacs and flavouring with various herbs to bring out the best flavour and aroma of the apricots. Enriched with a hint of almond, this amber coloured liqueur is one of Bols most popular liqueurs.

With a mild aroma of juicy apricots this distinctively flavoured liqueur is suited to being used in a variety of different cocktails. The light clean taste features apricot with a hint of Cognac and almond. 24% alc./vol. (48°proof)

Web: www.bols.com
Producer: Bols Royal Distilleries, Zoetermeer, The Netherlands. **UK distributor:** Maxxium UK Ltd, Stirling, Scotland.
Tel: 01786 430 500
Email: enquiries@maxxium.com

APRICOT FIZZ UPDATED ●●●●◐○

Glass: Collins
Garnish: Lemon wedge
Method: Shake first four ingredients with ice and strain into ice-filled glass, then top up with soda water.

2	shot(s)	Bols apricot brandy liqueur
1	shot(s)	Freshly squeezed orange juice
1¼	shot(s)	Freshly squeezed lime juice
¼	shot(s)	Sugar (gomme) syrup
Top up with		Soda water (club soda)

Comment: This low-alcohol, refreshing cocktail is perfect for a summer afternoon.

APRICOT MARTINI UPDATED ●●●○○

Glass: Martini
Garnish: Lemon zest twist
Method: Shake all ingredients with ice and fine strain into chilled glass.

1½	shot(s)	Plymouth gin
1	shot(s)	Bols Apricot brandy liqueur
¼	shot(s)	Freshly squeezed lemon juice
⅛	shot(s)	Grenadine syrup
3	dashes	Angostura aromatic bitters
¾	shot(s)	Chilled mineral water

Comment: This scarlet cocktail combines gin, apricot and lemon juice.

CLARIDGE

Glass: Martini
Garnish: Lemon zest twist
Method: Shake ingredients with ice and strain.

1½	shot(s)	Plymouth gin
1½	shot(s)	Cinzano Extra Dry vermouth
¾	shot(s)	Cointreau / triple sec
¾	shot(s)	Bols apricot brandy liqueur

Comment: Gin for the strength, Martini for dryness and liqueur to sweeten – an interesting combination.

GOLDEN SCREW UPDATED ●●●●◐○

Glass: Flute
Garnish: Physalis fruit
Method: Pour all ingredients into glass and then lightly stir.

½	shot(s)	Rémy Martin Cognac
½	shot(s)	Bols apricot brandy liqueur
1	shot(s)	Freshly squeezed orange juice
Top up with		Piper-Heidsieck Brut Champagne

Variant: With gin in place of brandy.
Comment: A favourite with Midas and others whose budgets extend beyond a Buck's Fizz or a Mimosa.

KATINKA

Glass: Martini
Garnish: Split lime wedge
Method: Shake ingredients with ice and strain into glass.

1	shot(s)	Absolut vodka
1	shot(s)	Bols Apricot brandy liqueur
1	shot(s)	Freshly squeezed lime juice
1/2	shot(s)	Sugar (gomme) syrup

Comment: Tart and tasty.

MAMBO

Glass: Collins
Garnish: Orange slice
Method: Shake ingredients with ice and strain into ice-filled glass.

1	shot(s)	Absolut vodka
1	shot(s)	Cointreau/Triple Sec
1	shot(s)	Bols apricot brandy liqueur
1/4	shot(s)	Campari
5	shot(s)	Freshly squeezed orange juice

Origin: Created by Nichole Colella.
Comment: A bitter orange, long, cooling drink.

MULES HIND LEG MARTINI

Glass: Martini
Garnish: Apricot slice on rim
Method: Shake all ingredients with ice and fine strain into chilled glass.

1	shot(s)	Plymouth gin
1	shot(s)	Bénédictine D.O.M. liqueur
1	shot(s)	Calvados or applejack brandy
1/4	shot(s)	Maple syrup
3/4	shot(s)	Bols apricot brandy liqueur
3/4	shot(s)	Chilled mineral water

Origin: My version of a classic recipe.
Comment: Apricot and maple syrup dominate this medium sweet drink.

PARADISE MARTINI

Glass: Martini
Garnish: Flamed orange zest twist
Method: Shake all ingredients with ice and fine strain into chilled glass.

2	shot(s)	Plymouth gin
3/4	shot(s)	Bols Apricot brandy liqueur
1 3/4	shot(s)	Freshly squeezed orange juice
3	dashes	Fee Brothers Orange bitters (optional)

Origin: An old, old recipe that in recent times has been revitalized by Dale DeGroff.
Comment: Wonderfully fruity cocktail that when well made beautifully harnesses and balances its ingredients.

PLAYMATE MARTINI

Glass: Martini
Garnish: Flamed orange zest twist
Method: Shake all ingredients with ice and strain into chilled glass.

1	shot(s)	Rémy Martin Cognac
1	shot(s)	Grand Marnier liqueur
1	shot(s)	Bols apricot brandy liqueur
1	shot(s)	Freshly squeezed orange juice
1/2	fresh	Egg white
4	dashes	Angostura aromatic bitters

Comment: Smooth and easy drinking.

RESOLUTE MARTINI

Glass: Martini
Garnish: Lemon zest twist
Method: Shake all ingredients with ice and fine strain into chilled glass.

2	shot(s)	Plymouth gin
1	shot(s)	Freshly squeezed lemon juice
1	shot(s)	Bols Apricot brandy liqueur
1/4	shot(s)	Sugar (gomme) syrup

Comment: Simple but tasty with all three flavours working in harmony.

SPEYSIDE MARTINI NEW

Glass: Martini
Garnish: Lemon zest twist
Method: Muddle grapes in base of shaker. Add other ingredients, shake with ice and fine strain into chilled glass.

7	fresh	Seedless white grapes
2	shot(s)	The Famous Grouse Scotch whisky
3/4	shot(s)	Bols apricot brandy liqueur
3/4	shot(s)	Freshly squeezed grapefruit juice

Origin: Discovered in 2004 at Indigo Yard, Edinburgh, Scotland.
Comment: Scotch, grape juice, apricot liqueur and grapefruit may seem an unlikely combo but they get on well together.

YELLOW BIRD UPDATED

Glass: Martini
Garnish: Banana slice on rim
Method: Shake all ingredients with ice and fine strain into chilled glass.

1 1/2	shot(s)	Mount Gay Eclipse golden rum
1/2	shot(s)	Bols crème de banane
1/4	shot(s)	Bols apricot brandy liqueur
2	shot(s)	Pressed pineapple juice
1/2	shot(s)	Freshly squeezed lime juice
1/2	shot(s)	Sugar (gomme) syrup
1/4	shot(s)	Galliano liqueur

Comment: A sweet and sour cocktail with four different fruits, rum and a splash of Galliano.

BOLS® BLACKBERRY LIQUEUR

The Latin words 'Semper Idem' inscribed on the coat of arms of the Bols family literally translate as 'always the same'. For the distillers at Bols this motto represents their goal to produce liqueurs of a consistently high quality. It is to that end that they apply their years of experience and knowledge.

Some cocktail recipe books state 'crème de mûre' instead of 'blackberry liqueur'. This comes from 'mûre', the French for blackberry, and 'crème' as in the French phrase 'crème de la crème', meaning 'best of the best'. In such cases you can use Bols Blackberry liqueur which is made from the finest fresh blackberries.

The intense blackberry flavour of this rich liqueur adds a concentrated fruit flavour to cocktails and can be used to boost the flavour when using fresh fruit in a drink.

Web: www.bols.com **Producer:** Bols Royal Distilleries, Zoetermeer, The Netherlands. **UK distributor:** Maxxium UK Ltd, Stirling, Scotland.
Tel: 01786 430 500 **Email:** enquiries@maxxium.com

BLACK & WHITE DAIQUIRI

Glass: Martini
Garnish: Blackberry in drink
Method: Muddle berries in base of shaker. Add other ingredients, shake with ice and fine strain into chilled glass.

12	fresh	Blackberries
2	shot(s)	Malibu coconut rum liqueur
1	shot(s)	Havana Club light rum
3/4	shot(s)	Bols blackberry liqueur
1/2	shot(s)	Freshly squeezed lime juice
1/2	shot(s)	Chilled water

Origin: I named this drink after the black berries and the white Malibu bottle.
Comment: Blackberries and coconut add depth to the classic Daiquiri.

BRAMBLE

Glass: Old-fashioned
Garnish: Blackberry & lemon slice
Method: Fill glass with crushed ice, add gin, lemon juice and sugar syrup and stir. Top up with more crushed ice. Then lace drink with creme de mûre by slowly pouring over fresh ice.

2	shot(s)	Plymouth gin
1 1/2	shot(s)	Freshly squeezed lemon juice
1/2	shot(s)	Sugar (gomme) syrup
1/2	shot(s)	Bols Blackberry liqueur

Origin: Created in the mid-80s by Dick Bradsell at Fred's Club, Soho, London, England.
Comment: A 1980s classic.

CONGO BLUE

Glass: Martini
Garnish: Lemon zest twist
Method: Shake ingredients with ice and strain into glass.

1 1/4	shot(s)	Zubrowka bison vodka
1/2	shot(s)	Midori melon liqueur
1	shot(s)	Pressed apple juice
1/2	shot(s)	Bols blackberry liqueur
1/4	shot(s)	Freshly squeezed lemon juice

Origin: Created in 1999 by Marc Dietrich at Atlantic Bar & Grill, London.
Comment: Although this drink is green, Marc tells me it is named after the beauty of the Congo sunset.

FOREST BREEZE

Glass: Collins
Garnish: Blackberry & raspberry
Method: Muddle blackberries and raspberries in base of shaker. Add next five ingredients, shake with ice and strain into ice-filled glass. Top up with soda water (club soda).

6	fresh	Blackberries
6	fresh	Raspberries
2	shot(s)	Absolut vodka
1/2	shot(s)	Chambord black raspberry liqueur
1/2	shot(s)	Bols blackberry liqueur
3	shot(s)	Cranberry juice
1/4	shot(s)	Freshly squeezed lime juice
	Top up with	Soda water (club soda)

Origin: Created in 2002 by Paul Mott at Waikiki, London, England.
Comment: The fresh fruity flavour will please your taste buds.

GODFREY

Glass: Rocks
Garnish: Three blackberries on drink
Method: Muddle blackberries in base of shaker.
Add other ingredients, shake with ice and fine
strain into glass filled with crushed ice.

6	fresh	Blackberries
1¹/₂	shot(s)	Rémy Martin Cognac
¹/₂	shot(s)	Grand Marnier liqueur
¹/₄	shot(s)	Bols blackberry liqueur
¹/₄	shot(s)	Freshly squeezed lemon juice
¹/₄	shot(s)	Sugar (gomme) syrup

Origin: Created by Salvatore Calabrese at the
Library Bar, Lanesborough Hotel, London,
England.
Comment: Well balanced with a rich blackberry
flavour.

HEDGEROW SLING

Glass: Sling
Garnish: Seasonal berries & lemon slice
Method: Shake first three ingredients with ice
and strain into ice-filled glass, then top up with
soda and pour crème de mûre on top.

2	shot(s)	Plymouth sloe gin
1	shot(s)	Freshly squeezed lemon juice
¹/₄	shot(s)	Sugar (gomme) syrup
¹/₂	shot(s)	Bols blackberry liqueur
Top up with		Soda water

Origin: Created by Brian Duell at Detroit, London,
England.
Comment: Citrus and berries with fizz and an
alcoholic float.

THE LEGEND UPDATED

Glass: Martini
Garnish: Blackberries on stick
Method: Shake all ingredients with ice and fine
strain into chilled glass.

2	shot(s)	Absolut vodka
1	shot(s)	Freshly squeezed lime juice
¹/₄	shot(s)	Bols blackberry liqueur
¹/₄	shot(s)	Sugar (gomme) syrup
4	dashes	Fee Brothers orange bitters

Origin: Created by Dick Bradsell for Karen
Hampsen at Legends, London, England.
Comment: The quality of orange bitters and
blackberry liqueur used dramatically affect the
taste of the drink.

PONTBERRY MARTINI UPDATED

Glass: Martini
Garnish: Blackberries
Method: Shake all ingredients with ice and fine
strain into chilled glass.

1¹/₂	shot(s)	Absolut vodka
¹/₂	shot(s)	Bols blackberry (crème de mûre) liqueur
2	shot(s)	Cranberry juice

Origin: Created by Dick Bradsell in the late 90s
for the opening of Agent Provocateur in Pont
Street, London, England.
Comment: A light, fruity, easy drinking cocktail.

SUMMER MARTINI

Glass: Martini
Garnish: Berries on a cocktail stick
Method: Muddle berries in base of shaker. Add
other ingredients; shake with ice and fine strain
into chilled glass.

3	fresh	Blackberries
3	fresh	Raspberries
3	fresh	Strawberries
¹/₂	shot(s)	Bols Blackberry liqueur
¹/₂	shot	Bols Raspberry (framboise) liqueur
¹/₂	shot	Bols Strawberry (fraise) liqueur
2	shot(s)	Plymouth gin
³/₄	shot(s)	Cinzano Extra Dry vermouth
2	dashes	Fee Brothers Orange bitters

Origin: Created in 2003 by Wayne Collins.
Comment: A drink which combines a trio of
summer berries with the classic aromatic Martini.

UNCLE VANYA

Glass: Martini
Garnish: Lime wedge on rim
Method: Shake all ingredients with ice and fine
strain into chilled glass.

1³/₄	shot(s)	Absolut vodka
1	shot(s)	Bols Blackberry liqueur
1	shot(s)	Freshly squeezed lime juice
¹/₂	shot(s)	Sugar (gomme) syrup
¹/₂	fresh	Egg white

Comment: Simple but great – smooth sweet 'n'
sour blackcurrant, although possibly a tad on
the sweet side for some.

VANILLA LAIKA

Glass: Collins
Garnish: Berries
Method: Shake all ingredients with ice and
strain into glass filled with crushed ice.

1¹/₂	shot(s)	Absolut Vanilia vodka
³/₄	shot(s)	Bols Blackberry (Crème de mûre) liqueur
¹/₄	shot(s)	Freshly squeezed lemon juice
³/₄	shot(s)	Sugar (gomme) syrup
4	shot(s)	Pressed apple juice

Origin: Created by Jake Burger in 2002 at
Townhouse, Leeds, England.
Comment: Vanilla berry fruit in a tall,
refreshing drink.

WIBBLE UPDATED

Glass: Martini
Garnish: Sprayed lemon zest twist
Method: Shake all ingredients with ice and fine
strain into chilled glass.

1	shot(s)	Plymouth gin
1	shot(s)	Plymouth sloe gin liqueur
1	shot(s)	Freshly squeezed grapefruit juice
¹/₄	shot(s)	Freshly squeezed lemon juice
¹/₈	shot(s)	Sugar (gomme) syrup
¹/₈	shot(s)	Bols blackberry (crème de mûre) liqueur

Origin: Created in 1999 by Dick Bradsell at The
Player, London, England.
Comment: As Dick says, 'It may make you
wobble, but it won't make you fall down.'
Complex and balanced.

BOLS BLUE® CURAÇAO

This vivid blue curaçao liqueur is probably the best known of the Bols range. Part of Remy Cointreau, Bols Royal Distilleries originated from a firm started in 1575 by a Dutchman called Lucas Bols. Prevented from distilling within the city walls due to the fire risk, Lucas distilled from a wooden shed outside Amsterdam. Today Bols is one of the largest liqueur producers in the world. Bols Blue is distilled from a blend of predominantly natural products from around the world – herbs, sweet red oranges, the characteristically flavourful bitter Curaçao oranges and the rare Kinnow oranges. This gives Bols Blue a fresh, yet complex orange scent and taste.

Bols Blue is frequently used by bartenders due to its distinctive deep blue colour and refreshing taste which features orange zest with a hint of spice. 21% alc./vol. (42°proof)

Web: www.bols.com **Producer:** Bols Royal Distilleries, Zoetermeer, The Netherlands. **UK distributor:** Maxxium UK Ltd, Stirling, Scotland.
Tel: 01786 430 500 **Email:** enquiries@maxxium.com

BABY BLUE MARTINI

Glass: Martini
Garnish: Orange zest twist
Method: Shake all ingredients with ice and fine strain into chilled glass.

1	shot(s)	Plymouth gin
1	shot(s)	Bols blue curaçao
1	shot(s)	Squeezed pink grapefruit juice
1	shot(s)	Pressed pineapple juice

Comment: Turquoise blue, easy drinking and fairly sweet.

BIKINI MARTINI UPDATED

Glass: Martini
Garnish: Orange zest
Method: Shake all ingredients with ice and fine strain into chilled glass.

2	shot(s)	Plymouth gin
3/4	shot(s)	Bols blue curaçao
1/4	shot(s)	Teichenné peach schnapps liqueur
1/4	shot(s)	Freshly squeezed lemon juice
3/4	shot(s)	Chilled water

Origin: Adapted from a cocktail created in 1999 by Dick Bradsell for an Agent Provocateur swimwear launch.
Comment: A vivid blue combination of lemon, orange and peach laced with gin.

BLUE COSMO

Glass: Martini
Garnish: Orange zest twist
Method: Shake all ingredients with ice and fine strain into chilled glass.

2	shot(s)	Absolut Citron vodka
3/4	shot(s)	Bols Blue curaçao
1 1/2	shot(s)	White cranberry & grape drink
1/4	shot(s)	Freshly squeezed lime juice

Comment: This blue rinsed drink may have sales appeal but sadly is not quite as good as a traditional red Cosmo.

BLUE LAGOON

Glass: Collins
Method: Blend ingredients with crushed ice and serve.

1	shot(s)	Plymouth gin
1	shot(s)	Absolut vodka
1	shot(s)	Bols Blue curaçao
1	shot(s)	Freshly squeezed lime juice
1	shot(s)	Sugar (gomme) syrup

Variation: Vodka, blue curaçao and lemonade on the rocks.
Origin: Created in the 1960's by Andy MacElhone (son of Harry of Harry's Bar, Paris).
Comment: Better than the film – not hard!

BLUE MARGARITA

Glass: Coupette
Garnish: Salt rim & lime wedge on rim
Method: Shake all ingredients with ice and fine strain into chilled glass.

2	shot(s)	Sauza Hornitos Tequila
1	shot(s)	Bols Blue Curaçao
1	shot(s)	Freshly squeezed lime juice
1/4	shot(s)	Sugar (gomme) syrup

Variation: Blend with crushed ice.
Comment: As the name suggests, a Margarita only blue.

BLUE STAR UPDATED

Glass: Martini
Garnish: Orange zest twist
Method: Shake all ingredients with ice and fine strain into chilled glass.

1 1/2	shot(s)	Plymouth gin
3/4	shot(s)	Cinzano Extra Dry vermouth
3/4	shot(s)	Freshly squeezed orange juice
1 1/2	shot(s)	Bols Blue curaçao

Comment: Gin, orange and a kick.

BLUE PASSION UPDATED

Glass: Old-fashioned
Garnish: Orange zest twist
Method: Shake all ingredients with ice and strain into glass filled with crushed ice.

1	shot(s)	Havana Club light rum
1	shot(s)	Bols Blue curaçao
1 3/4	shot(s)	Freshly squeezed lime juice
1	shot(s)	Sugar (gomme) syrup

Comment: This sweet and sour tangy drink is surprisingly good.

GREEN EYES

Glass: Martini
Garnish: Lime wedge on rim
Method: Shake ingredients with ice and strain into glass.

1 1/2	shot(s)	Absolut vodka
1/2	shot(s)	Bols blue curaçao
3	shot(s)	Freshly squeezed orange juice

Comment: A refreshing version of the classic Screwdriver.

BLUE RASPBERRY MARTINI

Glass: Martini
Garnish: Raspberries
Method: Shake all ingredients with ice and fine strain into chilled glass.

2	shot(s)	Absolut Raspberri Vodka
1/2	shot(s)	Bols Blue curaçao
3/4	shot(s)	Freshly squeezed lime juice
1/2	shot(s)	Sugar (gomme) syrup
3/4	shot(s)	Chilled water

Origin: Discovered in 2002 at The Sky Bar, Sunset Boulevard, Los Angeles, USA, where sour mix is used instead of fresh lime juice and sugar.
Comment: As turquoise-blue drinks go this one is surprisingly adult and tasty.

LOTUS MARTINI

Glass: Martini
Garnish: Mint leaf
Method: Muddle mint leaves with gin in base of shaker. Add other ingredients, shake with ice and strain into glass.

6	fresh	Fresh mint leaves
1 3/4	shot(s)	Plymouth gin
1/4	shot(s)	Grenadine syrup
1/4	shot(s)	Bols Blue curaçao
1 1/2	shot(s)	Lychee juice from tinned fruit

Origin: Created in 2001 by Martin Walander at Match Bar, London, England.
Comment: This violet coloured drink may have an unlikely list of ingredients, but boy does it look and taste good.

BLUE RIBAND UPDATED

Glass: Martini
Garnish: Cherry dropped into glass
Method: Stir all ingredients with ice and strain into chilled glass.

2	shot(s)	Plymouth gin
1	shot(s)	Cointreau / triple sec
1	shot(s)	Bols Blue curaçao

Origin: The 'Blue Riband' was awarded to the liner that made the fastest Atlantic crossing. This cocktail is thought to have been created on one of these ships.
Comment: A sweetened, blue rinsed, orange and gin Martini.

SWEDISH BLUE MARTINI

Glass: Martini
Garnish: Orange peel twist
Method: Shake ingredients with ice and strain into glass.

1 1/2	shot(s)	Absolut vodka
1/2	shot(s)	Bols Blue curaçao
1/2	shot(s)	Teichenné Peach schnapps liqueur
1/4	shot(s)	Freshly squeezed lime juice
1/4	shot(s)	Sugar (gomme) syrup
2	dashes	Fee Brothers Orange bitters

Origin: Timothy Schofield at Teatro, London, England.
Comment: A blue concoction with a sweet style.

BOLS® CHERRY BRANDY LIQUEUR

This richly flavoured liqueur is made from the juice of ripe, dark red cherries. Crushing the kernels while pressing the cherries enhances almond notes in the cherry juice and is very evident in the finished liqueur. Extracts of various carefully selected herbs and spices such as cinnamon and cloves produce a well-balanced liqueur. With its luscious cherry flavour and hints of almond and spice, this traditional liqueur is a versatile mixer.
24% alc./vol. (48°proof)

Web: www.bols.com
Producer: Bols Royal Distilleries, Zoetermeer, The Netherlands. **UK distributor:** Maxxium UK Ltd, Stirling, Scotland.
Tel: 01786 430 500
Email: enquiries@maxxium.com

AQUARIUS

Glass: Rocks
Method: Shake ingredients with ice and strain into ice-filled glass.

2	shot(s)	The Famous Grouse Scotch whisky
1	shot(s)	Bols cherry brandy liqueur
1½	shot(s)	Cranberry juice
¼	shot(s)	Sugar (gomme) syrup

Comment: The sweet cherry edge is balanced by the dryness of cranberry and Scotch.

BLOOD & SAND

Glass: Martini
Method: Shake ingredients with ice and strain into glass.

1	shot(s)	The Famous Grouse Scotch whisky
1	shot(s)	Bols Cherry brandy liqueur
1	shot(s)	Cinzano Rosso (sweet) vermouth
1	shot(s)	Freshly squeezed orange juice

Origin: Made for the premiere of the Rudolph Valentino film, Blood and Sand.
Comment: One of the best Scotch cocktails.

CANARIES

Glass: Hurricane
Garnish: Pineapple leaf.
Method: Shake ingredients with ice and strain into ice-filled glass.

1	shot(s)	Havana Club light rum
1	shot(s)	Cointreau / triple sec
1	shot(s)	Bols crème de banane
1	shot(s)	Bols cherry brandy liqueur
3	shot(s)	Pressed pineapple juice
3	shot(s)	Freshly squeezed orange juice

Comment: A long, fruity drink fit for consumption on a tropical beach.

CHERRY DAIQUIRI

Glass: Martini
Garnish: Cherry on rim
Method: Muddle cherries in base of shaker. Add other ingredients, shake vigorously with ice and fine strain into chilled glass.

8	fresh	Stoned cherries
2	shot(s)	Vanilla infused Havana Club rum
1	shot(s)	Bols cherry brandy liqueur
⅛	shot(s)	Maraschino syrup
½	shot(s)	Freshly squeezed lime juice
½	shot(s)	Chilled water

Comment: Cherry sweetness paired with Daiquiri sharpness.

CHERRY MASH SOUR

Glass: Old-fashioned
Garnish: Lemon twist & cherry
Method: Shake all ingredients with ice and strain into ice-filled glass.

2	shot(s)	Jack Daniel's Tennessee whiskey
½	shot(s)	Bols cherry brandy liqueur
¾	shot(s)	Freshly squeezed lemon juice
½	shot(s)	Sugar (gomme) syrup

Origin: Created by Dale DeGroff.
Comment: Tennessee whiskey soured with lemon and sweetened with cherry.

GIN SLING

Glass: Sling
Garnish: Split lemon wedge and cherry on stick
Method: Shake first three ingredients with ice and strain into ice-filled glass, then top up with soda water.

1	shot(s)	Plymouth gin
2	shot(s)	Bols cherry brandy liqueur
1	shot(s)	Freshly squeezed lemon juice
Top up with		Soda water (club soda)

Comment: Add sugar to taste.

●●●○○

NIGHTMARE MARTINI UPDATED

Glass: Martini
Garnish: Stemmed maraschino cherry
Method: Shake all ingredients with ice and fine strain into chilled glass.

1	shot(s)	Plymouth gin
1	shot(s)	Dubonnet Red
1/2	shot(s)	Bols cherry brandy liqueur
2	shot(s)	Freshly squeezed orange juice

Comment: I don't know why this drink is called a nightmare. It's pleasant enough, with hints of cherry.

●●●●○

RED NECK MARTINI

Glass: Martini
Garnish: Orange zest twist
Method: Shake all ingredients with ice and fine strain into chilled glass.

2	shot(s)	The Famous Grouse Scotch whisky
1	shot(s)	Dubonnet Red
1	shot(s)	Bols Cherry brandy liqueur

Origin: Created by Sylvain Solignac in 2002 at Circus Bar, London, England.
Comment: Nicely balanced, aromatic and not too sweet – the flavour of the Scotch shines through.

●●●●○

REMEMBER THE MAINE

Glass: Old-fashioned
Garnish: Stemmed cherry in drink
Method: Pour absinthe into ice-filled glass and top up with water. Separately, pour other ingredients into an ice-filled mixing glass and stir well. Discard absinthe, water and ice from glass. Finally strain contents of mixing glass into the now absinthe rinsed empty glass.

1	shot(s)	La Fée absinthe
Top up with		Chilled mineral water
2	shot(s)	Buffalo Trace Bourbon
3/4	shot(s)	Bols Cherry brandy liqueur
3/4	shot(s)	Cinzano Rosso (sweet) vermouth

Origin: Created in 2001 by Jason Fendick at Rockwell, London, England.
Comment: A modern twist on the Sazerac.

●●●●○

SINGAPORE SLING #1 UPDATED

Glass: Sling
Garnish: Split lemon wheel
Method: Shake first seven ingredients with ice and strain into ice-filled glass. Top up with soda and serve with straws.

1 1/2	shot(s)	Plymouth gin
1	shot(s)	Bols cherry brandy liqueur
1/2	shot(s)	Bénédictine D.O.M. liqueur
3/4	shot(s)	Freshly squeezed orange juice
3/4	shot(s)	Freshly squeezed lime juice
1/4	shot(s)	Rose's lime cordial
3	dashes	Angostura aromatic bitters
Top up with		Soda water (club soda)

Origin: Created sometime between 1911 and 1915 by Chinese-born Ngiam Tong Boon at the Long Bar in Raffles Hotel, Singapore.

Raffles Hotel is named after the colonial founder of Singapore, Sir Stamford Raffles, and was the Near East's ex-pat central. Everyone from Noel Coward to the Prince of Siam to Ernest Hemingway stayed and drank there - W. Somerset Maugham would cruise for plotlines in the Palm Court bar outside. It still sticks out of modern-day Singapore like a vast colonial Christmas cake.

Although there is little controversy as to who, where and roughly when the Singapore Sling was created, there is much debate over the original name and ingredients. 'Sling, comes from the German word 'schlingen', meaning 'to swallow., and Slings based on spirit mixed with sugar and water were popularly drunk in the late 1800s. However, cocktail books from the period include a similar concoction called the Straits Sling, which has various ingredients in common with the Singapore Sling. Whether these two drinks have merged over the years or the Singapore Sling was originally called the Straits Sling is unclear.

Considering the confusion, it's hardly surprising that there are many versions of this drink. However, it's generally accepted that a Singapore Sling should be based on gin and contain cherry brandy and Bénédictine liqueurs.
Comment: A gin fortified meld of citrus, cherries and spice.

●●●○○

TAINTED CHERRY UPDATED

Glass: Martini
Garnish: Maraschino cherry
Method: Shake all ingredients with ice and fine strain into chilled glass.

1 3/4	shot(s)	Absolut vodka
3/4	shot(s)	Bols cherry brandy liqueur
1 3/4	shot(s)	Freshly squeezed orange juice

Comment: Orange and cherry combine to produce a flavour rather like amaretto.

●●●●◐○

VANDERBILT UPDATED

Glass: Martini
Garnish: Maraschino cherry & lemon zest twist
Method: Stir all ingredients with ice and strain into chilled glass.

2	shot(s)	Rémy Martin Cognac
1 1/4	shot(s)	Bols Cherry brandy liqueur
4	dashes	Angostura aromatic bitters

Comment: Supercharged cherry brandy.

BOLS® CREME DE BANANE

The French term 'crème de' indicates that one particular flavour predominates in the liqueur; it does not imply that the liqueur contains cream. Many fruit liqueurs are described as 'crème de' followed by the name of a fruit. This refers to the liqueur's quality, as in the phrase 'crème de la crème'. Therefore crème de banane is a banana flavoured liqueur made by infusion and maceration of the fruit in neutral spirit.

Bols Crème de Banane is a clear yellow liqueur with the flavour of sun-ripened bananas, enhanced with a touch of soft vanilla and a hint of almond. Extracts of various carefully selected herbs and spices give this well-balanced liqueur its special taste.

Like many of the liqueurs in the Bols range, Crème de Bananes is extremely mixable and is found in a plethora of cocktails that use its exotic ripe banana flavour. 17% alc./vol. (34°proof)

Web: www.bols.com **Producer:** Bols Royal Distilleries, Zoetermeer, The Netherlands. **UK distributor:** Maxxium UK Ltd, Stirling, Scotland.
Tel: 01786 430 500 **Email:** enquiries@maxxium.com

BANANA BANSHEE

Glass: Collins
Garnish: Banana slice
Method: Blend ingredients with crushed ice and serve.

1¹/₂	shot(s)	Bols crème de banane
1¹/₂	shot(s)	Bols white crème de cacao
¹/₂	shot(s)	Cointreau/triple sec
1¹/₂	shot(s)	Double (heavy) cream
1¹/₂	shot(s)	Milk
¹/₂		Peeled banana

Comment: A very popular, long, creamy cocktail.

BANANA BLISS UPDATED ●●●○○

Glass: Martini
Garnish: Split banana chunk
Method: Stir all ingredients with ice and strain into chilled glass.

2	shot(s)	Bols crème de banane
2	shot(s)	Rémy Martin Cognac
1	shot(s)	Chilled water
2	dashes	Fee Brothers orange bitters

AKA: Golden Brown
Comment: Crème de banane and Cognac go shockingly well together.

BANANA COLADA

Glass: Hurricane
Garnish: Split banana chunk
Method: Blend ingredients with crushed ice and serve.

¹/₂	shot(s)	Bols crème de banane
2	shot(s)	Mount Gay Eclipse golden rum
¹/₂	fresh	Peeled banana
1	shot(s)	Double (heavy) cream
1	shot(s)	Coco López cream of coconut
4	shot(s)	Pressed pineapple juice

Comment: A Piña Colada with gold rum and banana.

BANANAS & CREAM ●●●●○

Glass: Collins
Garnish: Banana chunk on rim
Method: Blend all ingredients with crushed ice and serve with straws.

2	shot(s)	Bols crème de banane
1	shot(s)	Disaronno Originale amaretto
1	shot(s)	Baileys Irish Cream liqueur
1	shot(s)	Double (heavy) cream
2	shot(s)	Milk

Comment: Banana and cream frappé with hints of almond – one for a summer afternoon.

BANOFFEE MARTINI

Glass: Martini
Garnish: Dust with chocolate powder
Method: Muddle banana in base of shaker. Add other ingredients, shake with ice and fine strain into chilled glass.

¼	fresh	Banana
1½	shot(s)	Absolut Vanilia
¾	shot(s)	Teichenné butterscotch schnapps
¾	shot(s)	Bols crème de banane
1	spoon	Maple syrup
½	shot(s)	Double (heavy) cream
½	shot(s)	Milk

Origin: Adapted from a recipe created in 2002 by Barry Wilson, Zinc Bar & Grill, Edinburgh, Scotland.
Comment: Thick and rich, one for after the cheese course.

BEJA FLOR UPDATED

Glass: Martini
Garnish: Banana chunk on rim
Method: Shake all ingredients with ice and fine strain into chilled glass.

2	shot(s)	Sagatiba cachaça
1	shot(s)	Cointreau / triple sec
1	shot(s)	Bols crème de banane
½	shot(s)	Freshly squeezed lemon juice

Comment: Sharp and quite dry but with a sweet banana twang.

FRUIT SALAD

Glass: Collins
Garnish: Orange slice
Method: Shake ingredients with ice and strain into ice-filled glass.

2	shot(s)	Absolut vodka
¾	shot(s)	Bols crème de banane
4	shot(s)	Freshly squeezed orange juice
¾	shot(s)	Galliano liqueur
¼	shot(s)	Grenadine syrup

Comment: This variation on the Harvey Wallbanger tastes like Fruit Salad penny chews.

JUMPING JACK FLASH

Glass: Martini
Method: Shake all ingredients with ice and strain into glass.

1	shot(s)	Jack Daniel's Tennessee whiskey
1	shot(s)	Bols crème de banane
½	shot(s)	Galliano liqueur
1	shot(s)	Freshly squeezed orange juice
1	shot(s)	Pressed pineapple juice

Comment: The Galliano complements the banana; both mix well with the fruit juices and vanilla.

SAN FRANCISCO

Glass: Collins
Garnish: Pineapple wedge on rim
Method: Shake ingredients with ice and strain into ice-filled glass.

2	shot(s)	Absolut vodka
1	shot(s)	Cointreau / triple sec
1	shot(s)	Bols Crème de banane
2½	shot(s)	Freshly squeezed orange juice
2½	shot(s)	Pressed pineapple juice
¼	shot(s)	Grenadine syrup

Comment: Long, fruity drink laced with vodka.

SCREAMING BANANA BANSHEE

Glass: Hurricane
Garnish: Banana slice on rim
Method: Blend ingredients with crushed ice and serve.

1	shot(s)	Absolut vodka
¾	shot(s)	Bols Crème de banane
¾	shot(s)	Bols White crème de cacao
1½	shot(s)	Double (heavy) cream
1½	shot(s)	Milk
2	scoops	Vanilla ice cream

Comment: Choc, bananas and cream.

TOOTIE FRUITY LIFESAVER

Glass: Collins
Method: Shake ingredients with ice and strain into ice-filled glass.

1	shot(s)	Absolut vodka
1½	shot(s)	Bols Crème de banane
¾	shot(s)	Galliano liqueur
2	shot(s)	Cranberry juice
2	shot(s)	Pressed pineapple juice
2	shot(s)	Freshly squeezed orange juice

Comment: Aptly named fruity drink.

YELLOW BIRD UPDATED

Glass: Martini
Garnish: Banana slice on rim
Method: Shake all ingredients with ice and fine strain into chilled glass.

1½	shot(s)	Mount Gay Eclipse golden rum
½	shot(s)	Bols crème de banane
¼	shot(s)	Bols apricot brandy liqueur
2	shot(s)	Pressed pineapple juice
½	shot(s)	Freshly squeezed lime juice
½	shot(s)	Sugar (gomme) syrup
¼	shot(s)	Galliano liqueur

Comment: A sweet and sour cocktail with four different fruits, rum and a splash of Galliano.

BOLS® BROWN CRÈME DE CACAO

The finest roasted cacao beans are used to prepare Bols Brown crème de cacao. The cacao seeds are first broken open and then percolated. Various herbs are added to give the liqueur its own distinctive flavour. Please note that 'brown crème de cacao' liqueurs are sometimes alternatively named 'dark crème de cacao'.

Bols Crème de Cacao is perfect for adding a rich chocolate flavour to any cocktail. Choose between the lighter, more delicately flavoured white or this rich dark version. 24% alc./vol. (48°proof)

Web: www.bols.com
Producer: Bols Royal Distilleries, Zoetermeer, The Netherlands. **UK distributor:** Maxxium UK Ltd, Stirling, Scotland.
Tel: 01786 430 500
Email: enquiries@maxxium.com

APPLE STRUDEL MARTINI UPDATED

Glass: Martini
Garnish: Dust with cinnamon
Method: Shake first five ingredients with ice and strain into glass. Float cream.

1	shot(s)	Apple schnapps liqueur
1/2	shot(s)	Goldschläger Cinnamon schnapps
1/2	shot(s)	Bols white crème de cacao
1/2	shot(s)	Bols brown crème de cacao
1	shot(s)	Pressed apple juice
3/4	shot(s)	Double (heavy) cream

Variant: May also be served as a shooter in a shot glass.
Origin: Created in 1999 by Alex Kammerling, London, England.
Comment: This sweet dessert cocktail tastes just like mum's home-made apple pie with cream.

BLACK MARTINI UPDATED

Glass: Martini
Garnish: Float grated white chocolate
Method: Shake all ingredients with ice and fine strain into chilled glass.

1 1/2	shot(s)	Havana Club light rum
1 1/2	shot(s)	Bols brown crème de cacao liqueur
1 1/2	shot(s)	Espresso coffee (cold)

Origin: Created by yours truly in March 2004.
Comment: This flavoursome mix of coffee and chocolate is further enhanced if vanilla infused rum is used.

BRAZILIAN MONK

Glass: Hurricane
Method: Blend ingredients with crushed ice and serve.

1	shot(s)	Frangelico hazelnut liqueur
1	shot(s)	Kahlúa coffee liqueur
1	shot(s)	Bols brown crème de cacao
3	scoops	Vanilla ice cream

Comment: Nutty and rich – serve alfresco.

BRANDY ALEXANDER

Glass: Martini
Garnish: Sprinkle ground nutmeg
Method: Shake ingredients with ice and strain into glass.

1 1/2	shot(s)	Rémy Martin Cognac
1/2	shot(s)	Bols brown crème de cacao
1/2	shot(s)	Bols white crème de cacao
2	shot(s)	Double (heavy) cream

Comment: This classic blend of brandy and chocolate smoothed with cream is based on the original Alexander. Made with gin, this was a Prohibition favourite, as the cream, chocolate and nutmeg disguised the rough taste of homemade 'bathtub' gin. Creamy, subtle, spicy and rich.

CHOCOLATE PUFF

Glass: Old-fashioned
Garnish: Crumbled Cadbury's Flake bar
Method: Shake all ingredients with ice and strain into glass.

1	shot(s)	Mount Gay Eclipse golden rum
1	shot(s)	Bols brown crème de cacao
6	spoons	Natural yoghurt
2	zests	Fresh orange
1/4	shot(s)	Sugar (gomme) syrup

Origin: Created by Wayne Collins in 2002 for Maxxium UK.
Comment: Smooth as you like. The orange is surprisingly evident.

DEATH BY CHOCOLATE | FROZEN

Glass: Hurricane
Garnish: Chocolate shavings
Method: Blend ingredients with crushed ice and serve.

1	shot(s)	Absolut vodka
1½	shot(s)	Baileys Irish Cream liqueur
1	shot(s)	Bols brown crème de cacao
3	scoops	Chocolate ice cream

Comment: Unsophisticated but delicious.

DONNA'S CREAMY'TINI

Glass: Martini
Garnish: Cherry on rim
Method: Shake all ingredients with ice and fine strain into chilled glass.

1¼	shot(s)	Disaronno Originale amaretto
1¼	shot(s)	Bols cherry brandy liqueur
1¼	shot(s)	Bols brown crème de cacao
1¼	shot(s)	Double (heavy) cream

Origin: Adapted from a drink created in 2002 by Yannick Miseriaux at the Fifth Floor Bar, London, England.
Comment: A fine example of an alcoholic liquid pudding.

JAFFA MARTINI NEW

Glass: Martini
Garnish: Float mini Jaffa Cake
Method: Shake all ingredients with ice and fine strain into chilled glass.

1	shot(s)	Cointreau / triple sec
1	shot(s)	Bols brown crème de cacao
1/2	shot(s)	Absolut Mandrin vodka
1/2	shot(s)	Freshly squeezed lemon juice
1	shot(s)	Freshly squeezed orange juice
3	dashes	Fee Brothers orange bitters (optional)
1	whole	Egg

Origin: Created by yours truly in 2004. McVitie's Jaffa Cakes have a tangy orange jelly centre on a hardish sponge base, covered in dark chocolate.
　　Back in 1991 these tasty little snacks beat off UK Customs & Excise who sought to reclassify them as chocolate biscuits, which, unlike cakes, are categorised as luxuries and so subjected to Value Added Tax.
Comment: While the alcohol in this sweet, dessert-style Martini may be taxed to oblivion, thankfully the garnish, since it is technically a cake, remains tax free in the UK.

MOCHA MARTINI

Glass: Martini
Garnish: Dust centre with cocoa powder
Method: Shake first four ingredients with ice and fine strain into chilled glass. Float just half a shot of cream in centre of drink.

1	shot(s)	Buffalo Trace Bourbon
1½	shot(s)	Espresso coffee (cold)
1	shot(s)	Baileys Irish Cream liqueur
1	shot(s)	Bols brown crème de cacao
1/2	shot(s)	Double (heavy) cream

Comment: Made with great espresso coffee, this drink is a superb, richly flavoured balance of sweet and bitter.

MULATA DAIQUIRI

Glass: Martini
Garnish: Lime wedge on rim
Method: Shake all ingredients with ice and fine strain into chilled glass.

2	shot(s)	Appleton Estate V/X aged rum
1/2	shot(s)	Bols brown crème de cacao
1/2	shot(s)	Freshly squeezed lime juice
1/4	shot(s)	Sugar (gomme) syrup

Comment: A classic Daiquiri with aged rum and a hint of chocolate.

TIRAMISU MARTINI

Glass: Martini
Garnish: Chocolate powder dust
Method: Shake all ingredients with ice and strain into glass.

1	shot(s)	Rémy Martin Cognac
1/2	shot(s)	Kahlúa coffee liqueur
1/2	shot(s)	Bols Brown crème de cacao
1/2	shot(s)	Double (heavy) cream
1/2	shot(s)	Milk
1	fresh	Egg yolk
1	spoon	Mascarpone cheese

Origin: Created by Adam Ennis in 2001 at Isola, London, England.
Comment: The chef meets the bartender in this rich dessert cocktail.

TRIANGULAR MARTINI

Glass: Martini
Garnish: Toblerone chocolate on rim
Method: Stir honey with vodka in base of shaker so as to dissolve honey. Add other ingredients, shake with ice and fine strain into chilled glass.

2	spoons	Runny honey
1½	shot(s)	Absolut Vanilia vodka
1/2	shot(s)	Disaronno Originale amaretto
1¼	shot(s)	Bols brown crème de cacao
3/4	shot(s)	Double (heavy) cream
1/2	fresh	Egg white

Origin: Created by yours truly in 2003. The famous triangular Toblerone chocolate bar was invented in 1908 by the Swiss chocolate maker Theodor Tobler and the name is a blend of Tobler with Torrone, the Italian word for honey-almond nougat, one of its main ingredients.
Comment: Nibble at the garnish as you sip honeyed, chocolate and almond flavoured liquid candy.

BOLS® LYCHEE

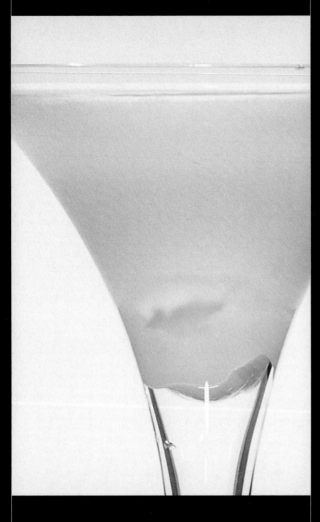

The lychee fruit originated in China and its name derives from the Cantonese 'lai ji'. Although the fruit is now also grown in India, South Africa, the West Indies and the United States, it remains decidedly oriental in flavour and image. The translucent, whitish flesh inside the knobbly pink shell has a distinctively eastern delicacy of flavour.

The fruit's wonderful taste coupled with the rise in popularity of East-West fusion cuisine has led to the creation of fusion cocktails such as the Lychee Martini. This liqueur from Bols harnesses and concentrates the rich aromatic qualities of lychee and enables the mixologist to easily add the fruit's flavour and scent to any combination. Bols Lychee has an unmistakable scent of freshly peeled lychee. Its flavour is gentle, smooth and intriguing. 17% alc./vol. (34°proof)

Web: www.bols.com **Producer:** Bols Royal Distilleries, Zoetermeer, The Netherlands. **UK distributor:** Maxxium UK Ltd, Stirling, Scotland.
Tel: 01786 430 500 **Email:** enquiries@maxxium.com

CHINA BLUE

Glass: Collins
Garnish: Orange slice in drink
Method: Shake all ingredients with ice and strain into ice-filled glass.

1	shot(s)	Bols Blue curaçao
1	shot(s)	Bols Lychee liqueur
4	shot(s)	Freshly squeezed grapefruit juice

Origin: Philip Duff tells me that he became aware of this drink in 1999 and that it is well-known along the Pacific Rim.
Comment: Looks sweet, but due to a generous splash of grapefruit is actually balanced and refreshing.

CHINA BLUE MARTINI

Glass: Martini
Garnish: Peeled lychee in drink
Method: Shake all ingredients with ice and fine strain into chilled glass.

1	shot(s)	Bols Blue curaçao
1	shot(s)	Bols Lychee liqueur
2	shot(s)	Freshly squeezed grapefruit juice
1/4	shot(s)	Freshly squeezed lemon juice

Origin: An almost inevitable short adaptation of the original long drink above.
Comment: This simple cocktail with its turquoise colour tastes more adult and interesting than it looks.

CHINESE COSMOPOLITAN NEW

Glass: Martini
Garnish: Flamed orange zest twist
Method: Shake all ingredients with ice and fine strain into chilled glass.

2	shot(s)	Krupnik honey liqueur
3/4	shot(s)	Bols lychee liqueur
1/2	shot(s)	Freshly squeezed lime juice
1	shot(s)	Cranberry juice

Origin: Discovered in 2003 at Raoul's Bar, Oxford, England.
Comment: Oriental in name and style – perhaps a tad sweeter than your standard Cosmo.

CHINESE WHISPER MARTINI NEW

Glass: Martini
Garnish: Lemon zest twist
Method: Muddle ginger in base of shaker. Add other ingredients, shake with ice and fine strain into chilled glass.

2	slices	Fresh root ginger (thumb-nail sized)
2	shot(s)	Absolut Citron vodka
1	shot(s)	Bols lychee liqueur
1/2	shot(s)	Freshly squeezed lime juice
1/4	shot(s)	Ginger syrup

Origin: Adapted from a recipe discovered in 2003 at Oxo Tower Bar, London, England.
Comment: There's more than a hint of ginger in this spicy Martini.

LYCHEE & BLACKCURRANT MARTINI NEW

●●●●○

Glass: Martini
Garnish: Peeled lychee in glass
Method: Shake all ingredients with ice and fine strain into chilled glass.

2	shot(s)	Plymouth gin
3/4	shot(s)	Bols lychee liqueur
1/4	shot(s)	Sisca crème de cassis
1/4	shot(s)	Rose's lime cordial
3/4	shot(s)	Chilled mineral water

Origin: Created by yours truly in 2004.
Comment: Light and fragrant.

LYCHEE & SAKE MARTINI NEW

●●●●○

Glass: Martini
Garnish: Peeled lychee in glass
Method: Stir all ingredients with ice and strain into chilled glass.

1 1/2	shot(s)	Plymouth gin
3/4	shot(s)	Bols lychee liqueur
2	shot(s)	Sake

Origin: Created by yours truly in 2004.
Comment: A soft Martini with subtle hints of sake and lychee.

LYCHEE MAC NEW

●●●◐○

Glass: Old-fashioned
Garnish: Peeled lychee in drink
Method: Shake all ingredients with ice and strain into ice-filled glass.

2 1/4	shot(s)	The Famous Grouse Scotch whisky
1	shot(s)	Bols lychee liqueur
3/4	shot(s)	Stone's green ginger wine

Origin: Created by yours truly in 2004.
Comment: Peaty Scotch with sweet lychee and hot ginger.

LYCHEE MARTINI

●●●●○

Glass: Martini
Garnish: Whole lychee from tin in drink
Method: Stir all ingredients with ice and strain into chilled glass.

2	shot(s)	Absolut vodka
1/2	shot(s)	Bols Lychee liqueur
2	shot(s)	Lychee syrup from tinned fruit

Origin: Rumoured to have been first made in 2001 at Clay, a Korean restaurant in New York City.
Comment: If you like lychee you'll like this delicate Martini.

MELLOW MARTINI

Glass: Martini
Garnish: Fresh lychee on a stick
Method: Shake ingredients with ice and strain into glass.

1 1/2	shot(s)	Absolut vodka
3/4	shot(s)	Bols Lychee liqueur
3/4	shot(s)	Bols crème de banane
2	shot(s)	Pressed pineapple juice

Comment: Fruity tropical flavour.

ORIENTAL TART NEW

●●●●○

Glass: Martini
Garnish: Peeled lychee in drink
Method: Shake all ingredients with ice and fine strain into chilled glass.

1 1/2	shot(s)	Plymouth gin
1	shot(s)	Bols lychee liqueur
2	shot(s)	Freshly squeezed golden grapefruit juice

Origin: Created by yours truly in 2004.
Comment: A sour, tart, fruity Martini with more than a hint of lychee.

PEAR DROP NEW

●●●◐○

Glass: Shot
Method: Shake all ingredients with ice and fine strain into chilled glass.

1/2	shot(s)	Absolut Citron vodka
1/2	shot(s)	Bols lychee liqueur
1/2	shot(s)	Xanté pear & cognac liqueur

Comment: Sweet, sticky and strong.

SUMMER ROSE MARTINI

●●●●○

Glass: Martini
Garnish: Red rose petal
Method: Stir first three ingredients with ice and strain into chilled glass. Pour grenadine into the centre of the drink. This should sink and settle to form a red layer in the base of the glass.

1 1/2	shot(s)	Absolut vodka
3/4	shot(s)	Bols White crème de cacao
1/2	shot(s)	Bols Lychee liqueur
1/2	shot(s)	Grenadine syrup

Origin: Created in 2003 by Davide Lovison at Isola Bar, London, England.
Comment: This red and white layered drink could have been named War of the Roses. Unless you've a sweet tooth don't mix the factions – sip from the chocolate and lychee top and stop when you hit red.

BOLS® RASPBERRY LIQUEUR

The French word for raspberry is 'framboise', so it is common to find cocktail recipe books referring to 'crème de framboise' for a raspberry liqueur. Bols Raspberry liqueur was introduced to answer the needs of modern bartenders for a quality liqueur based on the berry fruit most often used in their drinks.

Interestingly, the raspberry is related to the rose and its intense flavour lends itself to use in cocktails. To use raspberries as a cocktail ingredient, either purée the fruit in a blender or muddle them in the base of the shaker (or the glass the cocktail is to be served in). To further enhance the flavour add a splash of Bols Raspberry liqueur.

This liqueur delivers a rich raspberry flavour. The sugar content is well balanced to bring out and enhance the natural flavours of the fruit.

Web: www.bols.com **Producer:** Bols Royal Distilleries, Zoetermeer, The Netherlands.
UK distributor: Maxxium UK Ltd, Stirling, Scotland.
Tel: 01786 430 500 **Email:** enquiries@maxxium.com

CAROL CHANNING

Glass: Flute
Garnish: 2 raspberries.
Method: Shake first three ingredients with ice and strain into glass. Top up with Champagne.

1/2	shot(s)	Bols raspberry (framboise) liqueur
1/2	shot(s)	Framboise eau de vie
1/8	shot(s)	Sugar (gomme) syrup
Top up with		Piper-Heidsieck Brut Champagne

Origin: Created by Dick Bradsell in 1984 with the milliner Stephen Jones.
Comment: A popular new classic cocktail – the combination of raspberry eau-de-vie with the fizz is lethal.

GUYANAN RASPBERRY PUNCH

Glass: Collins
Garnish: Lime wedge & raspberries
Method: Shake ingredients with ice and strain.

2	shot(s)	Pusser's Navy rum
1	shot(s)	Bols raspberry (framboise) liqueur
3	shot(s)	Cranberry juice
3/4	shot(s)	Freshly squeezed lime juice
4	dashes	Angostura aromatic bitters
1/4	shot(s)	Sugar (gomme) syrup

AKA: Mui Rico
Comment: Very similar to Trader Vic's Shinglestain: rum and berries.

MRS ROBINSON

Glass: Old-fashioned
Garnish: Three raspberries
Method: Muddle raspberries in base of shaker. Add next four ingredients, shake with ice and strain into ice-filled glass. Top up with soda and stir.

8	fresh	Raspberries
2	shot(s)	Buffalo Trace Bourbon
1	shot(s)	Bols raspberry (framboise) liqueur
1/4	shot(s)	Freshly squeezed lemon juice
1/4	shot(s)	Sugar (gomme) syrup
Top up with		Soda water (club soda)

Origin: Created in 2000 by Max Warner at Long Bar, Sanderson, London, England.
Comment: Rich raspberry fruit laced with Bourbon.

RASPBERRY COLLINS

Glass: Collins
Garnish: Three raspberries & lemon slice
Method: Muddle raspberries in base of shaker. Add next five ingredients, shake with ice and strain into an ice-filled glass. Top up with soda, stir and serve with straws.

10	fresh	Raspberries
2	shot(s)	Plymouth gin
1 1/2	shot(s)	Freshly squeezed lemon juice
1/2	shot(s)	Bols Raspberry (framboise) liqueur
1/2	shot(s)	Sugar (gomme) syrup
3	dashes	Fee Brothers Orange bitters (optional)
Top up with		Soda water (club soda)

Variant: Raspberry Debonnaire
Origin: Created in 1999 by Cairbry Hill, London, England.
Comment: This fruity drink is the most popular modern adaptation of the classic Collins.

RASPBERRY COSMO NEW

Glass: Martini
Garnish: Raspberries on stick
Method: Shake all ingredients with ice and fine strain into chilled glass.

2	shot(s)	Absolut Citron vodka
3/4	shot(s)	Bols raspberry (framboise) liqueur
1 1/4	shot(s)	Cranberry juice
1/2	shot(s)	Freshly squeezed lime juice

Origin: Formula by yours truly in 2004.
Comment: Your classic Cosmo but with raspberry liqueur replacing orange liqueur.

RASPBERRY DEBONNAIRE

Glass: Collins
Garnish: Three raspberries & lemon slice
Method: Muddle raspberries in base of shaker. Add next five ingredients, shake with ice and strain into an ice-filled glass. Top up with soda, stir and serve with straws.

10	fresh	Raspberries
2	shot(s)	Absolut vodka
1 1/2	shot(s)	Freshly squeezed lemon juice
1/2	shot(s)	Bols Raspberry (framboise) liqueur
1/2	shot(s)	Sugar (gomme) syrup
3	dashes	Fee Brothers Orange bitters (optional)
Top up with		Soda water (club soda)

Variant: Raspberry Collins
Comment: If based on gin rather than vodka it would be a Raspberry Collins.

RASPBERRY MARTINI #2

Glass: Martini
Garnish: Raspberries
Method: Muddle raspberries in base of shaker. Add other ingredients, shake with ice and fine strain into chilled glass.

12	fresh	Raspberries
2 1/2	shot(s)	Absolut vodka
3/4	shot(s)	Bols Raspberry (framboise) liqueur
3/4	shot(s)	Sugar (gomme) syrup
4	dashes	Fee Brothers Orange bitters (optional)

Variant: Better made with vanilla vodka if you have it.
Origin: Created in 1997 by Dick Bradsell, London, England.
Comment: Rich raspberries fortified with vodka.

RASPBERRY MOCHA'TINI

Glass: Martini
Garnish: Three raspberries on stick
Method: Shake all ingredients with ice and fine strain into chilled glass.

1	shot(s)	Espresso coffee (cold)
1 1/2	shot(s)	Absolut Raspberri vodka
3/4	shot(s)	Bols Brown crème de cacao
3/4	shot(s)	Bols Raspberry (framboise) liqueur

Origin: Discovered in 2002 at Lot 61, New York City.
Comment: Sweet chocolate and raspberry tempered by dry coffee and vodka.

RED HOOKER

Glass: Martini
Garnish: Peach slice on rim
Method: Shake all ingredients with ice and fine strain into chilled glass.

1	shot(s)	Freshly extracted peach juice
2	shot(s)	Sauza Hornitos Tequila
1	shot(s)	Bols Raspberry (framboise) liqueur
3/4	shot(s)	Freshly squeezed lemon juice
1/4	shot(s)	Sugar (gomme) syrup

Comment: An appropriately named red fruity drink with more than a hint of Tequila.

SANGRIA MARTINI

Glass: Martini
Garnish: Quarter orange slice
Method: Shake all ingredients with ice and fine strain into chilled glass.

1	shot(s)	Red wine (Shiraz)
1	shot(s)	Freshly squeezed orange juice
1 3/4	shot(s)	Rémy Martin Cognac
1/2	shot(s)	Apple schnapps liqueur
1/2	shot(s)	Bols Raspberry (framboise) liqueur
1/2	shot(s)	Sugar (gomme) syrup

Origin: Created in 2003 by Angelo Vieira at Light Bar, St. Martins Hotel, London, England.
Comment: Brandy based and fruit laced – just like its namesake.

SUMMER MARTINI

Glass: Martini
Garnish: Berries on a cocktail stick
Method: Muddle berries in base of shaker. Add other ingredients; shake with ice and fine strain into chilled glass.

3	fresh	Blackberries
3	fresh	Raspberries
3	fresh	Strawberries
1/2	shot(s)	Bols Blackberry liqueur
1/2	shot	Bols Raspberry (framboise) liqueur
1/2	shot	Bols Strawberry (fraise) liqueur
2	shot(s)	Plymouth gin
3/4	shot(s)	Cinzano Extra Dry vermouth
2	dashes	Fee Brothers Orange bitters

Origin: Created in 2003 by Wayne Collins for Maxxium UK.
Comment: A drink which combines a trio of summer berries with the classic aromatic Martini.

WILD PROMENADE MARTINI

Glass: Martini
Garnish: Float 3 raspberries
Method: Muddle cucumber and raspberries in base of shaker. Add other ingredients, shake with ice and fine strain into ice-filled glass.

2	inch	Chopped cucumber
5	fresh	Raspberries
1 1/2	shot(s)	Absolut vodka
1/2	shot(s)	Absolut Raspberri vodka
1/2	shot(s)	Bols Raspberry (framboise) liqueur
1/4	shot(s)	Sugar (gomme) syrup

Origin: Created in 2002 by Mehdi Otmann at The Player, London, England.
Comment: Rich raspberry with green hints of cucumber.

BOLS® STRAWBERRY LIQUEUR

Bols are one of the largest and oldest producers of fine spirits and liqueurs in the world. Some of them even go back to the year 1575. However, this strawberry liqueur is a relatively new addition to the Bols range. It is a distillate of refreshing citrus fruit and real strawberry juice. The French word for strawberry is 'fraise' and cocktail recipes often call for the use of crème de fraise, or strawberry liqueur. Bols Strawberry liqueur is ideal for use in any recipe which calls for crème de fraise.

This liqueur has a rich ripe strawberry flavour with light hints of citrus fruit. It is great served chilled, in a cocktail, over strawberries or in a fruit salad. 17% alc./vol. (34°proof)

Web: www.bols.com
Producer: Bols Royal Distilleries, Zoetermeer, The Netherlands. **UK distributor:** Maxxium UK Ltd, Stirling, Scotland.
Tel: 01786 430 500
Email: enquiries@maxxium.com

BLACK FOREST GATEAU MARTINI

Glass: Martini
Garnish: Dust with cocoa powder
Method: Shake first four ingredients with ice and strain into chilled glass. Float cream on drink.

2	shot(s)	Absolut vodka
3/4	shot(s)	Chambord black raspberry liqueur
3/4	shot(s)	Bols strawberry (fraise) liqueur
1/4	shot(s)	Sisca crème de cassis
1	shot(s)	Double (heavy) cream

Origin: Created in 2002 at Hush, London, England.
Comment: Dessert by name and dessert by nature. Wonderfully moreish, naughty but very nice.

BLACK WIDOW UPDATED

Glass: Martini
Garnish: Liquorice
Method: Shake all ingredients with ice and fine strain into chilled glass.

1	shot(s)	Opal Nera black sambuca
1	shot(s)	Bols strawberry (fraise) liqueur
1	shot(s)	Malibu coconut rum liqueur
1/2	shot(s)	Double (heavy) cream
1/2	shot(s)	Milk

Comment: This sticky, fruity, liquorice cocktail tastes a little like an Allsort sweet.

BOURBON BLUSH

Glass: Martini
Garnish: Strawberry on rim
Method: Muddle strawberries in base of shaker. Add other ingredients, shake with ice and fine strain into chilled glass.

3	fresh	Strawberries
2	shot(s)	Buffalo Trace Bourbon
3/4	shot(s)	Bols strawberry (fraise) liqueur
1/4	shot(s)	Maple syrup

Origin: Created in 2003 by Simon King at MJU @ Millennium Hotel, London, England.
Comment: Strawberry and maple syrup combine brilliantly with Bourbon in this drink.

FRENCH SPRING PUNCH

Glass: Sling
Garnish: Strawberry
Method: Pour ingredients into ice-filled glass.

1	shot(s)	Rémy Martin Cognac
1/4	shot(s)	Bols strawberry (fraise) liqueur
1/4	shot(s)	Freshly squeezed lemon juice
1/4	shot(s)	Sugar (gomme) syrup
Top up with		Piper-Heidsieck Brut Champagne

Origin: Created by Dick Bradsell & Rodolphe Sorel.
Comment: Not as popular as the Russian Spring Punch.

JAYNE MANSFIELD

Glass: Flute
Garnish: Strawberry on rim
Method: Muddle strawberries in base of shaker. Add other ingredients, shake with ice and fine strain into glass.

4	fresh	Hulled strawberries
1	shot(s)	Havana Club light rum
1	shot(s)	Bols Strawberry (fraise) liqueur
1/4	shot(s)	Sugar (gomme) syrup
Top up with		Piper-Heidsieck Brut Champagne

Origin: Named after the Hollywood actress.
Comment: Champagne is made to go with strawberries.

STRAWBERRY COSMO NEW

Glass: Martini
Garnish: Strawberry on rim
Method: Shake all ingredients with ice and fine strain into chilled glass.

2	shot(s)	Absolut Citron vodka
3/4	shot(s)	Bols strawberry (fraise) liqueur
1 1/4	shot(s)	Cranberry juice
1/2	shot(s)	Freshly squeezed lime juice

Origin: Formula by yours truly in 2004.
Comment: Strawberry liqueur replaces the usual orange liqueur in this contemporary classic.

REGGAE RUM PUNCH

Glass: Collins
Garnish: Wedge of pineapple spiked with a maraschino cherry on rim
Method: Shake all ingredients with cubed ice and strain into a glass filled with crushed ice.

3/4	shot(s)	Freshly squeezed lime juice
3/4	shot(s)	Bols Strawberry (fraise) liqueur
1	shot(s)	Strawberry syrup
2	shot(s)	Wray & Nephew overproof rum
1 1/2	shot(s)	Pressed pineapple juice
2 1/2	shot(s)	Freshly squeezed orange juice

Origin: The most popular punch in Jamaica, where it is sold under different names with slightly varying ingredients. It always contains orange, pineapple and most importantly overproof rum.
Comment: A bright red drink with a frothy top.

THE STRAWBERRY ÉCLAIR

Glass: Shot
Method: Shake all ingredients with ice and fine strain into chilled glass.

1/2	shot(s)	Frangelico hazelnut liqueur
1/2	shot(s)	Bols Strawberry (fraise) liqueur
1/4	shot(s)	Freshly squeezed lime juice

Comment: This drink heralds from Australia where it is a popular shot.

ROSSINI NEW

Glass: Flute
Garnish: Strawberry on rim
Method: Muddle strawberries in base of shaker. Add strawberry liqueur, shake with ice and fine strain into glass. Top up with Prosecco and gently stir.

4	fresh	Strawberries
3/4	shot(s)	Bols strawberry (fraise) liqueur
Top up with		Prosecco sparkling wine

Origin: Named for the 19th century opera composer, this is one of the most popular Bellini variants in Venice.
Comment: Strawberries seem to complement Prosecco even better than peaches.

TRIFLE'TINI

Glass: Martini
Garnish: Crumbled Cadbury's Flake bar
Method: Muddle raspberries and strawberries in base of shaker. Add other ingredients apart from cream, shake with ice and fine strain into chilled glass. Lightly whip cream and layer over drink.

10	fresh	Raspberries
2	fresh	Strawberries
2	shot(s)	Rémy Martin Cognac
3/4	shot(s)	Disaronno Originale amaretto
1/2	shot(s)	Bols Strawberry (fraise) liqueur
1	shot(s)	Pedro Ximénez Sherry
1 1/2	shot(s)	Double (heavy) cream

Origin: Created in 2000 by Ian Baldwin at the GE Club, London, England.
Comment: Very rich – looks and tastes like trifle.

STRAWBERRY BLONDE MARTINI NEW

Glass: Martini
Garnish: Float basil leaf
Method: Muddle basil in mixing glass. Add other ingredients, stir with ice and fine strain into chilled glass.

4	fresh	Basil leaves
2 1/2	shot(s)	Absolut Kurant vodka
1/2	shot(s)	Cinzano Extra Dry vermouth
1/2	shot(s)	Bols strawberry (fraise) liqueur
1/8	shot(s)	Sugar (gomme) syrup

Origin: Adapted from a recipe discovered in 2003 at Oxo Tower Bar, London, England.
Comment: Blackcurrant vodka flavour dominates with hints of strawberry and basil.

WIMBLEDON MARTINI

Glass: Martini
Garnish: Strawberry on rim
Method: Shake all ingredients with ice and fine strain into chilled glass.

6	fresh	Hulled strawberries
1 1/2	shot(s)	Havana Club light rum
1 1/2	shot(s)	Bols Strawberry (fraise) liqueur
1/4	shot(s)	Sugar (gomme) syrup
1	shot(s)	Double (heavy) cream

Comment: Takes some getting through the strainer, but when you do it's simply strawberries and cream.

BOLS® WHITE CRÈME DE CACAO

A number of recipes require the chocolate flavour of crème de cacao but without the dark brown colour. In order to give this liqueur the taste without the dark colour, Bols extract the flavour of the finest roasted cacao beans by means of distillation instead of percolation. This process also gives Bols White crème de cacao a lighter flavour than Bols Brown crème de cacao.
Bols Crème de Cacao is perfect for adding a rich chocolate flavour to any cocktail. Choose between this lighter, more delicately flavoured white or the rich dark version.
24% alc./vol. (48°proof)

Web: www.bols.com
Producer: Bols Royal Distilleries, Zoetermeer, The Netherlands. **UK distributor:** Maxxium UK Ltd, Stirling, Scotland.
Tel: 01786 430 500
Email: enquiries@maxxium.com

BIRD OF PARADISE UPDATED

Glass: Martini
Garnish: Nutmeg dust
Method: Shake all ingredients with ice and fine strain into chilled glass.

1¼	shot(s)	Sauza Hornitos Tequila
¾	shot(s)	Bols white crème de cacao
½	shot(s)	Disaronno Originale amaretto
1	shot(s)	Double (heavy) cream
¾	shot(s)	Milk

Comment: If you like Tequila and creamy drinks, the two don't mix much better than this.

BRANDY ALEXANDER

Glass: Martini
Garnish: Sprinkle ground nutmeg
Method: Shake ingredients with ice and strain into glass.

1½	shot(s)	Rémy Martin Cognac
½	shot(s)	Bols brown crème de cacao
½	shot(s)	Bols white crème de cacao
2	shot(s)	Double (heavy) cream

Comment: This classic blend of brandy and chocolate smoothed with cream is based on the original Alexander. Made with gin, this was a Prohibition favourite, as the cream, chocolate and nutmeg disguised the rough taste of homemade 'bathtub' gin. Creamy, subtle, spicy and rich.

BUTTERSCOTCH MARTINI

Glass: Martini
Garnish: Butterscotch sweet
Method: Shake all ingredients with ice and fine strain into chilled glass.

2	shot(s)	Mount Gay Eclipse gold rum
¾	shot(s)	Teichenné butterscotch schnapps
¾	shot(s)	Bols white crème de cacao
⅛	shot(s)	Sugar (gomme) syrup
½	shot(s)	Chilled water

Comment: Sweet and suckable.

CHOCOLATE MARTINI

Glass: Martini
Garnish: White cacao & chocolate powder rim
Method: Shake all ingredients with ice and fine strain into chilled glass.

2	shot(s)	Absolut vodka
1	shot(s)	Bols white crème de cacao
1	shot(s)	Cinzano Extra Dry vermouth

Comment: Vodka and chocolate made more interesting with a hint of vermouth.

CHOCOLATE MINT MARTINI

Glass: Martini
Garnish: Chocolate powder rim
Method: Stir ingredients with ice and strain into glass.

2	shot(s)	Absolut vodka
1/2	shot(s)	White crème de menthe
1	shot(s)	Bols White crème de cacao
1/2	shot(s)	Cinzano Extra Dry vermouth

Comment: Tastes of after dinner mints.

DC MARTINI

Glass: Martini
Method: Stir all ingredients with ice and strain into glass.

2	shot(s)	Vanilla infused Appleton Estate V/X aged rum
1/4	shot(s)	Frangelico hazelnut liqueur
1/4	shot(s)	Bols white crème de cacao
1/4	shot(s)	Sugar (gomme) syrup
1/2	shot(s)	Chilled water

Origin: I discovered this in 2000 at Teatro, London, England.
Comment: Vanilla, chocolate and a hint of nut. Add more sugar to taste.

EASTER MARTINI

Glass: Martini
Garnish: Crumbled Flake bar
Method: Break away outer shells of cardamom pods and muddle inner seeds in base of shaker. Add other ingredients, shake with ice and fine strain into chilled glass.

4	pods	Green cardamom
2	shot(s)	Absolut Vanilia vodka
1	shot(s)	Bols white crème de cacao
1/4	shot(s)	Sugar (gomme) syrup
1/2	shot(s)	Chilled water
1/2	fresh	Egg white

Origin: Created in 2003 by Simon King at MJU Bar, Millennium Hotel, London, England.
Comment: A standard Chocolate Martini with extra interest thanks to the clever use of vanilla and cardamom. The egg was my own addition as it seemed appropriate for Easter.

LEMON CHIFFON PIE

Glass: Coupette
Garnish: Lemon wedge
Method: Blend ingredients with crushed ice and serve.

1	shot(s)	Havana Club light rum
1	shot(s)	Bols white crème de cacao
1	shot(s)	Freshly squeezed lemon juice
2	scoops	Vanilla ice cream

Comment: Creamy and tangy – like a lemon pie.

SAVANNAH NEW

●●●●◐○

Glass: Martini
Method: Shake all ingredients with ice and fine strain into chilled glass.

2	shot(s)	Plymouth gin
2	shot(s)	Freshly squeezed orange juice
1/4	shot(s)	Bols white crème de cacao
1/2	fresh	Egg white

Origin: Adapted from a recipe in the 1949 edition of Esquire's Handbook For Hosts.
Comment: Gin and orange with a hint of chocolate – smoothed by egg white.

SMARTINI

●●●●○

Glass: Martini
Garnish: Three Smarties in drink
Method: Shake all ingredients with ice and fine strain into chilled glass.

2	shot(s)	Absolut Citron vodka
1	shot(s)	Bols White crème de cacao
1/4	shot(s)	Sugar (gomme) syrup
3/4	shot(s)	Chilled mineral water
4	dashes	Fee Brothers Orange bitters

Comment: Citrus with a crispy chocolate edge.

SUPERMINTY-CHOCOLATINI

●●●●○

Glass: Martini
Garnish: Chocolate powder rim
Method: Shake all ingredients with ice and fine strain into chilled glass.

2	shot(s)	Absolut vodka
1	shot(s)	Bols White crème de cacao
1	shot(s)	White crème de menthe

Comment: Obviously but nicely flavoured.

TURKISH DELIGHT

●●●●○

Glass: Martini
Garnish: Turkish Delight on rim
Method: Stir honey and vodka in base of shaker so as to dissolve honey. Add other ingredients' shake with ice and fine strain into chilled glass.

2	spoons	Runny honey
1	shot(s)	Absolut vodka
1	shot(s)	Absolut Vanilia vodka
1/2	shot(s)	Bols White crème de cacao
1/8	shot(s)	Rosewater
3/4	shot(s)	Chilled water
1/2	fresh	Egg white

Origin: Created by yours truly in 2003.
Comment: Rosewater, honey, chocolate and vanilla provide a distinctly Turkish Delight flavour - fortified with vodka.

BUFFALO TRACE® BOURBON

For thousands of years wild buffalo carved their way across the wilderness of America, leaving huge paths in their wake. Early pioneers used these paths, or traces as they were later known, on their adventure westward to discover new lands. The largest of these traces, the Great Buffalo Trace, is situated north of the Kentucky River and it is here, where the trace crossed the river, that a settlement was established and distillation commenced in 1787. In 1857 a modern distillery was built on the site, the first to incorporate steam power and today, on this same site, stands Buffalo Trace Distillery, a family owned business producing over 25 different American whiskeys.

Buffalo Trace Kentucky Straight Bourbon Whiskey, the flagship whiskey of the distillery is made in batches of just 20-25 barrels using Indiana corn, rye and malted barley. It is laid down to age for 9-11 years, slowly maturing and developing the character-istics of a superb bourbon.

Jim Murray describes Buffalo Trace as 'one of the world's great whiskeys'. It has a light palate with well-integrated flavours including vanilla, ginger, clove, chocolate, espresso coffee, mint, aniseed and honey. 45% alc/vol.(90°proof)

Web: www.buffalotrace.com **Producer:** Buffalo Trace Distillery, Frankfort, Kentucky, USA. **UK distributor:** InSpirit Brands, London. **Tel:** 020 7377 9457 **Email:** info@inspiritbrands.com

APPLE MANHATTAN

Glass: Martini
Garnish: Apple slice on rim
Method: Shake all ingredients with ice and fine strain into chilled glass.

2	shot(s)	Buffalo Trace Bourbon
1½	shot(s)	Apple schnapps liqueur
½	shot(s)	Cinzano Rosso (sweet) vermouth

Origin: My take on a drink created by David Marsden at First on First in New York City and latterly popularised by Dale DeGroff. Traditionalists may want to stir this drink.
Comment: Rusty gold in colour, this is a flavoursome number for Bourbon lovers.

BOURBON BLUSH

Glass: Martini
Garnish: Strawberry on rim
Method: Muddle strawberries in base of shaker. Add other ingredients, shake with ice and fine strain into chilled glass.

3	fresh	Strawberries
2	shot(s)	Buffalo Trace Bourbon
¾	shot(s)	Bols strawberry (fraise) liqueur
¼	shot(s)	Maple syrup

Origin: Created in 2003 by Simon King at MJU @ Millennium Hotel, London, England.
Comment: Strawberry and maple syrup combine brilliantly with Bourbon in this drink.

BOURBON COOKIE

Glass: Old-fashioned
Garnish: Cinnamon dust
Method: Shake all ingredients with ice and fine strain into ice-filled glass.

2	shot(s)	Buffalo Trace Bourbon
½	shot(s)	Double (heavy) cream
½	shot(s)	Milk
½	shot(s)	Mango or passion fruit syrup
½	shot(s)	Teichenné butterscotch schnapps

Origin: Created in 2002 by Andres Masso, London, England.
Comment: Looks tame but packs a flavoursome punch.

BOURBON SMASH

Glass: Collins
Garnish: Lime wheel on rim
Method: Muddle raspberries in base of shaker. Add other ingredients, shake with ice and strain into ice-filled glass.

12	fresh	Raspberries
4	fresh	Torn mint leaves
2½	shot(s)	Buffalo Trace Bourbon
3½	shot(s)	Cranberry juice
1	shot(s)	Freshly squeezed lime juice
½	shot(s)	Sugar (gomme) syrup
2	dashes	Angostura aromatic bitters

Comment: This refreshing long drink has a sharp edge that adds to its appeal.

CASANOVA

Glass: Martini
Garnish: Crumble Flake bar over drink
Method: Shake all ingredients with ice and fine strain into chilled glass.

1¹/₂	shot(s)	Buffalo Trace Bourbon
³/₄	shot(s)	Blandy's Alvada Madeira
³/₄	shot(s)	Kahlúa coffee liqueur
³/₄	shot(s)	Double (heavy) cream
³/₄	shot(s)	Milk
¹/₈	shot(s)	Sugar (gomme) syrup

Comment: Rich, medium-sweet and creamy with a mocha coffee finish.

FOURTH OF JULY MARTINI

Glass: Martini
Garnish: Maraschino cherry on rim
Method: Pour Bourbon and Galliano into warm glass, ignite and sprinkle cinnamon while flaming. Shake coffee liqueur, orange juice and cream with ice and strain into glass with Bourbon and Galliano.

1	shot(s)	Buffalo Trace Bourbon
1	shot(s)	Galliano liqueur
1	shot(s)	Kahlúa coffee liqueur
1	shot(s)	Freshly squeezed orange juice
1	shot(s)	Double (heavy) cream

Comment: A wonderfully rich and tasty after dinner drink.

GINGERBREAD MARTINI NEW

Glass: Martini
Garnish: Slice of ginger
Method: Shake all ingredients with ice and fine strain into chilled glass.

1¹/₂	shot(s)	Buffalo Trace Bourbon
³/₄	shot(s)	Teichenné butterscotch schnapps
³/₄	shot(s)	Stone's green ginger wine
2	shot(s)	Pressed apple juice

Origin: Created by yours truly in 2004.
Comment: Sticky, warming and spicy.

GREAT MUGHAL MARTINI

Glass: Martini
Garnish: Lemon zest twist
Method: Muddle raisins in base of shaker. Add other ingredients, shake with ice and strain into glass.

20		Raisins
1¹/₂	shot(s)	Buffalo Trace Bourbon
¹/₄	shot(s)	Sugar (gomme) syrup
³/₄	shot(s)	Passion fruit syrup
¹/₄	shot(s)	Freshly squeezed lime juice
3	drops	Rosewater
1	shot(s)	Lime & lemongrass cordial

Origin: Created in 2001 by Douglas Ankrah for Red Fort, Soho, London, England.
Comment: Douglas' original recipe called for raisin infused Bourbon and we'd recommend you make this drink that way if time permits.

IRISH MANHATTAN

Glass: Martini
Garnish: Shamrock
Method: Stir all ingredients with ice and strain into chilled glass.

1¹/₂	shot(s)	Buffalo Trace Bourbon
1	shot(s)	Tuaca Italian liqueur
¹/₂	shot(s)	Grand Marnier liqueur
¹/₄	shot(s)	Vanilla syrup

Origin: Adapted from a drink discovered in 2001 at Detroit, London, England.
Comment: There's nothing Irish about this drink, but it's good all the same.

JULEP MARTINI

Glass: Martini
Garnish: Mint leaf
Method: Muddle mint in base of shaker. Add other ingredients, shake with ice and fine strain into chilled glass.

8	fresh	Mint leaves
2¹/₂	shot(s)	Buffalo Trace Bourbon
¹/₂	shot(s)	Sugar (gomme) syrup
³/₄	shot(s)	Chilled water

Origin: Adapted from a recipe created by Dick Bradsell.
Comment: A short variation on the classic Julep: sweetened Bourbon and mint.

KENTUCKY COLONEL

Glass: Old-fashioned
Garnish: Peach slice & mint sprig
Method: Shake all ingredients with ice and strain into glass filled with crushed ice.

1¹/₂	shot(s)	Buffalo Trace Bourbon
¹/₄	shot(s)	Southern Comfort liqueur
¹/₄	shot(s)	Cointreau / triple sec
1	shot(s)	Freshly extracted peach juice
¹/₂	shot(s)	Freshly squeezed lemon juice
¹/₂	shot(s)	Sugar (gomme) syrup

Origin: Created by Morgan Watson of Apartment, Belfast, Northern Ireland.
Comment: Peach and Bourbon with hints of orange and spice.

KENTUCKY DREAM

Glass: Old-fashioned
Garnish: Lemon zest twist
Method: Stir vanilla liqueur and Angostura bitters with two ice cubes in a glass. Add one shot of Bourbon and two more ice cubes. Stir some more and add another two ice cubes and another shot of Bourbon. Add last two ingredients, more ice cubes and stir lots more. The melting and stirring in of ice cubes is essential to the dilution and taste of the drink.

¹/₂	shot(s)	Teichenné vanilla schnapps
2	dashes	Angostura aromatic bitters
2	shot(s)	Buffalo Trace Bourbon
¹/₂	shot(s)	Bols apricot brandy liqueur
1	shot(s)	Pressed apple juice

Origin: Created in 2002 by Wayne Collins for Maxxium UK.
Comment: Tames Bourbon in a dream-like way and adds hints of apricot, vanilla and apple.

KENTUCKY MUFFIN

Glass: Rocks
Method: Muddle blueberries in base of shaker. Add other ingredients, shake with ice and strain into glass filled with crushed ice. Stir well and serve with two straws.

12	fresh	Blueberries
2	shot(s)	Buffalo Trace Bourbon
1	shot(s)	Pressed apple juice
1/2	shot(s)	Freshly squeezed lime juice
1/2	shot(s)	Sugar (gomme) syrup

Origin: Created in 2000 at Mash, London, England.
Comment: Blueberries, lime and apple combine and are fortified with Bourbon.

KENTUCKY PEAR

Glass: Martini
Garnish: Pear slice on rim
Method: Shake all ingredients with ice and fine strain into chilled glass.

1	shot(s)	Buffalo Trace Bourbon
1	shot(s)	Xanté pear liqueur
1	shot(s)	Freshly extracted pear juice
1	shot(s)	Pressed apple juice

Origin: Created in 2003 by Jes at The Cinnamon Club, London, England.
Comment: Pear, apple, vanilla and whiskey are partners in this richly flavoured drink.

LUCKY LINDY

Glass: Collins
Garnish: Lemon wheel
Method: Stir honey with Bourbon in base of shaker so as to dissolve honey. Add lemon juice, shake with ice and strain into ice-filled glass. Top up with 7-Up.

3	spoon(s)	Runny honey
2	shot(s)	Buffalo Trace Bourbon
1/2	shot(s)	Freshly squeezed lemon juice
Top up with		7-Up

Origin: Adapted from a drink discovered in 2003 at The Grange Hall, New York City.
Comment: A long refreshing drink that combines whisky, citrus and honey – a long chilled hot toddy without the spice.

MAGIC TRACE

Glass: Martini
Garnish: Lemon wedge on rim
Method: Shake ingredients with ice and strain into glass.

1	shot(s)	Buffalo Trace Bourbon
3/4	shot(s)	Drambuie liqueur
1/4	shot(s)	Cinzano Extra Dry vermouth
1	shot(s)	Freshly squeezed orange juice
1/4	shot(s)	Freshly squeezed lemon juice
1/4	shot(s)	Sugar (gomme) syrup

Comment: Very drinkable mix of strong flavours.

MAN-BOUR-TINI

Glass: Martini
Garnish: Orange zest twist
Method: Shake all ingredients with ice and fine strain into chilled glass.

1	shot(s)	Mandarine Napoléon liqueur
3/4	shot(s)	Buffalo Trace Bourbon
1/2	shot(s)	Freshly squeezed lime juice
2	shot(s)	Cranberry juice
1/4	shot(s)	Sugar (gomme) syrup

Origin: Created in 1999 by yours truly.
Comment: A rounded, fruity Bourbon based drink with a mandarin and lime sourness.

MANHATTAN DRY

Glass: Martini
Garnish: Lemon zest twist
Method: Stir all ingredients with ice and strain into chilled glass.

2 1/2	shot(s)	Buffalo Trace Bourbon
1	shot(s)	Cinzano Extra Dry vermouth
4	dashes	Angostura aromatic bitters

Variant: As for 'Manhattan Sweet'. Create an Oddball Manhattan by the addition of a few dashes of Chartreuse or blue curaçao.
Origin: A Nineteenth century classic of disputed origin.
Comment: A bone dry Manhattan for those with dry palates.

MANHATTAN PERFECT

Glass: Martini
Garnish: Twist of orange & cherry on stick
Method: Stir all ingredients with ice and strain into chilled glass.

2 1/2	shot(s)	Buffalo Trace Bourbon
1/2	shot(s)	Cinzano Rosso (sweet) vermouth
1/2	shot(s)	Cinzano Extra Dry vermouth
4	dashes	Angostura aromatic bitters

Variant: As for 'Manhattan Sweet'.
Comment: The Manhattan version most popularly served – medium dry.

MANHATTAN SWEET

Glass: Martini
Garnish: Twist of orange & cherry on stick
Method: Stir ingredients with ice and strain into chilled glass.

2 1/2	shot(s)	Buffalo Trace Bourbon
1	shot(s)	Cinzano Rosso (sweet) vermouth
1	spoon	Syrup from jar of maraschino cherries
4	dashes	Angostura aromatic bitters

Variant: Served over ice in an old-fashioned glass. Originally a rye drink, it is called a Rob Roy when Scotch is substituted, a Harvard when made with brandy (as in the Midwestern states of the US) or a Star Cocktail when made with applejack.
Comment: I must confess to preferring my Manhattans served sweet, perfect at a push. The Manhattan is complex, challenging and moreish. Best of all, it's available in a style to suit every palate.

MET MANHATTAN

Glass: Martini
Garnish: Orange zest twist
Method: Shake ingredients with ice and strain into glass.

2	shot(s)	Buffalo Trace Bourbon
1	shot(s)	Grand Marnier liqueur
³/₄	shot(s)	Teichenné butterscotch schnapps
1	dash	Fee Brothers orange bitters

Origin: The Met Bar, Metropolitan Hotel, London, England.
Comment: A Manhattan with orange interest.

MINT JULEP

Glass: Collins
Garnish: Mint sprig and slice of lemon
Method: Lightly muddle (only bruise) mint with Bourbon in base of shaker. (Crushing the leaves releases the bitter, inner juices. Discard stems, which are also bitter.) Place shaker and its contents in refrigerator with serving glass for at least two hours. Remove glass from refrigerator and half fill with crushed ice. Place sugar and Angostura into shaker base with Bourbon and mint. Shake with ice and strain into glass. Churn the drink with the crushed ice using a bar spoon. Top up the glass with more crushed ice so as to fill it and churn again. Serve with two long straws.

12	fresh	Mint leaves
2¹/₂	shot(s)	Buffalo Trace Bourbon
³/₄	shot(s)	Sugar (gomme) syrup
3	dashes	Angostura aromatic bitters

Comment: Serving this drink ice cold and giving the flavours in the mint time to marry with the Bourbon are key to the quality of the finished Julep. Hence, it's a drink that requires advance planning.

MISSISSIPPI PUNCH

Glass: Collins
Method: Shake all ingredients with cubed ice and strain into a glass filled with crushed ice.

1¹/₄	shot(s)	Sugar (gomme) syrup
³/₄	shot(s)	Freshly squeezed lemon juice
1¹/₂	shot(s)	Buffalo Trace Bourbon
³/₄	shot(s)	Rémy Martin Cognac
3	shot(s)	Chilled water

Comment: A beautifully balanced concoction.

MOCHA MARTINI

Glass: Martini
Garnish: Dust centre with cocoa powder
Method: Shake first four ingredients with ice and fine strain into chilled glass. Float just half a shot of cream in centre of drink.

1	shot(s)	Buffalo Trace Bourbon
1¹/₂	shot(s)	Espresso coffee (cold)
1	shot(s)	Baileys Irish Cream liqueur
1	shot(s)	Bols brown crème de cacao
¹/₂	shot(s)	Double (heavy) cream

Comment: Made with great espresso coffee, this drink is a superb, richly flavoured balance of sweet and bitter.

MRS ROBINSON

Glass: Old-fashioned
Garnish: Three raspberries
Method: Muddle raspberries in base of shaker. Add next four ingredients, shake with ice and strain into ice-filled glass. Top up with soda and stir.

8	fresh	Raspberries
2	shot(s)	Buffalo Trace Bourbon
1	shot(s)	Bols raspberry (framboise) liqueur
¹/₄	shot(s)	Freshly squeezed lemon juice
¹/₄	shot(s)	Sugar (gomme) syrup
Top up with		Soda water (club soda)

Origin: Created in 2000 by Max Warner at Long Bar, Sanderson, London, England.
Comment: Rich raspberry fruit laced with Bourbon.

NEW ORLEANS PUNCH

Glass: Collins
Method: Shake all ingredients with cubed ice and strain into a glass filled with crushed ice.

1¹/₂	shot(s)	Buffalo Trace Bourbon
³/₄	shot(s)	Appleton Estate V/X aged rum
1¹/₂	shot(s)	Chambord black raspberry liqueur
³/₄	shot(s)	Freshly squeezed lemon juice
3	shot(s)	Cold black camomile tea

Comment: Raspberry is the predominant flavour in this long drink.

OLD FASHIONED UPDATED

Glass: Old-fashioned
Garnish: Orange (or lemon) twist
Method: Stir one shot of Bourbon with two ice cubes in a glass. Add sugar syrup and Angostura and two more ice cubes. Stir some more and add another two ice cubes and another shot of Bourbon. Stir lots more so as to melt ice and add more ice. The melting and stirring in of ice cubes is essential to the dilution and taste of the drink.

2¹/₂	shot(s)	Buffalo Trace Bourbon
¹/₂	shot(s)	Sugar (gomme) syrup
3	dashes	Angostura aromatic bitters

Origin: Like the Martini, the glass this cocktail is served in has taken the name of the drink.
Comment: The Old Fashioned tames Bourbon, making it smooth and remarkably easy to drink.

WHISKEY SOUR UPDATED

Glass: Old-fashioned
Garnish: Cherry & lemon slice sail
Method: Shake all ingredients with ice and strain into ice-filled glass

2	shot(s)	Buffalo Trace Bourbon
³/₄	shot(s)	Freshly squeezed lemon juice
1	shot(s)	Sugar (gomme) syrup
¹/₂	fresh	Egg white
4	dashes	Angostura aromatic bitters

Comment: This recipe follows the classic sour proportions: three quarter part of the sour ingredient (lemon juice), one part of the sweet ingredient (sugar syrup) and two parts of the strong ingredient (whiskey) (3:4:8). I actually prefer mine sourer with 1 shot lemon juice and ¹/₂ shot sugar (4:2:8). You might want to experiment to find your preferred balance.

CAMPARI®

Renowned for its distinctive, bitter-sweet taste and vivid red colour, Campari was created in 1860 by Gaspare Campari from a secret recipe of herbs, plants and fruit which remains unchanged to this day . Available in over 190 countries world-wide, Campari reflects a world of passion, prestige and transgression.

Campari may be enjoyed at whatever time of day and a few fundamentals of preparation should always be rigorously followed for it to be appreciated at its fullest:

•Campari must always be served chilled to enhance its balanced taste.

•The bottle must be kept from direct sunlight and heat, ideally in a refrigerator .

•Campari must never be served with lemon but can be garnished with a slice or peel of orange.

To fully appreciate the unique taste of Campari as a long drink – why not try lime cordial & tonic, orange or grapefruit juice – always serve a 50ml measure.

Campari can also be enjoyed in a variety of exciting cocktails. **Web:** www.campari.com **Producer:** Campari SpA, Milan, Italy. **UK distributor:** FIOR Brands Ltd, Stirling, Scotland. **Tel:** 01786 406 360 **Email:** info@fiorbrands.co.uk

AMERICANO UPDATED

Glass: Collins
Garnish: Orange slice
Method: Pour Campari and vermouth into ice-filled glass and top up with soda. Stir and serve with straws.

2	shot(s)	Campari
2	shot(s)	Cinzano Rosso sweet vermouth
Top up with		Soda water

Origin: First served in the 1860s in Gaspare Campari's bar in Milan, this was originally known as the 'Milano-Torino' as Campari came from Milano (Milan) and Cinzano from Torino (Turin). It was not until Prohibition that the Italians noticed an influx of Americans who enjoyed the drink and, as a dubious compliment, dubbed the drink Americano.
Comment: A bitter, fizzy, long refreshing drink, which you'll love if you like Campari.

ANGERS ROSE UPDATED

Glass: Martini
Garnish: Pineapple wedge
Method: Shake all ingredients with ice and fine strain into chilled glass.

1	shot(s)	Cointreau / triple sec
1	shot(s)	Buffalo Trace Bourbon
2	shot(s)	Pressed pineapple juice
½	shot(s)	Campari
½	fresh	Egg white

Comment: This sweet and sour cocktail features orange, pineapple, Bourbon and the herbal bitterness of Campari.

BLOODHOUND UPDATED

Glass: Collins
Garnish: Lime wedge
Method: Shake all ingredients with ice and strain into ice-filled glass.

2	shot(s)	Campari
1	shot(s)	Absolut vodka
4	shot(s)	Freshly squeezed grapefruit juice

Comment: A dry, tart, refreshing long drink.

CUMBERSOME

Glass: Martini
Garnish: Physalis fruit
Method: Muddle cucumber in base of shaker. Add other ingredients, shake with ice and strain into a chilled Martini glass.

4	inch	Fresh chopped peeled cucumber
2	shot(s)	Plymouth gin
½	shot(s)	Campari
1	shot(s)	Freshly squeezed orange juice
½	shot(s)	Sugar (gomme) syrup

Origin: Created in 2002 by Shelim Islam at the GE Club, London, England.
Comment: Interesting and fresh as you like with a pleasant bitterness.

DOLCE-AMARO UPDATED

Glass: Martini
Garnish: Orange zest twist
Method: Stir all ingredients with ice and strain into chilled glass.

1¹/₂	shot(s)	Campari
1¹/₂	shot(s)	Cinzano Bianco vermouth
³/₄	shot(s)	Disaronno Originale amaretto

Comment: The very apt name translates as 'bitter-sweet'.

DOLCE HAVANA

Glass: Martini
Method: Shake all ingredients with ice and fine strain into chilled glass.

1¹/₄	shot(s)	Havana Club light rum
¹/₂	shot(s)	Campari
¹/₂	shot(s)	Cointreau / triple sec
1¹/₄	shot(s)	Freshly squeezed orange juice
1¹/₄	shot(s)	Freshly squeezed lime juice
¹/₈	shot(s)	Sugar (gomme) syrup

Origin: Created by Fabrizio Musorella in 2000 at the Library Bar, Lanesborough Hotel, London, England.
Comment: A melange of Mediterranean fruit.

JASMINE UPDATED

Glass: Martini
Garnish: Lemon zest twist
Method: Shake all ingredients with ice and fine strain into chilled glass.

1	shot(s)	Plymouth gin
¹/₂	shot(s)	Campari
¹/₂	shot(s)	Cointreau / triple sec
1	shot(s)	Freshly squeezed lemon juice
¹/₂	shot(s)	Sugar (gomme) syrup
³/₄	shot(s)	Chilled mineral water

Origin: Created by Alex Turner in 2001.
Comment: The distinctive flavour of Campari is enhanced by lemon and orange.

MILANESE

Glass: Old-fashioned
Garnish: Orange zest twist
Method: Shake all ingredients with ice and strain into glass filled with ice.

1¹/₂	shot(s)	Campari
¹/₂	shot(s)	Galliano liqueur
1	shot(s)	Freshly squeezed lemon juice
¹/₃	shot(s)	Almond (Orgeat) syrup

Origin: Created by Alex Turner in 2001, London, England.
Comment: Also works well served long and topped with soda.

MONZA UPDATED

Glass: Collins
Garnish: Slice of apple
Method: Cut passion fruit in half and scoop out flesh into shaker. Add other ingredients, shake with ice and strain into ice-filled glass.

1	fresh	Passion fruit
2	shot(s)	Absolut vodka
2	shot(s)	Campari
2	shot(s)	Pressed apple juice
¹/₄	shot(s)	Sugar (gomme) syrup

Origin: A cocktail promoted by Campari and named after the Italian Grand Prix circuit.
Comment: If you like Campari you'll love this.

NEGRONI UPDATED

Glass: Old-fashioned
Garnish: Orange zest twist
Method: Stir all ingredients with ice and strain into ice-filled glass.

1¹/₂	shot(s)	Plymouth gin
1¹/₂	shot(s)	Campari
1¹/₂	shot(s)	Cinzano Rosso (sweet) vermouth

Variant: Serve in a Collins glass topped with soda water (club soda).
Origin: This variation on the Americano takes its name from Count Camillo Negroni. In the mid-1920s, while drinking at the Casoni Bar in Florence, Italy, he is said to have asked for an Americano 'with a bit more kick'.
Comment: Bitter and dry, but very tasty.

SPRITZ AL BITTER NEW

Glass: Old-fashioned
Garnish: Orange zest twist
Method: Pour ingredients into ice-filled glass and stir.

1¹/₂	shot(s)	Campari
1¹/₂	shot(s)	Unoaked Chardonnay wine
Top up with		Soda water (club soda)

Origin: The origins of this Venetian speciality date back to the end of the 19th century when the Austrians ruled the city.
Comment: Basically a white wine Spritzer with a splash of Campari – dry and very refreshing.

TRIPLE ORANGE MARTINI

Glass: Martini
Garnish: Orange zest twist
Method: Shake all ingredients with ice and fine strain into chilled glass.

1	shot(s)	Absolut vodka
1	shot(s)	Grand Marnier liqueur
¹/₄	shot(s)	Campari
2	shot(s)	Freshly squeezed orange juice
¹/₂	fresh	Egg white

Origin: I created this drink in 1998.
Comment: A trio of orange flavours. The bitter orange of Campari adds character and balance.

CINZANO® EXTRA DRY VERMOUTH

Over 250 years and world recognition have made Cinzano a cult beverage for today's root conscious consumer. Remarkably rich in culture, full of historical soul yet still as contemporary on the lips of the world's youth as it was 200 years ago. Graceful, moody, ambitious, intellectual, low key but by no means passive, Cinzano makes a very modern statement not to be taken lightly. All the richness of Italian culture with a delightful modern twist. From the vineyards surrounding Turin to the chic lounge-bars of Manhattan or Tokyo, Cinzano the 'original' Vermouth with universal appeal has been adopted by connoisseurs across the globe.

Created in 1757 in Italy according to a traditional method that is still used today, Cinzano Extra Dry is a unique blend of selected high quality wines, herbs and spices appreciated worldwide for its delicate bouquet and sophisticated crispy taste.

Enjoy Cinzano Extra Dry neat over ice, in creative cocktails or as a refreshing long drink with one of your favourite mixers such as lemonade, tonic or soda water.

Web: www.campari.com **Producer:** Francesco Cinzano & C.ia S.p.A – Milano-Italy. **UK distributor:** Fior Brands Ltd, Stirling, Scotland. **Tel:** 01786 406 360 **Email:** info@fiorbrands.co.uk

ARNAUD MARTINI

Glass: Martini
Garnish: Blackberry on rim
Method: Stir all ingredients with ice and strain into chilled glass.

1¹/₂	shot(s)	Plymouth gin
1¹/₂	shot(s)	Cinzano Extra Dry vermouth
1¹/₂	shot(s)	Sisca crème de cassis

Origin: A classic (retro) cocktail named after the stage actress Yvonne Arnaud.
Comment: An interesting balance of blackcurrant, vermouth and gin. Sweet palate and dry finish.

BAMBOO UPDATED

Glass: Martini
Garnish: Orange zest twist
Method: Stir all ingredients with ice and strain into chilled glass.

2	shot(s)	Tio Pepe Fino Sherry
2	shot(s)	Cinzano Extra Dry vermouth
¹/₄	shot(s)	Cointreau / triple sec
3	dashes	Fee Brothers Orange bitters

Variant: East Indian
Origin: A classic and all but forgotten cocktail from the 1940s.
Comment: Dry, refined and subtle - for sophisticated palates only.

BARTENDER'S MARTINI NEW

Glass: Martini
Garnish: Orange zest twist
Method: Shake all ingredients with ice and fine strain into chilled glass.

1	shot(s)	Plymouth gin
1	shot(s)	Tio Pepe Fino Sherry
1	shot(s)	Dubonnet Red
1	shot(s)	Cinzano Extra Dry vermouth
¹/₂	shot(s)	Grand Marnier liqueur

Comment: This classic cocktail resembles an aromatic Martini. Hints of Sherry and orange are followed by a dry finish.

CLARIDGE

Glass: Martini
Garnish: Lemon zest twist
Method: Shake ingredients with ice and strain.

1¹/₂	shot(s)	Plymouth gin
1¹/₂	shot(s)	Cinzano Extra Dry vermouth
³/₄	shot(s)	Cointreau / triple sec
³/₄	shot(s)	Bols apricot brandy liqueur

Comment: Gin for the strength, Martini for dryness and liqueur to sweeten – an interesting combination.

CORONATION NEW

Glass: Collins
Garnish: Maraschino cherry
Method: Stir first five ingredients with ice and strain into ice-filled glass. Top up with soda, stir and serve with straws.

1	shot(s)	Tio Pepe Fino Sherry
1	shot(s)	Cinzano Extra Dry vermouth
2	shot(s)	Sauvignon Blanc / unoaked Chardonnay wine
1/4	shot(s)	Maraschino liqueur
2	dashes	Angostura aromatic bitters
Top up with		Soda water (club soda)

Comment: Light and aromatic.

DRY MARTINI TRADITIONAL

Glass: Martini
Garnish: Olive on stick or lemon zest twist
Method: Stir vermouth with ice in a mixing glass and strain to discard excess vermouth, leaving only a coating on the ice. Pour gin into mixing glass containing coated ice, stir and strain into a chilled glass.

3/4	shot(s)	Cinzano Extra Dry vermouth
2 1/2	shot(s)	Plymouth gin
3	dashes	Fee Brothers orange bitters (optional)

Variant: The proportion of gin to vermouth is a matter of taste, some say 7 to 1, others that one drop is sufficient. We recommend you ask the drinker how they would like their Martini, in the same manner you might ask how they have their steak. If the drinker orders a 'Sweet Martini' use sweet red vermouth rather than dry and use a cherry as garnish instead of an olive. A 'Wet Martini' is a Martini with extra vermouth - don't strain the vermouth out.
Variant: A 'Dickens' is a Martini without a twist, a 'Gibson' is Martini with an onion instead of an olive or a twist and a 'Franklin Martini' is named after Franklin Roosevelt and has two olives.
Origin: Although Martini vermouth is commonly used to make this recipe, the name is coincidental. It is said that this cocktail was invented in 1911 by a New York bartender called Martini di Arma di Taggia who was the head bartender at the fashionable Knickerbocker Hotel and that a French vermouth (Noilly Prat) was originally used with orange bitters.
Comment: If a Martini is shaken it becomes a 'Bradford'. Shaken Martinis taste very different due to further dilution and the air bubbles shaking introduces to the drink.

EAST INDIAN UPDATED

Glass: Martini
Garnish: Olive on stick
Method: Stir all ingredients with ice and strain into chilled glass.

2	shot(s)	Tio Pepe Fino Sherry
2	shot(s)	Cinzano Extra Dry vermouth
1/4	shot(s)	Sugar (gomme) syrup
3	dashes	Fee Brothers orange bitters

Variant: Bamboo
Comment: Dry and pretty flat (like much of India) but perfectly balanced with subtle hints of orange zest.

SLOPPY JOE

Glass: Martini
Method: Shake ingredients with ice and strain into glass.

1	shot(s)	Havana Club light rum
1	shot(s)	Cinzano Extra Dry vermouth
1/4	shot(s)	Cointreau / triple sec
1	shot(s)	Freshly squeezed lime juice
1/2	shot(s)	Sugar (gomme) syrup
1/4	shot(s)	Grenadine syrup

Comment: Nicely balanced.

SUNSHINE COCKTAIL

Glass: Martini
Garnish: Pineapple wedge on rim
Method: Shake all ingredients with ice and fine strain into chilled glass.

1 1/2	shot(s)	Havana Club light rum
1 1/2	shot(s)	Cinzano Extra Dry vermouth
1 1/2	shot(s)	Pressed pineapple juice
1/8	shot(s)	Grenadine syrup

Origin: Adapted from a recipe in my 1949 copy of Esquire's Handbook For Hosts.
Comment: Light, fruity and a tad on the sweet side, but could well brighten your day.

TEXSUN NEW

Glass: Martini
Garnish: Lemon zest twist
Method: Shake all ingredients with ice and fine strain into chilled glass.

1 1/2	shot(s)	Buffalo Trace Bourbon
1 1/2	shot(s)	Cinzano Extra Dry vermouth
1 1/2	shot(s)	Freshly squeezed pink grapefruit juice

Origin: Adapted from a recipe in the 1949 edition of Esquire's Handbook For Hosts.
Comment: Bone dry with fruity herbal hints.

20TH CENTURY MARTINI

Glass: Martini
Garnish: Stemmed cherry on rim
Method: Shake ingredients with ice and strain into glass.

1 1/2	shot(s)	Plymouth gin
1	shot(s)	Cinzano Extra Dry vermouth
1	shot(s)	Bols White crème de cacao
3/4	shot(s)	Freshly squeezed lemon juice
1/4	shot(s)	Cherry syrup

Comment: Very simple, but this bizarre mix of sweet, sour, dryness and strength works well.

WET MARTINI

Glass: Martini
Garnish: Olive or twist?
Method: Stir all ingredients with ice and strain into chilled glass.

3	shot(s)	Plymouth gin
1 1/2	shot(s)	Cinzano Extra Dry vermouth

Origin: A generous measure of vermouth to three of gin, hence the name 'Wet' Martini.
Comment: Reputed to be a favourite of HRH Prince Charles.

CINZANO® ROSSO VERMOUTH

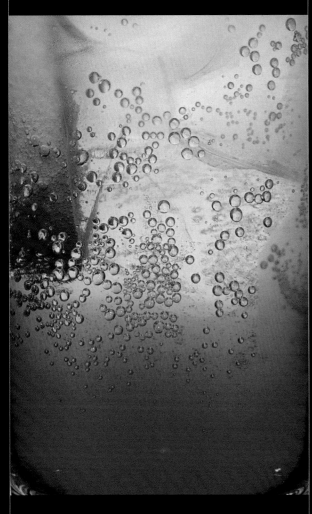

1757. In the back of their herbal store, Giovanni Giacomo Cinzano and his partner Carlo Stefano created a vermouth that was to become famous for its delicate and complex bouquet. Turin – the herbal epicentre at the time – had given birth to a wine enriched with herbs from the local hillsides. Graceful, refined and poetic, this was and still is one of the most successful reflections of Italian culture. This ambitious and desirable drink, which conjures up scenes of the romantic Italian lifestyle, has gained world popularity, and is today a true statement of timeless authenticity and originality.

Made according to a traditional method that is still used today, Cinzano Rosso is a sweet red vermouth made with a unique blend of selected high quality wines and 35 herbs and spices.

Cinzano Rosso has a rich, round and sweetly aromatic flavour and can be drunk as a traditional aperitif or used as an ingredient of classic or modern cocktails.

Web: www.campari.com **Producer:** Francesco Cinzano & C.ia S.p.A – Milano-Italy. **UK distributor:** Fior Brands Ltd, Stirling, Scotland. **Tel:** 01786 406 360 **Email:** info@fiorbrands.co.uk

AMERICANO UPDATED

Glass: Collins
Garnish: Orange slice
Method: Pour Campari and vermouth into ice-filled glass and top up with soda. Stir and serve with straws.

2	shot(s) **Campari**
2	shot(s) **Cinzano Rosso sweet vermouth**
Top up with **Soda water**	

Origin: First served in the 1860s in Gaspare Campari's bar in Milan, this was originally known as the 'Milano-Torino' as Campari came from Milano (Milan) and Cinzano from Torino (Turin). It was not until Prohibition that the Italians noticed an influx of Americans who enjoyed the drink and, as a dubious compliment, dubbed the drink Americano.
Comment: A bitter, fizzy, long refreshing drink, which you'll love if you like Campari.

BLOOD & SAND

Glass: Martini
Method: Shake ingredients with ice and strain into glass.

1	shot(s) **The Famous Grouse Scotch whisky**
1	shot(s) **Bols Cherry brandy liqueur**
1	shot(s) **Cinzano Rosso sweet vermouth**
1	shot(s) **Freshly squeezed orange juice**

Origin: Made for the premiere of the Rudolph Valentino film, Blood and Sand.
Comment: One of the best Scotch cocktails.

BOBBY BURNS

Glass: Martini
Garnish: Stemmed maraschino cherry in drink
Method: Shake all ingredients with ice and fine strain into chilled glass.

1¹/₂	shot(s) **The Famous Grouse Scotch whisky**
1¹/₂	shot(s) **Cinzano Rosso sweet vermouth**
¹/₄	shot(s) **Bénédictine D.O.M. liqueur**

Comment: Strictly speaking this drink should be stirred, but I prefer mine shaken so that's how it appears here.

BOMBAY UPDATED

Glass: Martini
Garnish: Orange zest twist
Method: Stir all ingredients with ice and strain into chilled glass.

1³/₄	shot(s) **Rémy Martin Cognac**
1¹/₂	shot(s) **Cinzano Rosso sweet vermouth**
³/₄	shot(s) **Grand Marnier liqueur**
¹/₂	shot(s) **Chilled water**
¹/₄	shot(s) **Pernod anis**

Origin: My adaptation of a classic.
Comment: A smooth, complex, Sazerac-style Martini.

BRONX UPDATED

Glass: Martini
Garnish: Cherry on rim
Method: Shake all ingredients with ice and fine strain into chilled glass.

1¹/₂	shot(s)	Plymouth gin
³/₄	shot(s)	Cinzano Extra Dry vermouth
³/₄	shot(s)	Cinzano Rosso sweet vermouth
1¹/₂	shot(s)	Freshly squeezed orange juice
2	dashes	Angostura aromatic bitters (optional)

Variant: 1/ Bloody Bronx – made with the juice of a blood orange. 2/ Golden Bronx – with the addition of an egg yolk. 3/ Silver Bronx - with the addition of egg white. Also see the Abbey Martini.
Origin: Created in 1906 by Johnny Solon, a bartender at New York's Waldorf-Astoria Hotel (the Empire State Building occupies the site today) and named after the newly opened Bronx Zoo.
Comment: A serious, dry, complex cocktail – less bitter than many of its era, but even with the modern formula above, still quite challenging to today's palate.

DEVIL'S MANHATTAN UPDATED

Glass: Martini
Garnish: Lemon zest twist
Method: Stir all ingredients with ice and strain into chilled glass.

2	shot(s)	Buffalo Trace Bourbon
1	shot(s)	Southern Comfort liqueur
1	shot(s)	Cinzano Rosso (sweet) vermouth
4	dashes	Angostura aromatic bitters

Comment: A Manhattan with a shot of Comfort.

FLYING SCOTSMAN UPDATED

Glass: Old-fashioned
Method: Stir all ingredients with ice and strain into ice-filled glass.

2	shot(s)	The Famous Grouse Scotch whisky
2	shot(s)	Cinzano Rosso (sweet) vermouth
¹/₄	shot(s)	Sugar (gomme) syrup
4	dashes	Angostura aromatic bitters

Comment: Sweetened Scotch with plenty of spice: like a homemade whisky liqueur.

GIN AND IT

Glass: Rocks
Garnish: Squeeze orange wedge over drink and drop into drink.
Method: Pour ingredients into ice-filled glass and stir.

1¹/₂	shot(s)	Plymouth gin
1¹/₂	shot(s)	Cinzano Rosso (sweet) vermouth

Origin: The name is short for 'Gin and Italian', a reference to the sweet vermouth which was traditionally Italian while French vermouth was dry.
Comment: An old school version of the classic Martini.

MANHATTAN SWEET

Glass: Martini
Garnish: Twist of orange & cherry on stick
Method: Stir ingredients with ice and strain into chilled glass.

2¹/₂	shot(s)	Buffalo Trace Bourbon
1	shot(s)	Cinzano Rosso (sweet) vermouth
1	spoon	Syrup from jar of maraschino cherries
4	dashes	Angostura aromatic bitters

Variant: Served over ice in an old-fashioned glass. Originally a rye drink, it is called a Rob Roy when Scotch is substituted, a Harvard when made with brandy (as in the Midwestern states of the US) or a Star Cocktail when made with applejack. Also see MAnhattan Perfect and Manhattan Dry.
Comment: I must confess to preferring my Manhattans served sweet, perfect at a push. The Manhattan is complex, challenging and moreish. Best of all, it's available in a style to suit every palate.

PICCA UPDATED

Glass: Martini
Garnish: Stemmed maraschino cherry
Method: Shake all ingredients with ice and strain into chilled glass.

1¹/₂	shot(s)	The Famous Grouse Scotch whisky
1	shot(s)	Galliano liqueur
1	shot(s)	Cinzano Rosso vermouth
³/₄	shot(s)	Chilled mineral water

Comment: Bittersweet whisky.

ROB ROY

Glass: Martini
Garnish: Cherry & orange zest twist (discard orange)
Method: Stir all ingredients with ice and strain into chilled glass.

2	shot(s)	Famous Grouse Scotch whisky
1	shot(s)	Cinzano Rosso (sweet) vermouth
2	dashes	Angostura aromatic bitters
¹/₈	shot(s)	Maraschino syrup (optional)

Variant: Affinity
Origin: A classic (retro) cocktail of unknown origins, but thought to have been created circa 1940 and named after a Broadway show.
Comment: A Sweet Manhattan made with Scotch in place of Bourbon. The dry, peaty whisky and bitters ensure it's not too sweet.

VOODOO

Glass: Collins
Garnish: Cinnamon sprinkled over a flame
Method: Shake and strain into an ice filled glass.

2	shot(s)	Appleton Estate V/X aged rum
1	shot(s)	Cinzano Rosso vermouth
4	shot(s)	Pressed apple juice
1	shot(s)	Freshly squeezed lime juice
1	shot(s)	Sugar (gomme) syrup

Origin: Created in 2002 by Alex Kammerling, London, England.
Comment: The rich flavour of the aged rum marries well with apple and lime juice.

COINTREAU®

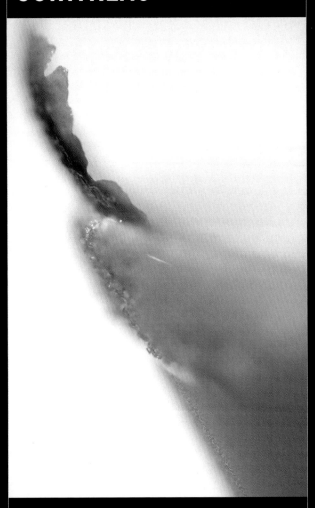

The distilling firm of Cointreau was started in 1849 by two brothers, Adolphe and Edouard-Jean Cointreau, who were confectioners in Angers. The liqueur we know today was created by Edouard Cointreau, the son of Edouard-Jean, and first marketed in the 1870s. Cointreau should not be confused with other liqueurs labelled mere 'triple secs'. This term is a confusing one as it means 'triple dry' and they tend to be very sweet. Where cocktail recipes call for the use of triple sec, we recommend Cointreau, which is made from the fragrant peels of bitter and sweet oranges, carefully grown and meticulously selected for their quality from the Caribbean. A versatile cocktail ingredient, Cointreau can also be served straight over ice or mixed with fruit juices, tonic or lemonade.

The mainstay of many classic recipes, Cointreau has a luscious, ripe taste featuring bitter orange, zesty, citrus hints, a splash of orange juice and a hint of spice. 40% alc./vol. (80°proof)

Web: www.cointreau.com **Producer:** Remy Cointreau, Angers, France. **UK distributor:** Maxxium UK Ltd, Stirling, Scotland. **Tel:** 01786 430 500 **Email:** enquiries@maxxium.com

APPLE CART

Glass: Martini
Garnish: Apple slice on rim
Method: Shake all ingredients with ice and fine strain into chilled glass.

2	shot(s)	Calvados or applejack brandy
3/4	shot(s)	Cointreau / triple sec
1/2	shot(s)	Freshly squeezed lemon juice
1/2	shot(s)	Sugar (gomme) syrup
1/2	shot(s)	Chilled water

AKA: Calvados Sidecar
Origin: This classic (retro) cocktail is an adaptation of the even older Sidecar.
Comment: A serious combination of apple with orange and sweet with sour.

BALALAIKA UPDATED

Glass: Martini
Garnish: Orange zest twist
Method: Shake all ingredients with ice and fine strain into chilled glass.

1 1/2	shot(s)	Absolut vodka
1 1/2	shot(s)	Cointreau / triple sec
1 1/2	shot(s)	Freshly squeezed lemon juice

Comment: Richly flavoured with orange and lemon.

BREAKFAST MARTINI

Glass: Martini
Garnish: Slice of toast on rim
Method: Stir marmalade with gin in base of shaker until it dissolves. Add other ingredients, shake with ice and fine strain into chilled glass.

1	spoon	Orange marmalade (rindless)
1 3/4	shot(s)	Plymouth gin
3/4	shot(s)	Cointreau / triple sec
3/4	shot(s)	Freshly squeezed lemon juice
3/4	shot(s)	Sugar (gomme) syrup

Origin: Created in the late 1990s by Salvatore Calabrese at the Library Bar, London, England, this is very similar to the Marmalade Cocktail created in the 1920s by Harry Craddock and published in The Savoy Cocktail Book.
Comment: The success or failure of this tangy drink is partly reliant on the quality of marmalade used.

COSMOPOLITAN #1 UPDATED

Glass: Martini
Garnish: Flamed orange zest twist
Method: Shake all ingredients with ice and fine strain into chilled glass.

1 1/2	shot(s)	Absolut Citron vodka
1	shot(s)	Cointreau / triple sec
1 1/4	shot(s)	Cranberry juice
1/4	shot(s)	Freshly squeezed lime juice
3	dashes	Fee Brothers orange bitters
1/2	spoon	Rose's lime cordial

AKA: Stealth Martini
Comment: The balance of citrus, berry fruit and sweetness is perfect. There are many recipes for the Cosmopolitan, although the core ingredients of vodka, cranberry, triple sec and lime remain the same.

ELEGANTE MARGARITA

Glass: Coupette
Garnish: Lime wedge & salted rim (optional)
Method: Shake all ingredients with ice and strain into glass.

1¹/₂ shot(s)	Sauza Hornitos Tequila
¹/₂ shot(s)	Cointreau / triple sec
¹/₂ shot(s)	Rose's lime cordial
³/₄ shot(s)	Freshly squeezed lime juice
¹/₂ shot(s)	Sugar (gomme) syrup

Origin: Created in 1999 by Robert Plotkin and Raymon Flores of BarMedia, USA.
Comment: One of the best Margarita recipes around. Richly endowed with flavour.

FLORIDITA MARGARITA

Glass: Coupette
Garnish: Lime wedge & salted rim (optional)
Method: Shake all ingredients with ice and strain into glass.

1¹/₂ shot(s)	Sauza Hornitos Tequila
¹/₂ shot(s)	Cointreau / triple sec
¹/₂ shot(s)	Cranberry juice
¹/₄ shot(s)	Rose's lime cordial
1¹/₂ shot(s)	Freshly squeezed grapefruit juice
³/₄ shot(s)	Freshly squeezed lime juice
¹/₂ shot(s)	Sugar (gomme) syrup

Origin: Created in 1999 by Robert Plotkin and Raymon Flores of BarMedia, USA.
Comment: A blush coloured Margarita-style drink with a well-matched amalgamation of flavours.

MARGARITA STRAIGHT UP

Glass: Coupette
Garnish: Salt rim & lime wedge
Method: Shake ingredients with ice and strain into chilled glass.

2 shot(s)	Sauza Hornitos Tequila
1 shot(s)	Cointreau / triple sec
1 shot(s)	Freshly squeezed lime juice

Variant: Margaritas made with premium Tequilas are sometimes referred to as 'Deluxe' or 'Cadillac' Margaritas.
Comment: The classic blend of citrus orange and agave with a salt tang.

OH GOSH

Glass: Martini
Garnish: Flamed Lemon zest twist
Method: Shake all ingredients long and vigorously with cubed ice and strain into glass.

1¹/₂ shot(s)	Havana Club light rum
1 shot(s)	Cointreau / triple sec
¹/₂ shot(s)	Freshly squeezed lime juice
¹/₄ shot(s)	Sugar (gomme) syrup
³/₄ shot(s)	Chilled mineral water

Origin: Created by Tony Conigliaro in 2001 at Isola, Knightsbridge, London, England. He named the drink after a customer who ordered a Daiquiri style drink with a difference – when the drink was served he took one sip and uttered "Oh gosh!".
Comment: A very subtle twist on a classic Daiquiri, but don't knock it until you've tried it as it harnesses citrus flavour from orange, lemon and lime - sublime.

OPAL MARTINI UPDATED

Glass: Martini
Garnish: Flamed orange zest twist
Method: Shake all ingredients with ice and fine strain into chilled glass.

1¹/₂ shot(s)	Plymouth gin
³/₄ shot(s)	Cointreau / triple sec
1¹/₂ shot(s)	Freshly squeezed orange juice

Origin: The combination of gin and orange dates back at least as far as 1906, when the Bronx was created. The mixture made a surprising comeback in the wonderful world of rap, when Snoop Doggy Dogg hymned 'Gin 'n' Juice'.
Comment: Simple but effective.

SIDECAR

Glass: Martini
Garnish: Sugar rim
Method: Shake all ingredients with ice and fine strain into chilled glass.

1¹/₂ shot(s)	Rémy Martin Cognac
1 shot(s)	Cointreau / triple sec
1 shot(s)	Freshly squeezed lemon juice
³/₄ shot(s)	Chilled mineral water

Variation: Apple Cart
Origin: Legend has it that this drink was created by Harry MacElhone at his Harry's New York Bar in Paris after the First World War and was named after an eccentric army captain who used to be chauffeur-driven to the bar in a motorcycle sidecar. However, in Harry's own book he credits the drink to MacGarry of Buck's Club, London.
Comment: This wonderful classic relies on the sugar rim to take the edge off the sourness of the drink. If serving without a sugared rim add a quarter shot of sugar syrup to compensate.

STORK CLUB NEW

Glass: Martini
Garnish: Orange zest twist
Method: Shake all ingredients with ice and fine strain into chilled glass.

¹/₄ shot(s)	Plymouth gin
¹/₄ shot(s)	Cointreau / triple sec
¹/₄ shot(s)	Freshly squeezed orange juice
¹/₂ shot(s)	Freshly squeezed lime juice

Comment: Orange and gin with a souring splash of lime juice.

SUNSTROKE UPDATED

Glass: Martini
Garnish: Orange zest twist (round)
Method: Shake all ingredients with ice and fine strain into chilled glass.

1 shot(s)	Absolut vodka
1 shot(s)	Cointreau / triple sec
2³/₄ shot(s)	Freshly squeezed pink grapefruit juice

Comment: Fresh, fruity and balanced. One to sip in the shade.

FINLANDIA® CRANBERRY VODKA

Finland is famous not only for its 600,000 saunas but also for its pollution free countryside. Finns are justly proud of their clean, uncontaminated and sparsely populated country and it's this natural purity that lies at the heart of the Finlandia brand. Finlandia is made from Finnish six-row barley using continuous stills. The water used is taken from a natural spring, which is so clean that no purification is required. This purity of water and distillation also negates the need to charcoal filter the finished vodka, a practice common in other brands.

Launched in the autumn of 1994, Finlandia Cranberry vodka is based on Finlandia's clean tasting vodka. Originally red coloured to emphasise its flavour and distinguish it from the original vodka, in 2002 new contemporary packaging was introduced and with it came a colourless cranberry vodka with a much improved flavour.

Cranberry is one of the most used juices in cocktail making and so it follows that cranberry flavoured vodka is a very versatile mixer. Complex cranberry flavour with hints of peach and honeyed cherries. 40% alc./vol. (80°proof)

Web: www.finlandia-vodka.com **Producer:** Primalco Ltd, Helsinki, Finland. **UK distributor:** Bacardi-Martini Ltd **Tel:** 02380 635 252
Email: see finlandia-vodka.com

APPLE & CRANBERRY PIE'TINI

Glass: Martini
Garnish: Cinnamon dust
Method: Shake first four ingredients with ice and fine strain into chilled glass. Float cream on surface of drink by pouring over back of dessertspoon.

1½	shot(s)	Finlandia Cranberry vodka
¾	shot(s)	Apple schnapps liqueur
1	shot(s)	Cranberry juice
½	shot(s)	Freshly squeezed lime juice
¾	shot(s)	Double (heavy) cream

Origin: I created this drink in 2003 for Finlandia.
Comment: Sip apple and cranberry through a creamy cinnamon layer.

CHOCOLATE 'N' CRANBERRY MARTINI

Glass: Martini
Garnish: White cacao & cocoa powder rim
Method: Shake all ingredients with ice and fine strain into chilled, rimmed glass.

1	shot(s)	Finlandia Cranberry vodka
1	shot(s)	Absolut Vanilia vodka
½	shot(s)	Bols white crème de cacao
1	shot(s)	Cinzano Extra Dry vermouth
1	shot(s)	Cranberry juice

Origin: I created this drink in 2003 for Finlandia.
Comment: The chocolate rim makes this vanilla and cranberry vodka laced drink.

CRANBERRY & MINT MARTINI

Glass: Martini
Garnish: Float mint leaf
Method: Lightly muddle mint in base of shaker. Add other ingredients, shake with ice and fine strain into chilled glass.

8	fresh	Mint leaves
2	shot(s)	Finlandia cranberry vodka
2	shot(s)	Cranberry juice
¼	shot(s)	Grenadine syrup

Origin: Created by yours truly in 2003.
Comment: This little red number combines the dryness of cranberry, the sweetness of cherry and the fragrance of mint.

CRANBERRY SAUCE

Glass: Martini
Garnish: Dried cranberries in base of glass
Method: Shake all ingredients with ice and fine strain into chilled glass.

2	shot(s)	Finlandia cranberry vodka
2	shot(s)	Cranberry juice
1	shot(s)	Lapponia cranberry liqueur

Origin: Created in 2003 by yours truly for Finlandia.
Comment: Rich, fruity flavour but with that customary dry cranberry finish.

FINITALY

Glass: Martini
Garnish: Blueberry or raspberry on rim
Method: Shake all ingredients with ice and fine strain into chilled glass.

1½	shot(s)	Finlandia Cranberry vodka
½	shot(s)	Cinzano Rosso (sweet) vermouth
½	shot(s)	Chambord black raspberry liqueur
1	shot(s)	Chilled water

Origin: Created by Michael Mahe at Hush, London, England.
Comment: A simple, berry led Martini.

FINNBERRY MARTINI

Glass: Martini
Garnish: Cranberries
Method: Shake all ingredients with ice and strain into glass.

2	shot(s)	Finlandia Cranberry vodka
2	shot(s)	Lingonberry or cranberry juice
1	shot(s)	Lapponia Cloudberry liqueur

Origin: I created this in 2002 after a trip to Finland with Finlandia vodka.
Comment: This rich berry Martini can be varied by using other berry liqueurs in the Lapponia range – try using two with a half shot of each.

THE JUXTAPOSITION

Glass: Martini
Garnish: Two pineapple wedges on rim
Method: Stir honey with vodka in base of shaker so as to dissolve honey. Add other ingredients, shake with ice and fine strain into chilled glass.

2	shot(s)	Finlandia Cranberry vodka
2	spoons	Runny honey
1	shot(s)	Pressed pineapple juice
¾	shot(s)	Freshly squeezed lime juice
3	dashes	Angostura aromatic bitters

Origin: Adapted from a long drink created in 2003 by Michael Butt and Giles Looker of Soulshakers, England. The name means to place things side by side, hence the garnish.
Comment: Tangy and complex and smoothed by foaming pineapple.

LAGO COSMO

Glass: Martini
Garnish: Flamed orange zest twist
Method: Shake all ingredients with ice and fine strain into chilled glass.

1½	shot(s)	Finlandia cranberry vodka
¾	shot(s)	Cointreau / triple sec
1¾	shot(s)	Freshly squeezed orange juice
¼	shot(s)	Freshly squeezed lime juice
½	shot(s)	Sugar (gomme) syrup

Origin: Discovered in 2003 at Nectar @ Bellagio, Las Vegas, USA.
Comment: A Cosmo with cranberry vodka in place of citrus vodka and orange juice in place of cranberry juice.

NUTTY BERRY'TINI

Glass: Martini
Garnish: Float mint leaf
Method: Shake all ingredients with ice and fine strain into chilled glass.

2	shot(s)	Finlandia Cranberry vodka
½	shot(s)	Bols Cherry brandy liqueur
½	shot(s)	Frangelico hazelnut liqueur
¼	shot(s)	Luxardo Maraschino liqueur
1	shot(s)	Cranberry juice
½	shot(s)	Freshly squeezed lime juice

Origin: Created by yours truly in 2003.
Comment: Cranberry vodka and juice, sweetened with cherry liqueur, dried with lime juice and flavoured with hazelnut.

SPICED CRANBERRY MARTINI

Glass: Martini
Garnish: Cranberry juice & cinnamon rim
Method: Muddle cloves in base of shaker. Add other ingredients, shake with ice and fine strain into chilled glass.

7	dried	Cloves
1	shot(s)	Finlandia cranberry vodka
1	shot(s)	Pusser's Navy rum
2	shot(s)	Cranberry juice
½	shot(s)	Sugar (gomme) syrup

Origin: Created in 2003 by yours truly for Finlandia.
Comment: The cloves add a festive note to this red, vaguely Martini styled drink.

SPICY FINN

Glass: Martini
Garnish: Blueberry or raspberry on rim
Method: Muddle ginger in base of shaker. Add other ingredients, shake with ice and fine strain into chilled glass.

3	slices	Root ginger (thumb nail sized)
2	shot(s)	Finlandia Cranberry vodka
½	shot(s)	Campari
½	shot(s)	Sugar (gomme) syrup
1	shot(s)	Chilled mineral water

Origin: Created by Michael Mahe at Hush, London, England.
Comment: Cranberry vodka, Campari and ginger with a dash of gomme to sweeten things up.

TARRABERRY'TINI

Glass: Martini
Garnish: Tarragon sprig
Method: Muddle tarragon in base of shaker. Add other ingredients, shake with ice and fine strain into chilled glass.

1	fistful	Fresh tarragon
1½	shot(s)	Finlandia Cranberry vodka
¼	shot(s)	Pernod anis
2	shot(s)	Cranberry juice
¼	shot(s)	Freshly squeezed lemon juice

Origin: I created this drink in 2003 for Finlandia.
Comment: Cranberry with subtle hints of tarragon and lemon.

FINLANDIA® LIME VODKA

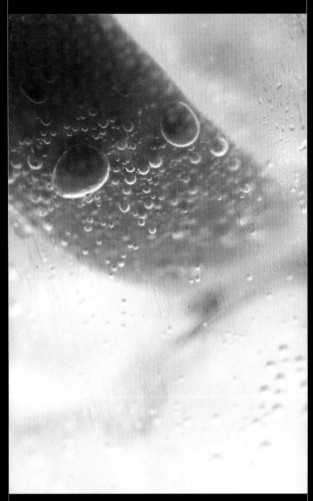

Finlandia vodka has something of a reputation for its clean flavour. This neutral base spirit is flavoured with essential lime oils to produce Finlandia Lime vodka.

The white reindeer prominently shown on the bottle originate from a Finnish legend about a beautiful young girl transformed into a fearsome white reindeer by a spell. The girl's boyfriend receives a fatal wound trying to kill the reindeer but his blood breaks the spell and the reindeer becomes a girl again. The couple are said to have fallen into eternal sleep. Thus many Finns believe it is lucky to see the sun, the moon and a white reindeer at once.

Finlandia lime has a perky lime/lemon zest flavour with hints of lemon sherbet, lemon drops, barley notes and some vodka spice. Being crystal clear adds to its versatility as a mixer. 40% alc./vol. (80°proof)

Web. www.finlandia-vodka.com **Producer:** Primalco Ltd, Helsinki, Finland. **UK distributor:** Bacardi-Martini Ltd. **Tel:** 02380 635 252 **Email:** see finlandia-vodka.com

BLIMEY

Glass: Rocks
Garnish: Lime wedge
Method: Muddle blackberries in glass. Fill glass with crushed ice, add other ingredients and stir.

8	fresh	Blackberries
2	shot(s)	Finlandia Lime vodka
1	shot(s)	Freshly squeezed lime juice
3/4	shot(s)	Sisca crème de cassis
1/8	shot(s)	Sugar (gomme) syrup

Origin: I created this drink in 2002 and Tarja Tuunanen, UK Finlandia brand manager, named it.
Comment: This blackberry and lime blend is both fruity and aptly named.

GRASSY FINNISH NEW

Glass: Martini
Garnish: Lemongrass
Method: Chop up lemongrass and muddle in base of shaker. Add other ingredients, shake with ice and fine strain into chilled glass.

1	stem	Fresh lemongrass
2	shot(s)	Finlandia lime vodka
1	shot(s)	Krupnik honey liqueur
1/4	shot(s)	Sugar (gomme) syrup

Origin: Created in 2003 by Gerard McCurry at Revolution, UK.
Comment: Like Finland, this drink is clean, green, wooded and safe, but deep down there's plenty of spice.

FRISKY LEMONADE

Glass: Collins
Garnish: Lime wedge squeezed & dropped into drink
Method: Pour ingredients into ice-filled glass and stir.

2	shot(s)	Finlandia lime vodka
1/2	shot(s)	Cinzano Extra Dry vermouth
Top up with		Lemonade / 7-Up

Origin: Created by Aaron Rudd in 2002 at Home, London, England.
Comment: Reminiscent of alcoholic lemon barley water.

KEY LIME

Glass: Coupette
Garnish: Split lime wedge
Method: Blend ingredients without ice and serve.

1	shot(s)	Absolut Vanilia vodka
1	shot(s)	Finlandia Lime vodka
1/2	shot(s)	Sugar (gomme) syrup
1/2	shot(s)	Rose's lime cordial
3	scoops	Vanilla ice cream

Comment: Tangy, smooth and rich! Alcoholic ice cream for the grown-up palate.

LIME BREEZE

Glass: Collins
Garnish: Lime wedge on rim
Method: Pour ingredients into ice-filled glass and stir.

2	shot(s)	Finlandia Lime vodka
4	shot(s)	Cranberry juice
2	shot(s)	Freshly squeezed grapefruit juice

Comment: A lime driven Sea Breeze.

LIME SOUR

Glass: Old-fashioned
Garnish: Lime wedge on rim
Method: Shake all ingredients with ice and strain into ice-filled glass.

2	shot(s)	Finlandia Lime vodka
1¼	shot(s)	Freshly squeezed lime juice
¼	shot(s)	Sugar (gomme) syrup
½	fresh	Egg white

Comment: Fresh egg white gives this drink a wonderfully frothy top and smoothes the alcohol and the citrus tang of the lime juice.

LIMERICK

Glass: Collins
Garnish: Lime wedge squeezed over drink
Method: Shake first three ingredients with ice and strain into ice-filled glass. Top up with soda water and lightly stir.

2	shot(s)	Finlandia lime vodka
1	shot(s)	Freshly squeezed lime juice
½	shot(s)	Sugar (gomme) syrup
Top up with		Soda water (club soda)

Origin: I created this twist on the classic Vodka Rickey in 2002.
Comment: Refreshing lime cooler.

LIMESTONE BREEZE UPDATED

Glass: Collins
Garnish: Lime wedge on rim
Method: Pour ingredients into ice-filled glass and stir.

2	shot(s)	Finlandia lime vodka
¾	shot(s)	Disaronno Originale amaretto
3½	shot(s)	Pressed apple juice

Origin: Created in 2002 by yours truly.
Comment: A richly flavoured long drink with a sweet edge.

LIMEY COSMO

Glass: Martini
Garnish: Lime wedge on rim
Method: Shake all ingredients with ice and strain into glass.

1½	shot(s)	Finlandia lime vodka
1	shot(s)	Cointreau / triple sec
1¼	shot(s)	Cranberry juice
¼	shot(s)	Freshly squeezed lime juice
½	shot(s)	Rose's lime cordial

Comment: If you like Cosmopolitans, you'll love this zesty alternative.

LIMEY MARTINI

Glass: Martini
Garnish: Lime twist
Method: Shake all ingredients with ice and strain into glass.

1¾	shot(s)	Finlandia lime vodka
½	shot(s)	Freshly squeezed lime juice
½	shot(s)	Sugar (gomme) syrup
1	spoon	Rose's lime cordial
3	dash(es)	Angostura aromatic bitters
1	shot(s)	Chilled mineral water

Origin: I created this drink and named it after the British naval tradition of mixing lime juice with spirits in an attempt to prevent scurvy. This practice gained British sailors the nickname 'limeys'. Angostura was also popular with sailors as it was said to ward off chronic stomach complaints.
Comment: A rust coloured drink with a delicate sour flavour.

LIMEY MULE

Glass: Collins
Garnish: Lime wedge squeezed & dropped in drink
Method: Pour ingredients into ice-filled glass and stir.

1¾	shot(s)	Finlandia lime vodka
1	shot(s)	Freshly squeezed lime juice
½	shot(s)	Sugar (gomme) syrup
Top up with		Ginger ale

Comment: Made with plain vodka this drink is a Moscow Mule. This variant uses lime flavoured vodka.

MOLOTOV COCKTAIL

Glass: Martini
Garnish: Lemon zest
Method: Shake all ingredients with ice and fine strain into chilled glass.

1½	shot(s)	Finlandia Lime vodka
1¼	shot(s)	Parfait Amour liqueur
½	shot(s)	Freshly squeezed lemon juice
½	shot(s)	Opal Nera black sambuca

Origin: I created this drink after a visit to the Rajamäki distillery, where Finlandia is bottled. At the start of the Second World War the plant was used to produce Molotov cocktails, inflammatory bombs with which the Finns put hundreds of Soviet tanks out of action.
I selected the ingredients to represent the four liquids used in the wartime weapon. Finlandia lime, which is clear, stands for alcohol, parfait amour shares the purple hue of paraffin, lemon juice represents gasoline and black sambuca replaces tar.
Comment: This inky cocktail combines sweet and sour with hints of liquorice and is as potent as its name suggests.

THOSE DRINKS I'VE SAMPLED RECENTLY ARE GRADED AS FOLLOWS:

● DISGUSTING　●○ PRETTY AWFUL　●● BEST AVOIDED
●●○ DISAPPOINTING　●●● ACCEPTABLE　●●●○ GOOD
●●●● RECOMMENDED　●●●●○ HIGHLY RECOMMENDED
●●●●● OUTSTANDING / EXCEPTIONAL

FRANGELICO® HAZELNUT LIQUEUR

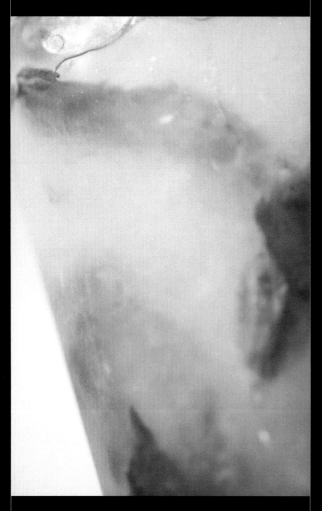

This Italian liqueur is produced from berries, herbs and hazelnuts. It is said to be named after a monk named Fra Angelico who lived as a hermit in the Piedmont area in the 17th century. His knowledge and understanding of nature inspired him to produce many fine foods and unique drinks, including the drink that bears his name. Frangelico uses the region's wild hazelnuts infused with herbs and berries. The brand was officially launched in the USA in 1978 and is now the world's third largest selling Italian liqueur. Frangelico is instantly recognisable by its eye-catching monk-shaped bottle and rope tie.

Frangelico has a rich and balanced flavour, now essential to many popular cocktails. The taste is complex, and as well as the obvious hazelnut, includes cheesecake base, butter and hints of espresso, citrus and vanilla. 24% alc./vol. (48°proof)

Web: www.frangelico.com **Producer:** Barbero 1981 S.p.A. (Cantrell & Cochrane), Canale D'Alba, Italy. **UK distributor:** Inspirit Brands, London. **Tel:** 020 7377 9457
Email: Info@inspiritbrands.com

CRIMSON TIDE NEW

●●●●○

Glass: Old-fashioned
Garnish: Raspberries
Method: Muddle raspberries in base of shaker. Add other ingredients, shake with ice and strain into glass filled with crushed ice.

7	fresh	Raspberries
1¼	shot(s)	Absolut Kurant vodka
1	shot(s)	Frangelico hazelnut liqueur
½	shot(s)	Chambord black raspberry liqueur
¼	shot(s)	Freshly squeezed lime juice

Comment: A medium-sweet tidal wave of flavours.

CUPPA JOE NEW

●●●●○

Glass: Martini
Garnish: Lemon zest twist
Method: Shake all ingredients with ice and fine strain into chilled glass.

1½	shot(s)	Absolut vodka
1½	shot(s)	Frangelico hazelnut liqueur
1½	shot(s)	Espresso coffee (cold)

Origin: Created in 2003 at Cellar Bar, New York City, USA.
Comment: Nutty coffee fortified with vodka – well balanced.

FRIAR TUCK

Glass: Martini
Garnish: Sprinkle ground nutmeg
Method: Shake ingredients with ice and strain into glass.

1	shot(s)	Frangelico hazelnut liqueur
1	shot(s)	Bols brown crème de cacao
1	shot(s)	Double (heavy) cream
1	shot(s)	Milk

Variant: With Amaretto and ice cream.
Comment: Round, jolly and creamy with chocolate and hazelnut.

FRUIT & NUT MARTINI NEW

●●●●○

Glass: Martini
Garnish: Orange zest twist & almond flakes
Method: Shake all ingredients with ice and fine strain into chilled glass.

1	shot(s)	Absolut Vanilia vodka
1	shot(s)	Frangelico hazelnut liqueur
½	shot(s)	Pedro Ximénez Sherry
1	shot(s)	Cranberry juice
½	shot(s)	Freshly squeezed orange juice

Origin: Created by yours truly in 2004.
Comment: A rich Christmas pudding of a Martini.

GINGER NUT

Glass: Collins
Garnish: Lemon wedge
Method: Pour ingredients into ice-filled glass and stir.

1½	shot(s)	Frangelico hazelnut liqueur
1½	shot(s)	Absolut Citron vodka
Top up with		Jamaican Ginger beer

Comment: A long refreshing meld of strong flavours.

GIUSEPPE'S HABIT

Glass: Martini
Garnish: Star anise
Method: Spray the oils from two lemon zest twists into the cocktail shaker, wipe them around the rim of the glass and drop them into the shaker. Pour other ingredients into shaker, shake with ice and fine strain into glass.

2	twists	Lemon zest
1½	shot(s)	Galliano liqueur
¾	shot(s)	Frangelico hazelnut liqueur
¾	shot(s)	Cointreau / triple sec
1¼	shot(s)	Pressed apple juice

Origin: Created in 2002 by Leon Stokes at Zinc Bar & Grill, Birmingham, England.
Comment: An intriguing drink that combines hazelnut, orange, apple, aniseed and peppermint.

HAZEL'ITO

Glass: Collins
Method: Muddle mint in base of glass. Add other ingredients, fill glass with crushed ice and churn drink with bar spoon to mix.

12	fresh	Mint leaves
2	shot(s)	Havana Club light rum
2	shot(s)	Frangelico hazelnut liqueur
1	shot(s)	Freshly squeezed lime juice
½	shot(s)	Sugar (gomme) syrup

Created: Created in January 2002 by Adam Wyartt.
Comment: Looks like a Mojito but has a nutty twang courtesy of Frangelico.

HAZELNUT MARTINI

Glass: Martini
Garnish: Chocolate powder rim
Method: Stir ingredients with ice and strain into glass.

½	shot(s)	Frangelico hazelnut liqueur
2	shot(s)	Absolut vodka
½	shot(s)	Bols white crème de cacao
¾	shot(s)	Sugar (gomme) syrup
½	shot(s)	Chilled mineral water

Comment: A hazelnut vodkatini with a hint of chocolate.

MAD MONK MILKSHAKE

Glass: Collins
Garnish: Tie cord around glass
Method: Shake ingredients with ice and strain into ice-filled glass.

2	shot(s)	Frangelico hazelnut liqueur
1	shot(s)	Baileys Irish Cream liqueur
¼	shot(s)	Kahlúa coffee liqueur
2	shot(s)	Double (heavy) cream
2	shot(s)	Milk

Variant: Blend instead of shaking and serve frozen.
Comment: Long and creamy with hazelnut and coffee.

MONK'S CANDY BAR

Glass: Martini
Garnish: Sprinkle with nutmeg
Method: Shake ingredients with ice and strain into glass.

1½	shot(s)	Frangelico hazelnut liqueur
1	shot(s)	Teichenné butterscotch schnapps
¾	shot(s)	Kahlúa coffee liqueur
1	shot(s)	Double (heavy) cream
1	shot(s)	Milk

Comment: Hazelnut, butterscotch and coffee mixed with milk and cream makes a cocktail reminiscent of a candy bar.

MONK'S HABIT

Glass: Collins
Garnish: Tie strip of orange rind and float on drink.
Method: Shake ingredients with ice and strain into glass.

1	shot(s)	Havana Club light rum
½	shot(s)	Cointreau / triple sec
1	shot(s)	Frangelico hazelnut liqueur
3½	shot(s)	Pressed pineapple juice
¼	shot(s)	Grenadine syrup

Comment: Fruit and nut laced with rum.

NUTTY NASHVILLE

Glass: Martini
Garnish: Lemon zest twist
Method: Stir honey with Bourbon in base of shaker so as to dissolve honey. Add other ingredients, shake with ice and fine strain into chilled glass.

2	spoon(s)	Runny honey
2	shot(s)	Buffalo Trace Bourbon
1	shot(s)	Frangelico hazelnut liqueur
1	shot(s)	Krupnik honey liqueur

Origin: Created in 2001 by Jason Fendick at Rockwell, Trafalgar Hotel, London, England.
Comment: Bourbon and hazelnut smoothed and rounded by honey.

GALLIANO®

Galliano is a vibrant, golden, vanilla flavoured liqueur from Italy, easily recognised by its distinctive, tall fluted bottle, inspired by Roman columns. Invented in 1896, Galliano is made from over 30 ingredients including star anise, lavender, ginger and vanilla. A noted cocktail ingredient, Galliano's signature drink is the Harvey Wallbanger. Apparently, Harvey was a surfer at Manhattan Beach, California, and his favourite drink was a Screwdriver with added Galliano. One day in the late 60s, while celebrating winning a surfing competition, he staggered from bar to bar, banging his surf board on the walls and so the cocktail was born. The versatility of Galliano ensures that it can be enjoyed in cocktails as a long drink and works particularly well as a hot shot with coffee and cream.

The lovely smell of Galliano is reminiscent of a pack of Tic-Tac sweets, while its smooth vanilla taste is complimented by peppermint and spicy with cinnamon, ginger, nutmeg and citrus. 30% alc./vol. (60°proof)

Web: www.galliano.com **Producer:** Remy Cointreau, Angers, France.
UK distributor: Maxxium UK Ltd, Stirling, Scotland.
Tel: 01786 430 500 **Email:** enquiries@maxxium.com

ADAM AND EVE UPDATED

Glass: Old-fashioned
Garnish: Lemon zest twist
Method: Shake all ingredients with ice and strain into ice-filled glass.

2	shot(s)	Buffalo Trace Bourbon
¹/₂	shot(s)	Galliano liqueur
¹/₂	shot(s)	Sugar (gomme) syrup
4	dashes	Angostura aromatic bitters

Comment: Lovers of the Sazerac will appreciate this herbal, Bourbon-laced concoction.

BARTENDER'S ROOT BEER

Glass: Collins
Garnish: Lime wedge on rim
Method: Pour first three ingredients into ice-filled glass and top up with cola.

1	shot(s)	Galliano liqueur
1	shot(s)	Kahlúa coffee liqueur
¹/₄	shot(s)	Freshly squeezed lime juice
Top up with		Cola

Comment: Not quite the root of all evil, but tasty all the same.

BOSSANOVA #1

Glass: Collins
Garnish: Split lime wedge
Method: Shake ingredients with ice and strain into ice-filled glass.

2	shot(s)	Havana Club light rum
³/₄	shot(s)	Galliano liqueur
³/₄	shot(s)	Bols apricot brandy liqueur
4	shot(s)	Pressed apple juice
1	shot(s)	Freshly squeezed lime juice
¹/₂	shot(s)	Sugar (gomme) syrup

Comment: Apple juice with the added zing of rum, Galliano, apricot brandy and lime.

FRUIT SALAD

Glass: Collins
Garnish: Orange slice
Method: Shake ingredients with ice and strain into ice-filled glass.

2	shot(s)	Absolut vodka
³/₄	shot(s)	Bols crème de banane
4	shot(s)	Freshly squeezed orange juice
³/₄	shot(s)	Galliano liqueur
¹/₄	shot(s)	Grenadine syrup

Comment: This variation on the Harvey Wallbanger tastes like Fruit Salad penny chews.

GOLDEN DREAM MARTINI

Glass: Martini
Garnish: Sponge biscuit on rim
Method: Shake all ingredients with ice and fine strain into glass.

1	shot(s)	Cointreau / triple sec
1	shot(s)	Galliano liqueur
2	shot(s)	Freshly squeezed orange juice
1	shot(s)	Double (heavy) cream

Comment: Tastes remarkably like syllabub.

HARVEY WALLBANGER

Glass: Collins
Garnish: Orange slice in drink
Method: Pour vodka and orange into ice-filled glass and stir, then float Galliano on top of drink.

2	shot(s)	Absolut vodka
4	shot(s)	Freshly squeezed orange juice
3/4	shot(s)	Galliano liqueur

Origin: Harvey was a surfer at Manhattan Beach, California. His favourite drink was a Screwdriver with added Galliano. One day in the late 60s, while celebrating winning a surfing competition, he staggered from bar to bar, banging his surfboard on the walls and so a contemporary classic got its name.
Comment: Hugely popular in the saeventies.

HOT SHOT

Glass: Shot
Method: Pour Galliano into glass, then layer coffee and float cream.

3/4	shot(s)	Galliano liqueur
3/4	shot(s)	Espresso coffee (hot)
Float		Lightly whipped cream

Comment: A winter warmer for Galliano fans.

JUMPING JACK FLASH

Glass: Martini
Method: Shake all ingredients with ice and strain into glass.

1	shot(s)	Jack Daniel's Tennessee whiskey
1	shot(s)	Bols crème de banane
1/2	shot(s)	Galliano liqueur
1	shot(s)	Freshly squeezed orange juice
1	shot(s)	Pressed pineapple juice

Comment: The Galliano complements the banana; both mix well with the fruit juices and vanilla.

PERFECT JOHN

Glass: Martini
Method: Shake ingredients with ice and strain into glass.

1	shot(s)	Absolut vodka
1	shot(s)	Cointreau / triple sec
3	shot(s)	Freshly squeezed orange juice
1/2	shot(s)	Galliano liqueur

Comment: A straight-up Harvey Wallbanger with Cointreau.

PICCA **UPDATED**

Glass: Martini
Garnish: Stemmed maraschino cherry
Method: Shake all ingredients with ice and strain into chilled glass.

1 1/2	shot(s)	The Famous Grouse Scotch whisky
1	shot(s)	Galliano liqueur
1	shot(s)	Cinzano Rosso vermouth
3/4	shot(s)	Chilled mineral water

Comment: Bittersweet whisky.

ROCKY MOUNTAIN ROOTBEER

Glass: Collins
Method: Fill glass with ice, add vodka and Galliano, then top up with cola and stir.

2	shot(s)	Absolut vodka
3/4	shot(s)	Galliano liqueur
Top up with		Cola

Comment: Aptly named.

TOOTIE FRUITY LIFESAVER

Glass: Collins
Method: Shake ingredients with ice and strain into ice-filled glass.

1	shot(s)	Absolut vodka
1 1/2	shot(s)	Bols Crème de banane
3/4	shot(s)	Galliano liqueur
2	shot(s)	Cranberry juice
2	shot(s)	Pressed pineapple juice
2	shot(s)	Freshly squeezed orange juice

Comment: Aptly named fruity drink.

NEW	A DRINK NEW TO DIFFORDS GUIDE.
UPDATED	ENTRY CHANGED SINCE LAST VOLUME.

GRAND MARNIER® CORDON ROUGE

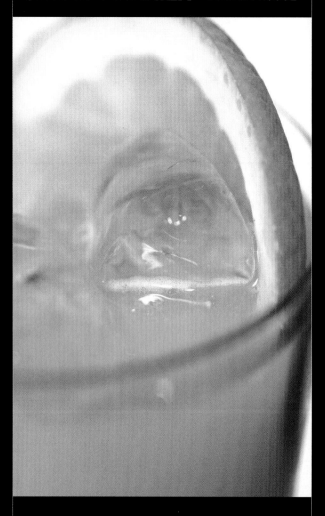

Grand Marnier is one of the best known and most widely sold premium liqueurs in the world. With a Cognac base, its unique flavour and delicate aromas come from the maceration and distillation of tropical, bitter orange peels.

Founded in 1827 by Jean Baptiste Lapostolle, Grand Marnier is still a family-run business today and continues to use traditional production methods and the original Grand Marnier recipe.

Despite its traditional credentials and heritage, Grand Marnier is also recognised as an international, classic brand which enjoys a large and loyal worldwide following, particularly in the United States where cocktail culture began. Following that trend, Grand Marnier has become an essential ingredient for flavoursome, stylish mixed drinks across the increasingly popular cocktail bar scene in the UK.

It is silky rich with a zesty, juicy flavour, good underlying bite of bitter orange and hints of marmalade and Cognac richness at the edges, making it the perfect cocktail partner. A highly mixable spirit, Grand Marnier enhances and adds depth and complexity to premium cocktails and long drinks.

A superb cocktail ingredient which features in many classic and contemporary recipes. 40% alcohol / vol. 80 proof.

Web: www.grand-marnier.com
Producer: Marnier-Lapostolle (Société des Produits), Paris, France
UK Distributor: Fior Brands Ltd **Tel:** 01786 406 360

B-52 SHOT

Glass: Shot
Method: Layer in glass by carefully pouring ingredients in the following order.

¹/₂	shot(s)	Kahlúa coffee liqueur
¹/₂	shot(s)	Baileys Irish Cream liqueur
¹/₂	shot(s)	Grand Marnier liqueur

Origin: Named after B-52 bombers in Vietnam.
Comment: Probably the best-known and most popular shot.

BASIL GRANDE

Glass: Martini
Garnish: Dust with black pepper & float basil leaf
Method: Muddle strawberries and basil leaves in shaker base. Add other ingredients, shake with ice and fine strain into glass.

4	fresh	Hulled strawberries
5	fresh	Basil leaves
1	shot(s)	Absolut vodka
1	shot(s)	Chambord black raspberry liqueur
1	shot(s)	Grand Marnier liqueur
3	shot(s)	Cranberry juice

Origin: Created in 2001 by Jamie Wilkinson at Living Room, Manchester, England.
Comment: Fruity, with interest courtesy of the basil and grind of pepper.

BIARRITZ NEW

Glass: Old-fashioned
Garnish: Orange slice & cherry (orange sail)
Method: Shake all ingredients with ice and strain into ice-filled glass.

2	shot(s)	Rémy Martin Cognac
1	shot(s)	Grand Marnier liqueur
³/₄	shot(s)	Freshly squeezed lemon juice
¹/₂	fresh	Egg white
3	dashes	Angostura aromatic bitters

Comment: Basically a brandy sour with a little something extra from the orange liqueur.

BLUEBERRY TEA UPDATED

Glass: Toddy
Garnish: Lemon slice & cinnamon stick
Method: Pour first two ingredients into glass, top up with hot tea and stir.

³/₄	shot(s)	Disaronno Originale amaretto
³/₄	shot(s)	Grand Marnier liqueur
Top up with		Black breakfast tea (hot)

Comment: This does indeed taste just as described on the tin.

NEW	A DRINK NEW TO DIFFORDS GUIDE.
UPDATED	ENTRY CHANGED SINCE LAST VOLUME.

BOMBAY UPDATED

Glass: Martini
Garnish: Orange zest twist
Method: Stir all ingredients with ice and strain into chilled glass.

1³/₄	shot(s)	Rémy Martin Cognac
1¹/₂	shot(s)	Cinzano Rosso sweet vermouth
³/₄	shot(s)	Grand Marnier liqueur
¹/₂	shot(s)	Chilled water
¹/₄	shot(s)	Pernod anis

Origin: My adaptation of a classic.
Comment: A smooth, complex, Sazerac-style Martini.

COSMOPOLITAN DELIGHT

Glass: Martini
Garnish: Flamed orange zest twist
Method: Shake all ingredients with ice and fine strain into chilled glass.

1¹/₂	shot(s)	Rémy Martin Cognac
¹/₂	shot(s)	Grand Marnier liqueur
1¹/₄	shot(s)	Shiraz Red wine
³/₄	shot(s)	Freshly squeezed lemon juice
¹/₄	shot(s)	Almond (orgeat) syrup
¹/₄	shot(s)	Sugar (gomme) syrup

Origin: Adapted from Dale DeGroff's book, 'The Craft of the Cocktail'. He credits the original recipe to a 1902 book by Charlie Paul.
Comment: No relation to the modern Cosmopolitan, this is a mellow, balanced blend of citrus, brandy and red wine.

DRAMATIC MARTINI UPDATED

Glass: Martini
Garnish: Grate nutmeg over drink
Method: Shake all ingredients with ice and fine strain into chilled glass.

1	shot(s)	Tuaca liqueur
1	shot(s)	Grand Marnier liqueur
1	shot(s)	Baileys Irish Cream liqueur
1	shot(s)	Milk

Comment: Creamy and sweet with orangey herbal notes.

GRANDE CHAMPAGNE COSMO

Glass: Martini
Garnish: Flamed orange zest twist
Method: Shake all ingredients with ice and fine strain into chilled glass.

2	shot(s)	Rémy Martin Cognac
³/₄	shot(s)	Grand Marnier liqueur
¹/₂	shot(s)	Freshly squeezed lemon juice
1	shot(s)	Cranberry juice

Comment: 'Grande Champagne' refers to the top cru of the Cognac region: this drink is suitably elite.

GRAND COSMOPOLITAN

Glass: Martini
Garnish: Flamed orange zest twist
Method: Shake ingredients with ice and strain into glass.

1¹/₂	shot(s)	Absolut Citron vodka
³/₄	shot(s)	Grand Marnier liqueur
1¹/₂	shot(s)	Cranberry juice
¹/₂	shot(s)	Freshly squeezed lime juice
¹/₂	shot(s)	Freshly squeezed lemon juice
¹/₂	shot(s)	Sugar (gomme) syrup
¹/₄	shot(s)	Rose's lime cordial
2	dashes	Fee Brothers orange bitters

Comment: One of the more complicated and most recent versions of this modern classic. Heavily promoted by Grand Marnier and rightly so.

GRAND MIMOSA

Glass: Flute
Garnish: Strawberry on rim
Method: Shake orange juice and Grand Marnier with ice and strain into chilled glass. Top up with Champagne.

1	shot(s)	Grand Marnier liqueur
2	shot(s)	Freshly squeezed orange juice
Top up with		Piper-Heidsieck Brut Champagne

Origin: The Mimosa, a blend of orange and Champagne, was created in 1925 at the Ritz Hotel, Paris, and named after the Mimosa plant - probably because of its trembling leaves, rather like the gentle fizz of this mixture. The Grand Mimosa as shown here benefits from the addition of Grand Marnier liqueur.
Comment: As its name suggests, the orange of Grand Marnier heavily influences this drink. Basically a Buck's Fizz with more of a kick.

MET MANHATTAN

Glass: Martini
Garnish: Orange zest twist
Method: Shake ingredients with ice and strain into glass.

2	shot(s)	Buffalo Trace Bourbon
1	shot(s)	Grand Marnier liqueur
³/₄	shot(s)	Teichenné butterscotch schnapps
1	dash	Fee Brothers orange bitters

Origin: The Met Bar, Metropolitan Hotel, London, England.
Comment: A Manhattan with added interest.

RED LION

Glass: Martini
Garnish: Orange slice on rim
Method: Shake all ingredients with ice and fine strain into chilled glass.

1¹/₄	shot(s)	Plymouth gin
1¹/₄	shot(s)	Grand Marnier liqueur
1	shot(s)	Freshly squeezed orange juice
1	shot(s)	Freshly squeezed lemon juice
¹/₈	shot(s)	Grenadine syrup

Origin: My take on a classic cocktail created in 1933 for the Chicago World Fair.
Comment: Rich, tangy orange flavour.

JACK DANIEL'S® TENNESSEE WHISKEY

In 1866 Jasper Newton (Jack) Daniel established his distillery in the small town of Lynchburg, Tennessee, close to a limestone cave flowing with pure spring water. Today, Jack's whiskey is still made with that same iron-free spring water at the same site, America's oldest registered distillery.

A mash bill consisting of 80% corn, 8% rye and 12% malted barley is distilled to produce a clear spirit which is slowly dripped through large vats of densely packed hard sugar maple charcoal. It is this extra process that sets Jack Daniels apart from Bourdon whiskies.
The charcoal mellowed spirit is then aged in new white charred oak barrels for over four years before being reduced to bottling strength using cave spring water and bottled in the distinctive square bottle.

This charcoal mellowed whiskey has buttery corn on the cob notes with vanilla, gingerbread and caffè latte flavours.
40% alc./vol. (80°proof)

Web: www.jackdaniels.com **Producer:** Jack Daniel Distillery (Brown-Forman), Lynchburg, Tennessee, USA.
UK distributor: Bacardi-Martini, Southampton.
Tel: 02380 318 288

CHERRY MASH SOUR

Glass: Old-fashioned
Garnish: Lemon twist & cherry
Method: Shake all ingredients with ice and strain into ice-filled glass.

2	shot(s)	Jack Daniel's Tennessee whiskey
1/2	shot(s)	Bols cherry brandy liqueur
3/4	shot(s)	Freshly squeezed lemon juice
1/2	shot(s)	Sugar (gomme) syrup

Origin: Created by Dale DeGroff when Beverage Manager at the Rainbow Room Promenade Bar, New York City.
Comment: The rich flavour of Tennessee whiskey soured with lemon and sweetened with cherry liqueur.

CICADA COCKTAIL

Glass: Martini
Garnish: Grate fresh nutmeg
Method: Shake all ingredients with ice and fine strain into chilled glass.

2	shot(s)	Jack Daniel's Tennessee whiskey
1	shot(s)	Disaronno Originale amaretto
1/2	shot(s)	Double (heavy) cream
3/4	shot(s)	Sugar (gomme) syrup

Origin: Those familiar with the Grasshopper cocktail (named for its green colour) will understand why this one is called the Cicada (they're a bit browner).
Comment: Smoothed whisky with more than a hint of almond.

JACK PUNCH UPDATED

Glass: Collins
Garnish: Pineapple wedge on rim
Method: Cut passion fruit in half and scoop seeds and flesh into shaker. Add other ingredients, shake with ice and strain into ice-filled glass.

1	fresh	Passion fruit
2	shot(s)	Jack Daniel's Tennessee whiskey
1/2	shot(s)	Cuarenta Y Tres (Licor 43) liqueur
3	shot(s)	Pressed pineapple juice
1/8	shot(s)	Sugar (gomme) syrup
4	dashes	Angostura aromatic bitters

Origin: Adapted from a recipe created in 2002 at Townhouse, London, England.
Comment: Vanilla hints in Jack Daniel's and Licor 43 combine to dominate this fruity long drink.

JACKTINI

Glass: Martini
Method: Shake all ingredients with ice and strain into glass.

1	shot(s)	Jack Daniel's Tennessee whiskey
1	shot(s)	Mandarine Napoléon liqueur
1 3/4	shot(s)	Freshly squeezed lemon juice
1/2	shot(s)	Sugar (gomme) syrup

Comment: A citrus bite and a smooth Tennessee whisky draw enhanced with mandarine.

JUMPING JACK FLASH

Glass: Martini
Method: Shake all ingredients with ice and strain into glass.

1	shot(s)	Jack Daniel's Tennessee whiskey
1	shot(s)	Bols crème de banane
1/2	shot(s)	Galliano liqueur
1	shot(s)	Freshly squeezed orange juice
1	shot(s)	Pressed pineapple juice

Comment: The Galliano complements the banana; both mix well with the fruit juices and vanilla.

LYNCHBURG LEMONADE

Glass: Collins
Garnish: Lemon wheel in glass
Method: Shake first three ingredients with ice and strain into ice-filled glass, then top up with 7-Up.

1 1/2	shot(s)	Jack Daniel's Tennessee whiskey
1	shot(s)	Cointreau / triple sec
1	shot(s)	Freshly squeezed lemon juice
Top up with	7-Up

Variant: With three dashes Angostura bitters.
Origin: Created for the Jack Daniel's distillery in, yep, you guessed it, Lynchburg, Tennessee.
Comment: Tangy, light and very easy to drink, this benefits from the sweet, flavoursome edge of Tennessee whiskey.

MISSISSIPPI SCHNAPPER

Glass: Martini
Garnish: Flamed orange twist
Method: Shake all ingredients with ice and fine strain into chilled glass.

2	shot(s)	Jack Daniel's Tennessee whiskey
3/4	shot(s)	Teichenné peach schnapps liqueur
1/2	shot(s)	Cointreau / triple sec
1/4	shot(s)	Freshly squeezed lime juice
1/4	shot(s)	Sugar (gomme) syrup

Origin: Created in 1999 by Dan Cottle at Velvet, Manchester, England.
Comment: Orange predominates with peach sweetness balanced by whiskey and lime.

MOUNTAIN SIPPER

Glass: Old-fashioned
Garnish: Orange zest twist
Method: Shake all ingredients with ice and strain into ice-filled glass.

2	shot(s)	Jack Daniel's Tennessee whisky
1	shot(s)	Cointreau / triple sec
1	shot(s)	Cranberry juice
1	shot(s)	Freshly squeezed grapefruit juice
1/8	shot(s)	Sugar (gomme) syrup

Comment: Fruity citrus flavours balance the richness of the whiskey.

RASPBERRY LYNCHBURG

Glass: Collins
Garnish: Raspberries on drink
Method: Shake first three ingredients with ice and strain into ice-filled glass. Top up with lemonade and drizzle Chambord around surface of drink. This will fall through the drink leaving coloured threads.

2	shot(s)	Jack Daniel's Tennessee whiskey
3/4	shot(s)	Freshly squeezed lime juice
1/4	shot(s)	Sugar (gomme) syrup
Top up with	Lemonade / Sprite / 7-Up
3/4	shot(s)	Chambord black raspberry liqueur

Origin: Created in 1992 by Wayne Collins at Roadhouse, London, England.
Comment: This variation on a Lynchburg Lemonade has a complex sweet and sour flavour laced with whiskey.

TENNESSEE ICED TEA

Glass: Sling
Garnish: Lemon wedge on rim
Method: Shake first six ingredients with ice and strain into ice-filled glass. Top up with cola.

1	shot(s)	Jack Daniel's Tennessee whiskey
1/2	shot(s)	Havana Club light rum
1/2	shot(s)	Absolut vodka
1/2	shot(s)	Cointreau / triple sec
3/4	shot(s)	Freshly squeezed lemon juice
1/3	shot(s)	Sugar (gomme) syrup
Top up with	Cola

Comment: JD and cola with extra interest courtesy of several other spirits and lemon juice.

TENNESSEE RUSH

Glass: Collins
Method: Shake ingredients with ice and strain into ice-filled glass.

2	shot(s)	Jack Daniel's Tennessee whiskey
1	shot(s)	Mandarine Napoléon liqueur
4	shot(s)	Cranberry juice
1	shot(s)	Freshly squeezed lime juice
1/4	shot(s)	Sugar (gomme) syrup

Comment: This ruby red cocktail is long, refreshing and not too sweet.

TOLLEYTOWN PUNCH

Glass: Collins
Garnish: Cranberries, orange and lemon slices
Method: Shake first four ingredients with ice and strain into ice-filled glass. Top up with ginger ale.

2	shot(s)	Jack Daniel's Tennessee whiskey
3	shot(s)	Cranberry juice
1/2	shot(s)	Pressed pineapple juice
1/2	shot(s)	Freshly squeezed orange juice
Top up with	Ginger ale

Origin: A drink promoted by Jack Daniel's. Tolleytown lies just down the road from Lynchburg.
Comment: A fruity long drink with a dry edge that also works well made in bulk and served from a punch bowl.

MIDORI® MELON LIQUEUR

Midori is flavoured with extracts of honeydew melons and can rightly claim to be the original melon liqueur. Midori's vibrant green colour, light melon taste and great versatility has ensured its demand in bars worldwide. Launched in 1978 at New York's famed Studio 54 nightclub, Midori was shaken within sight of the cast of Saturday Night Fever. That same year, Midori won first prize in the U.S. Bartenders Guild Annual Championship.

The name 'Midori' is Japanese for green and it is owned by Suntory, Japan's leading producer and distributor of alcoholic beverages.

Midori is one of the most noted modern day cocktail ingredients due to its vibrant colour and flavour, being: fruity, luscious, lightly syrupy while retaining freshness, with honeyed melon and a hint of green apple. It is also great simply served long with sparkling apple juice or cranberry juice. 20% alc./vol. (40°proof)

Web: www.midori-world.com **Producer:** Suntory Limited, Japan.
UK distributor: FIOR Brands Ltd, Stirling, Scotland.
Tel: 01786 406 360 **Email:** info@fiorbrands.co.uk

COOL MARTINI

Glass: Martini
Method: Shake ingredients with ice and strain into glass.

2	shot(s)	Midori melon liqueur
1	shot(s)	Sauza Hornitos Tequila
2	shot(s)	Cranberry juice

Comment: Tastes nothing like the ingredients - which include melon, Tequila and cranberry juice. Try it and see if you taste toffee. Whatever, it's enjoyable and complex.

E.T.

Glass: Shot
Method: Layer ingredients by carefully pouring in the following order.

1/2	shot(s)	Midori melon liqueur
1/2	shot(s)	Baileys Irish Cream liqueur
1/2	shot(s)	Absolut vodka

Comment: Fortified creamy melon.

EVITA UPDATED

Glass: Martini
Garnish: Orange zest twist
Method: Shake all ingredients with ice and fine strain into chilled glass.

2	shot(s)	Absolut vodka
1/2	shot(s)	Midori melon liqueur
1 1/2	shot(s)	Freshly squeezed orange juice
1/2	shot(s)	Freshly squeezed lime juice

Comment: A tasty, lime green, medium-sweet combination of melon, orange and lime.

JAPANESE SLIPPER

Glass: Martini
Garnish: Sugar rim
Method: Shake ingredients with ice and strain into glass.

1 1/2	shot(s)	Sauza Hornitos Tequila
1 3/4	shot(s)	Midori melon liqueur
3/4	shot(s)	Freshly squeezed lime juice
1/2	shot(s)	Sugar (gomme) syrup

Comment: A vivid green combination of melon and Tequila with a hint of lime.

KILLER PUNCH

Glass: Collins
Garnish: Lime wedge in drink
Method: Shake all ingredients with ice and strain into ice-filled glass.

1	shot(s)	Absolut vodka
1/2	shot(s)	Midori melon liqueur
1/2	shot(s)	Disaronno Originale amaretto
1/2	shot(s)	Freshly squeezed lime juice
4	shot(s)	Cranberry juice

Comment: Pretty soft, sweet and fruity as killers go.

KOOLAID

Glass: Collins
Garnish: Lime wedge on rim
Method: Shake all ingredients with ice and strain into ice-filled glass.

1½	shot(s)	Absolut vodka
¾	shot(s)	Midori melon liqueur
¾	shot(s)	Disaronno Originale amaretto
½	shot(s)	Freshly squeezed lime juice
2	shot(s)	Cranberry juice
1	shot(s)	Freshly squeezed orange juice

Origin: A drink with unknown origins that emerged and morphed during the 1990s.
Comment: Tangy liquid marzipan with hints of melon, cranberry and orange juice.

L.A. ICED TEA

Glass: Sling
Garnish: Split lime wedge
Method: Shake first seven ingredients with ice and strain into glass, then top up with soda water.

½	shot(s)	Absolut vodka
½	shot(s)	Plymouth gin
½	shot(s)	Havana Club light rum
½	shot(s)	Cointreau / triple sec
½	shot(s)	Midori melon liqueur
1	shot(s)	Freshly squeezed lime juice
½	shot(s)	Sugar (gomme) syrup
Top up with		Soda water (club soda)

Comment: The lasting flavour is that of midori.

MELON DAIQUIRI

Glass: Martini
Garnish: Melon slice on rim
Method: Muddle melon in base of shaker. Add other ingredients, shake with ice and fine strain into chilled glass.

2	cups	Diced honeydew melon
2	shot(s)	Havana Club light rum
½	shot(s)	Midori melon liqueur
½	shot(s)	Freshly squeezed lime juice
⅛	shot(s)	Sugar (gomme) syrup

Comment: A classic Daiquiri with the gentle touch of melon.

MELON MARGARITA

Glass: Coupette
Garnish: Melon balls on stick
Method: Muddle melon in base of shaker. Add other ingredients, shake with ice and fine strain into chilled glass.

1	cup	Diced honeydew melon
2	shot(s)	Sauza Hornitos Tequila
1	shot(s)	Midori melon liqueur
1	shot(s)	Freshly squeezed lime juice

Comment: Looks like stagnant pond water but tastes fantastic.

MELON MARTINI #1

Glass: Martini
Garnish: Split lime wedge
Method: Shake ingredients with ice and strain into glass.

2¼	shot(s)	Absolut vodka
1	shot(s)	Midori melon liqueur
½	shot(s)	Freshly squeezed lime juice
¼	shot(s)	Sugar (gomme) syrup

Comment: Bright green, lime and melon with more than a hint of vodka.

MELONCHOLY MARTINI

Glass: Martini
Method: Shake all ingredients with ice and strain into glass.

1	shot(s)	Absolut vodka
1	shot(s)	Midori melon liqueur
½	shot(s)	Cointreau / triple sec
½	shot(s)	Malibu coconut rum liqueur
1	shot(s)	Pressed pineapple juice
¾	shot(s)	Double (heavy) cream
¼	shot(s)	Freshly squeezed lime juice

Origin: Created in 2002 by Daniel O'Brien at Ocean Bar, Edinburgh, Scotland.
Comment: A tad on the sweet side, but the flavours in this smooth, lime-green drink combine surprisingly well.

SOURPUSS MARTINI

Glass: Martini
Garnish: Physalis (Cape gooseberry) on rim
Method: Shake all ingredients with ice and fine strain into chilled glass.

1	shot(s)	Absolut Citron vodka
½	shot(s)	Midori melon liqueur
½	shot(s)	Sourz Sour Apple liqueur
2	shot(s)	Pressed apple juice

Origin: Created in 2001 by Colin 'Big Col' Crowden at Time, Leicester, England.
Comment: A lime-green, flavourful cocktail balancing sweet and sour.

TROPICAL CREAM

Glass: Martini
Garnish: Kiwi fruit on rim
Method: Shake all ingredients with ice and fine strain into chilled glass.

½	shot(s)	Havana Club light rum
1	shot(s)	Midori melon liqueur
½	shot(s)	Frangelico hazelnut liqueur
½	shot(s)	Teichenné peach schnapps liqueur
½	shot(s)	Malibu coconut rum liqueur
1	shot(s)	Freshly squeezed orange juice
1	shot(s)	Double (heavy) cream

Comment: A velvety, smooth, fruity cocktail.

MOUNT GAY ECLIPSE® GOLDEN RUM

Mount Gay is believed to be the oldest rum brand name. The distillery has origins dating back to at least 1703 (some say 1663), which makes it the oldest rum distillery in the world. The Mount Gay Rum Estate lies on a ridge in the northernmost parish of Barbados (St. Lucy). Originally called Mount Gilboa, the estate was renamed in 1801 to honor the death of Sir John Gay Alleyne, the longstanding manager of the estate (a Mount Alleyne already existed at the time).
Mount Gay rums are distilled from molasses using both continuous, fractional distillation and traditional copper pot stills. These two different distillates are blended together with Barbadian underground spring water before being aged in American white oak barrels which have previously been used to age Bourbon.

Eclipse is a light-bodied rum particularly suited to mixing. Its elegant palate includes cooked fruit, citrus zest, gingerbread, caramel sauce and vanilla custard with hints of butterscotch garnish. 40% alc./vol. (80°proof)

Web: www.mountgay.com **Producer:** Mount Gay Distilleries Ltd, Exmouth Gap, Brandons St-Michael, Barbados.
UK distributor: Maxxium UK Ltd, Stirling, Scotland.
Tel: 01786 430 500 **Email:** enquiries@maxxium.com

AIR MAIL NEW

●●●●●◐

Glass: Martini
Garnish: Mint leaf
Method: Stir honey with rum in base of shaker until honey dissolves. Add lemon and orange juice, shake with ice and fine strain into chilled glass. Top up with Champagne.

1	shot(s)	Mount Gay Eclipse golden rum
2	spoons	Runny honey
1/2	shot(s)	Freshly squeezed lime juice
1/2	shot(s)	Freshly squeezed orange juice
Top up with		Piper-Heidsieck Brut Champagne

Comment: Rum, honey and a touch of citrus freshness make this classic one of the better Champagne cocktails.

CLUB COCKTAIL UPDATED

●●●●○

Glass: Martini
Garnish: Stemmed maraschino cherry in drink
Method: Stir all ingredients with ice and fine strain into chilled glass.

2	shot(s)	Mount Gay Eclipse golden rum
1/2	shot(s)	Cinzano Rosso (sweet) vermouth
1/2	shot(s)	Cinzano Extra Dry vermouth
1/2	shot(s)	Maraschino syrup
4	dashes	Angostura aromatic bitters
3/4	shot(s)	Chilled mineral water

Origin: David Embury once wrote, "There are as many Club Cocktails as there are clubs." I based this one on a drink created by Michael Butt in 2002 at Milk & Honey, London, England.
Comment: An aromatic, spirited, classical cocktail.

CUBAN MASTER

Glass: Collins
Method: Shake ingredients with ice and strain into glass.

1 1/2	shot(s)	Mount Gay Eclipse golden rum
1	shot(s)	Rémy Martin Cognac
2	shot(s)	Freshly squeezed orange juice
2	shot(s)	Pressed pineapple juice
1/2	shot(s)	Freshly squeezed lemon juice
1/2	shot(s)	Sugar (gomme) syrup

Origin: I based this on a drink created by an old master Cantinero (bartender) I met in Cuba.
Comment: A long fruity medium dry cocktail based on rum and brandy – would make a good punch.

DAIQUIRI NATURAL UPDATED

●●●●○

Pronounced: Dye-Ker-Ree
Glass: Martini
Garnish: Lime wedge
Method: Shake all ingredients with ice and fine strain into chilled glass.

2	shot(s)	Mount Gay Eclipse golden rum
1/2	shot(s)	Freshly squeezed lime juice
1/4	shot(s)	Sugar (gomme) syrup
3/4	shot(s)	Chilled mineral water

Origin: Mr Jennings Cox, an American engineer who was working at a mine near Santiago, Cuba, created the Daiquiri in 1896.
Comment: The classic proportions of a Daiquiri are 8 parts rum to 2 parts lime to 1 part sugar (as above). A deliciously simple, clean, refreshing sour drink, this is a must-try.

FOUR W DAIQUIRI

●●●●●○

Glass: Martini
Garnish: Grapefruit wedge on rim
Method: Shake all ingredients with ice and fine strain into chilled glass.

2	shot(s)	Mount Gay Eclipse golden rum
1½	shot(s)	Freshly squeezed grapefruit juice
¾	shot(s)	Maple syrup
2	dashes	Angostura aromatic bitters
½	shot(s)	Chilled water

Origin: My version of an old drink created by Herb Smith and popularised by his friend Oscar at the Waldorf, New York City.
Comment: The oomph of rum, the sourness of grapefruit and the richness of maple syrup aromatised by bitters.

HONEYSUCKLE DAIQUIRI

●●●●●

Glass: Martini
Garnish: Mint leaf
Method: Stir honey with rum in base of shaker until honey dissolves. Add lemon and orange juice, shake with ice and fine strain into chilled glass.

2	shot(s)	Mount Gay Eclipse golden rum
4	spoons	Runny honey
1	shot(s)	Freshly squeezed lemon juice
1	shot(s)	Freshly squeezed orange juice

Origin: Adapted from a recipe in David Embury's 'The Fine Art Of Mixing Drinks'.
Comment: Honey – I love it!

MOJITO

●●●●●

Glass: Collins
Garnish: Mint sprig
Method: Muddle mint in base of glass. Add rum, sugar and lime juice. Half fill glass with crushed ice and churn (stir) with bar spoon. Fill glass to brim with more crushed ice and churn some more. Top up with soda, stir and serve with straws.

12	fresh	Mint leaves
2	shot(s)	Mount Gay Eclipse golden rum
1	shot(s)	Freshly squeezed lime juice
¼	shot(s)	Sugar (gomme) syrup
Top up with		Soda water (club soda)

Comment: When well made, this Cuban classic is one of the world's greatest and most refreshing cocktails.

OH GOSH!

●●●●●

Glass: Martini
Garnish: Flamed lemon zest twist
Method: Shake all ingredients long and vigorously with cubed ice and strain into glass.

1½	shot(s)	Mount Gay Eclipse golden rum
1	shot(s)	Cointreau / triple sec
½	shot(s)	Freshly squeezed lime juice
¼	shot(s)	Sugar (gomme) syrup
¾	shot(s)	Chilled mineral water

Origin: Created by Tony Conigliaro in 2001 at Isola, Knightsbridge, London, England.
Comment: A very subtle twist on a classic Daiquiri, but don't knock it until you've tried it as it harnesses citrus flavour from orange, lemon and lime - sublime.

PASSION FRUIT DAIQUIRI UPDATED

●●●●○

Glass: Martini
Garnish: Lime wedge on rim
Method: Cut passion fruit in half and scoop out flesh into shaker. Add other ingredients, shake with ice and fine strain into chilled glass.

2	fresh	Passion fruit
2	shot(s)	Mount Gay Eclipse golden rum
½	shot(s)	Freshly squeezed lime juice
½	shot(s)	Sugar (gomme) syrup

Origin: Formula by yours truly in 2004.
Comment: The rum character comes through in this fruity cocktail.

PINA COLADA

●●●●●

Glass: Hurricane
Garnish: Split pineapple wedge & cherry on stick
Method: Blend ingredients with crushed ice and serve.

2	shot(s)	Mount Gay Eclipse gold rum
3	shot(s)	Pressed pineapple juice
1	shot(s)	Coco López cream of coconut
½	shot(s)	Double (heavy) cream

Origin: Two Puerto Rican bartenders compete the ownership of this drink: Ramon Marrero Pérez & Don Ramon Patas Minyot.
Comment: This is a truly wonderful creamy, fruity concoction, with a real depth of flavour and not half as sticky as the world would have you believe. But can you face the bar call?

PINEAPPLE & CARDAMOM DAIQUIRI

●●●●●

Glass: Martini
Garnish: Pineapple wedge on rim
Method: Break away outer shells of cardamom pods and muddle inner seeds in base of shaker. Add other ingredients, shake with ice and fine strain into chilled glass.

4	pods	Green cardamom
2	shot(s)	Mount Gay Eclipse golden rum
1¾	shot(s)	Pressed pineapple juice
¼	shot(s)	Freshly squeezed lime juice
¼	shot(s)	Sugar (gomme) syrup

Origin: Adapted from Henry Besant's Pineapple & Cardamom Martini.
Comment: One of the tastiest Daiquiris I've tried.

UNCLE VANYA

●●●●●

Glass: Martini
Method: Shake all ingredients with ice and fine strain into glass.

2	shot(s)	Vanilla infused Mount Gay Eclipse golden rum
½	shot(s)	Freshly squeezed lime juice
¼	shot(s)	Sugar (gomme) syrup
¾	shot(s)	Chilled mineral water

Tip: Flavour rum by slicing four vanilla pods down their length and placing in bottle. Replace cap and leave for at least a week, shaking periodically.
Comment: A fantastic drink of flavour and balance.

OPAL BIANCA® SAMBUCA

In 1999, some ten years after launching his very successful Opal Nera black Sambuca, Alessandro Francoli set out to create the ultimate clear Sambuca. The result - Opal Bianca - is made using the finest natural ingredients including star anise, green anise, elderberries, elderflowers and lemon peel. It possesses an exceptional smoothness. The modern bottle, designed to compliment the existing packaging of Opal Nera, reflects the fact that this is not just another traditional clear Italian sambuca.

Opal Bianca has a rich aniseed and black liquorice flavour with hints of spicy elderberry and fresh citrus. 38% alc./vol. (76°proof)

Web: www.opalnera.com **Producer:** Fratelli Francoli S.p.A., Ghemme, Corso Romagnano, Italy. **UK distributor:** Inspirit Brands, London. **Tel:** 020 7377 9457 **Email:** info@inspiritbrands.com

ANIS'TINI

Glass: Martini
Garnish: Star anise
Method: Muddle star anise in base of shaker. Add other ingredients, shake with ice and fine strain into chilled glass.

2	dried	Star anise
1	shot(s)	Absolut vodka
³/₄	shot(s)	Opal Bianca white sambuca
¹/₂	shot(s)	Pernod anis
1¹/₂	shot(s)	Chilled mineral water

Origin: Discovered in 2002 at Lot 61, New York City.
Comment: Specs of star anise are evident in this aniseedy Martini.

ALL WHITE FRAPPÉ

Glass: Old-fashioned
Garnish: Lemon zest
Method: Blend all ingredients with ³/₄ scoop crushed ice and serve with short straws.

1	shot(s)	Opal Bianca white sambuca
1	shot(s)	Bols white crème de cacao
1	shot(s)	Peppermint schnapps
1	shot(s)	Freshly squeezed lemon juice

Comment: Aniseed, chocolate, peppermint and lemon juice are an unlikely but tasty combination for summer afternoons.

BUMBLE BEE

Glass: Shot
Method: Layer by carefully pouring ingredients in the following order.

¹/₂	shot(s)	Kahlúa coffee liqueur
¹/₂	shot(s)	Opal Bianca white sambuca
¹/₂	shot(s)	Baileys Irish Cream liqueur

Comment: A B-52 with a liquorice kick.

CRÈME DE CAFÉ

Glass: Rocks
Method: Shake ingredients with ice and strain into ice-filled glass.

1	shot(s)	Kahlúa coffee liqueur
³/₄	shot(s)	Mount Gay Eclipse golden rum
³/₄	shot(s)	Opal Bianca white sambuca
1	shot(s)	Double (heavy) cream
1	shot(s)	Milk

Comment: Coffee predominates over the creaminess with hints of aniseed and rum.

NEW	A DRINK NEW TO DIFFORDS GUIDE.
UPDATED	ENTRY CHANGED SINCE LAST VOLUME.

FLATLINER

Glass: Shot
Method: Pour sambuca into chilled shot glass. Carefully pour Tequila so as to float on sambuca. Lastly drip pepper sauce onto drink. This will sink through Tequila to form an orange line on top of sambuca.

³/₄	shot(s)	Opal Bianca white sambuca
³/₄	shot(s)	Sauza Hornitos Tequila
8	drops	Tabasco pepper sauce

Comment: A serious combination of sweetness, strength and heat.

GLASS TOWER UPDATED

●●●○○

Glass: Collins
Method: Shake first five ingredients with ice and strain into ice-filled glass, then top up with 7-Up and stir.

1	shot(s)	Absolut vodka
1	shot(s)	Havana Club light rum
¹/₂	shot(s)	Cointreau / triple sec
¹/₂	shot(s)	Teichenné peach schnapps
¹/₄	shot(s)	Opal Bianca white sambuca
Top up with		7-Up or lemonade

Comment: A heady, slightly sweet combination of spirits and liqueurs.

RAGING BULL

Glass: Shot
Method: Combine coffee liqueur and Tequila in glass then float sambuca.

¹/₂	shot(s)	Kahlúa coffee liqueur
¹/₂	shot(s)	Sauza Hornitos Tequila
¹/₂	shot(s)	Opal Bianca white sambuca

Comment: Coffee and sambuca – always a good combination.

SILVER BULLET MARTINI

●●●○○

Glass: Martini
Garnish: Lemon zest twist
Method: Shake all ingredients with ice and fine strain into chilled glass.

2	shot(s)	Plymouth gin
1	shot(s)	Opal Bianca white sambuca
1	shot(s)	Freshly squeezed lemon juice
¹/₂	shot(s)	Sugar (gomme) syrup

Origin: A pre-1930s gin based drink that originally used Kümmel. Now more often based on vodka and made (as here) with sambuca.
Comment: A sweet but balanced combination of aniseed, gin and lemon.

SLIPPERY NIPPER

Glass: Shot
Method: Layer in glass by carefully pouring ingredients in the following order.

¹/₄	shot(s)	Grenadine syrup
³/₄	shot(s)	Opal Bianca white sambuca
³/₄	shot(s)	Baileys Irish Cream liqueur

Comment: The infamous red, clear and brown shot.

TICK-TACK MARTINI UPDATED

●●●○○

Glass: Martini
Garnish: Three Tic-Tac mints
Method: Stir all ingredients with ice and strain into chilled glass.

2	shot(s)	Absolut vodka
¹/₂	shot(s)	Opal Bianca white sambuca
¹/₂	shot(s)	White crème de menthe

Origin: Created in 2001 by Rodolphe Sorel.
Comment: Strangely enough, tastes like a Tic-Tac mint.

TYPHOON

Glass: Rocks
Method: Stir ingredients with ice and strain into ice-filled glass.

1	shot(s)	Plymouth gin
1	shot(s)	Opal Bianca white sambuca
¹/₂	shot(s)	Rose's lime cordial

Comment: Great for sambuca lovers.

VENETO UPDATED

●●●●○

Glass: Martini
Garnish: Lemon zest twist
Method: Shake all ingredients with ice and fine strain into chilled glass.

2	shot(s)	Rémy Martin Cognac
¹/₂	shot(s)	Opal Bianca white sambuca
¹/₂	shot(s)	Freshly squeezed lemon juice
¹/₈	shot(s)	Sugar (gomme) syrup
¹/₂	shot(s)	Egg white

Comment: A serious, Stinger-like drink.

THOSE DRINKS I'VE SAMPLED RECENTLY ARE GRADED AS FOLLOWS:

● DISGUSTING ●● PRETTY AWFUL ●● BEST AVOIDED
●●● DISAPPOINTING ●●● ACCEPTABLE ●●●○ GOOD
●●●● RECOMMENDED ●●●●○ HIGHLY RECOMMENDED
●●●●● OUTSTANDING / EXCEPTIONAL

OPAL NERA® BLACK SAMBUCA

In 1989 Alessandro Francoli was on his honeymoon in America, when he took time out to present his company's traditional Italian grappa and Sambucas to a potential buyer. He noticed the interest the buyer showed in a coffee Sambuca, and this dark liqueur set Alessandro thinking. He experimented with different flavours combined with traditional Sambuca and created Opal Nera, a black coloured Sambuca with a hint of lemon. The unique colouring of Opal Nera comes from the rich, purple-blackness of elderberries, a key ingredient in all Sambucas, macerating the skins of which lends Opal its seductive and unmistakable colour.

Opal Nera Sambuca is a favourite with many bartenders due to its colour and flavour which includes: aniseed, soft black liquorice, light spice of elderberry and lemon zest. 40% alc./vol. (80°proof)

Web: www.opalnera.com **Producer:** Fratelli Francoli S.p.A., Ghemme, Corso Romagnano, Italy. **UK distributor:** Inspirit Brands, London. **Tel:** 020 7377 9457
Email: info@inspiritbrands.com

ALESSANDRO

Glass: Martini
Method: Shake all ingredients with ice and fine strain into chilled glass.

2	shot(s)	Opal Nera black sambuca
3/4	shot(s)	Plymouth gin
3/4	shot(s)	Double (heavy) cream
3/4	shot(s)	Milk

Comment: Hints of aniseed, elderflower and gin emerge from this grey, creamy drink.

BLACK DREAM

Glass: Shot
Method: Layer in glass by carefully pouring ingredients in the following order.

1/2	shot(s)	Baileys Irish Cream liqueur
1/2	shot(s)	Opal Nera black sambuca

Comment: Fairly similar to the Slippery Nipper..

BLACK JACK

Glass: Shot
Method: Layer in glass by carefully pouring ingredients in the following order.

1	shot(s)	Opal Nera black sambuca
1	shot(s)	Jack Daniel's Tennessee whiskey

Comment: Great - if you like sambuca!

BLACK NUTS NEW

Glass: Shot
Method: Layer in glass by carefully pouring in the following order.

3/4	shot(s)	Opal Nera black sambuca
3/4	shot(s)	Frangelico hazelnut liqueur

Comment: It's something of a challenge to get the Frangelico to float on the black sambuca. If you store the Opal Nera in a freezer and the Frangelico at room temperature, this helps.

BLACK WIDOW UPDATED

Glass: Martini
Garnish: Liquorice
Method: Shake all ingredients with ice and fine strain into chilled glass.

1	shot(s)	Opal Nera black sambuca
1	shot(s)	Bols strawberry (fraise) liqueur
1	shot(s)	Malibu coconut rum liqueur
1/2	shot(s)	Double (heavy) cream
1/2	shot(s)	Milk

Comment: This sticky, fruity, liquorice cocktail tastes a little like an Allsort sweet.

FLAMING FERRARI

A flaming drink to be downed in one this requires an assistant to help the drinker consume the concoction.

Step 1.
Glass: Martini
Method: Layer ingredients in glass by carefully pouring in the following order.

¹/₂	shot(s)	Grenadine syrup
1	shot(s)	Galliano liqueur
1	shot(s)	Opal Nera black sambuca
1	shot(s)	Green Chartreuse

Step 2.
Glass: Two shot glasses.
Method: Pour each ingredient into its own shot glass.

1	shot	Grand Marnier liqueur
1	shot	Pusser's Navy rum

Step 3.
Method: Ignite the contents of the Martini glass. Give two long straws to the drinker and instruct them to drink the contents of the Martini glass in one gulp. As they do so, slowly pour the contents of the two shot glasses into the flaming Martini glass.
Comment: Not recommended if you want to remember the rest of the evening and please be careful – alcohol and fire is a dangerous mixture.
Variant: Flaming Lamborghini with coffee liqueur and blue curaçao in the shot glasses.

LIQUORICE ALL SORT

Glass: Collins
Garnish: Liquorice Allsort sweet
Method: Shake first four ingredients with ice and strain into ice-filled glass. Then top up with lemonade.

1	shot(s)	Opal Nera black sambuca
1	shot(s)	Bols crème de banane
1	shot(s)	Bols Strawberry (fraise) liqueur
1	shot(s)	Bols Blue curaçao
Top up with		Lemonade/ 7-Up

Origin: George Bassett (1818-1886), a manufacturer of a variety of liquorice sweets, did not invent the Liquorice Allsort that carries his name. The famous sweet was invented 15 years after George died by one of Bassett's salesmen who accidentally dropped a tray of sweets that had been laid out in neat rows. They fell in a muddle and the Liquorice Allsort was born.
Comment: This aptly named semi-sweet drink has a strong liquorice flavour with hints of fruit.

LIQUORICE MARTINI NEW

Glass: Martini
Garnish: Piece of liquorice
Method: Stir all ingredients with ice and strain into chilled glass.

2	shot(s)	Plymouth gin
¹/₄	shot(s)	Opal Nera black sambuca
¹/₈	shot(s)	Sugar (gomme) syrup

Origin: Created in 2003 by Jason Fendick of Gorgeous Group, London, England.
Comment: Violet coloured, liquorice flavoured and slightly sweetened gin.

MOLOTOV COCKTAIL

Glass: Martini
Garnish: Lemon zest
Method: Shake all ingredients with ice and fine strain into chilled glass.

1¹/₂	shot(s)	Finlandia Lime vodka
1¹/₄	shot(s)	Parfait Amour liqueur
¹/₂	shot(s)	Freshly squeezed lemon juice
¹/₂	shot(s)	Opal Nera black sambuca

Origin: I created this drink after a visit to the Rajamäki distillery, where Finlandia is bottled. At the start of the Second World War the plant was used to produce Molotov cocktails, inflammatory bombs with which the Finns put hundreds of Soviet tanks out of action.
I selected the ingredients to represent the four liquids used in the wartime weapon. Finlandia lime, which is clear, stands for alcohol, parfait amour shares the purple hue of paraffin, lemon juice represents gasoline and Opal Nera replaces tar.
Comment: This inky cocktail combines sweet and sour with hints of liquorice and is as potent as its name suggests.

OIL SLICK

Glass: Shot
Method: Shake ingredients with ice and strain into glass.

³/₄	shot(s)	Opal Nera black sambuca
³/₄	shot(s)	Baileys Irish Cream liqueur

Comment: Whiskey cream and liquorice.

PURPLE FLIRT #2 NEW

Glass: Old-fashioned
Garnish: Orange sail
Method: Shake all ingredients with ice and strain into ice-filled glass.

1	shot(s)	Gosling's Black Seal rum
¹/₄	shot(s)	Bols Blue curaçao
1	shot(s)	Pressed pineapple juice
¹/₂	shot(s)	Freshly squeezed lemon juice
¹/₄	shot(s)	Grenadine syrup
¹/₂	fresh	Egg white

Comment: This popular drink is more brown than purple. It tastes OK, anyway.

REDBACK

Glass: Shot
Garnish: Split cherry on rim
Method: Pour sambuca into glass, then pour advocaat down the side of glass.

1	shot(s)	Opal Nera black sambuca
¹/₂	shot(s)	Warninks advocaat

Comment: An impressive looking shot and a good taste too.

PASSOA® PASSION FRUIT LIQUEUR

The passion fruit was first discovered in South America by Spanish missionaries in the 1500s. They first noticed the amazing flowers of the fruit in the jungle. Nobody knows exactly why it became known as the passion fruit. Was it because the crown-like flower reminded people of the thornbush of Christ's Passion? Or because of its supposed qualities as an aphrodisiac?

Passoã is a passion fruit flavoured liqueur launched in the Netherlands in 1986 and is now the second biggest liqueur brand in Holland and the third biggest in Belgium. The matt black Passoã bottle features a brightly coloured tropical motif of palm trees suggesting its tropical fruit taste. While Passoã is widely used in cocktails, it is also great served over ice with two thirds orange or grapefruit juice.

Passoã is a superbly versatile mixer with a flavour profile that boasts balanced passion fruit and grapefruit with hints of cherries and a honeyed, citrus garnish. 20% alc./vol. (40°proof)

Web: www.passoa.com **Producer:** Cointreau, Angers, France.
UK distributor: Maxxium UK Ltd, Stirling, Scotland.
Tel: 01786 430 500 **Email:** enquiries@maxxium.com

APPLE OF MY EIRE

Glass: Martini
Garnish: Clove
Method: Muddle cloves and cinnamon in base of shaker, add Drambuie and continue to muddle. Add the rest of the ingredients and shake with ice. Strain into glass.

7	whole	Cloves
1/4	spoon	Ground cinnamon
1	shot(s)	Drambuie liqueur
1	shot(s)	Passoã passion fruit liqueur
1/2	shot(s)	Grand Marnier liqueur
3/4	shot(s)	Pressed apple juice
3/4	shot(s)	Cranberry juice

Origin: Adapted from a recipe created by Elaine in 2002 at Living Room, Liverpool, England. The original uses a blend of apple purée with cloves and cinnamon.
Comment: Cinnamon and cloves combine with a veritable fruit basket to produce a drink reminiscent of cold mulled wine – very refreshing.

BAY OF PASSION UPDATED

Glass: Collins
Garnish: Maraschino cherry
Method: Shake all ingredients with ice and strain into ice-filled glass.

1	shot(s)	Passoã passion fruit liqueur
1	shot(s)	Absolut vodka
3 1/2	shot(s)	Cranberry juice
2	shot(s)	Pressed pineapple juice

Comment: Variation on a Bay Breeze - fruity with a tropical tinge.

CHILL BREEZE

Glass: Collins
Garnish: Split lime wheel
Method: Shake ingredients with ice and strain into ice-filled glass.

2	shot(s)	Passoã passion fruit liqueur
1	shot(s)	Absolut vodka
1	shot(s)	Bols cherry brandy liqueur
4	shot(s)	Cranberry juice

Comment: Long, dry passion and cherry – good!

CHINESE PASSION

Glass: Collins
Garnish: Orange slice in glass
Method: Shake ingredients with ice and strain into ice-filled glass.

1	shot(s)	Passoã passion fruit liqueur
1 1/2	shot(s)	Buffalo Trace Bourbon
1 1/2	shot(s)	Teichenné peach schnapps liqueur
3	shot(s)	Freshly squeezed orange juice

Comment: Bizarrely, an element of Chinese flavour.

CRIME OF PASSION SHOT

Glass: Shot
Method: Shake ingredients with ice and strain into glass.

¹/₂	shot(s)	Bols cherry brandy liqueur
1	shot(s)	Passoã passion fruit liqueur
¹/₂	shot(s)	Absolut vodka

Comment: Passion, cherry and vodka - hardly criminal.

EXOTIC PASSION UPDATED

●●●●◐○

Glass: Collins
Garnish: Strawberry
Method: Shake all ingredients with ice and strain into ice-filled glass.

1¹/₂	shot(s)	Absolut vodka
1	shot(s)	Passoã passion fruit liqueur
1	shot(s)	Bols strawberry (fraise) liqueur
2	shot(s)	Pressed pineapple juice
2	shot(s)	Freshly squeezed grapefruit juice

Comment: Bittersweet and floral - one for the poolside.

PALM SPRINGS

●●●●◐○

Glass: Collins
Garnish: Apple slice & mint sprig
Method: Shake all ingredients with ice and strain into glass filled with crushed ice.

4	fresh	Mint leaves
1	shot(s)	Passoã passion fruit liqueur
1	shot(s)	Mount Gay Eclipse golden rum
¹/₄	shot(s)	Freshly squeezed lime juice
1	shot(s)	Pressed apple juice
2	shot(s)	Cranberry juice

Comment: Sweet and aromatic.

PASS-ON-THAT

Glass: Collins
Method: Shake ingredients with ice and strain into ice-filled glass.

1	shot(s)	Passoã passion fruit liqueur
1	shot(s)	Absolut vodka
3	shot(s)	Passion fruit juice
3	shot(s)	Cranberry juice

Comment: Passion fruit and berries.

PASSBOUR COOLER

Glass: Collins
Garnish: Orange slice in glass
Method: Shake ingredients with ice and strain into ice-filled glass.

1	shot(s)	Passoã passion fruit liqueur
1	shot(s)	Bols cherry brandy liqueur
1	shot(s)	Buffalo Trace Bourbon
5	shot(s)	Cranberry juice

Comment: Interesting cherry and Bourbon flavours with subtle passion fruit in the background.

PASSOVER

Glass: Collins
Garnish: Orange slice in glass
Method: Shake ingredients with ice and strain into ice-filled glass.

2	shot(s)	Passoã passion fruit liqueur
1	shot(s)	Absolut vodka
6	shot(s)	Freshly squeezed grapefruit juice

Comment: Grapefruit complements the flavour of Passoã.

PINK PASSION

Glass: Martini
Garnish: Cherry on rim
Method: Shake ingredients with ice and strain into glass.

³/₄	shot(s)	Passoã passion fruit liqueur
³/₄	shot(s)	Bols cherry brandy liqueur
³/₄	shot(s)	Buffalo Trace Bourbon
2	shot(s)	Cranberry juice
¹/₂	shot(s)	Coconut milk

Comment: Interesting and varied flavours.

SAIGON SLING

●●●●●○

Glass: Sling
Method: Shake first seven ingredients and top up with ginger ale

1¹/₂	shot(s)	Plymouth gin
³/₄	shot(s)	Ginger & lemongrass cordial
¹/₂	shot(s)	Krupnik honey liqueur
³/₄	shot(s)	Freshly squeezed lime juice
1	shot(s)	Pressed pineapple juice
¹/₄	shot(s)	Passoã passion fruit liqueur
2	dash(es)	Peychaud's aromatic bitters
Top up with		Ginger ale

Origin: Created in 2001 by Rodolphe Manor for a London bartenders competition.
Comment: A wonderful and adult fusion of flavours.

PIPER-HEIDSIECK CUVÉE BRUT®

The Champagne house of Piper-Heidsieck takes its name from its founder, Florens-Louis Heidsieck, who originally moved to Reims to be a cloth merchant but instead discovered his love for wine-making. He started making his own Champagne in 1780 and founded his own house five years later when he had already become an expert at his art, so much so that he was granted the honour of personally presenting his wine to Queen Marie-Antoinette.

Piper-Heidsieck harvest and separately vinify wines from fifty carefully selected vineyards. It is this technique which enables Piper-Heidsieck cuvée brut to develop its delicious aromas and flavour. This exceptionally well balanced Champagne is fresh and lively, with light aromas of citrus fruit, apple, pear and spring flowers.

Piper-Heidsieck adds a certain joie de vivre to any cocktail and so in keeping with this we recommend serving in luxurious flutes to enhance the aroma and preserve the wine's sparkle.

Web: www.piper-heidsieck.com **Producer:** Champagne Piper-Heidsieck, Reims, France. **UK distributor:** Maxxium UK Ltd, Stirling. **Tel:** 01786 430 500 **Email:** enquiries@maxxium.com

AUTUMN PUNCH

Glass: Sling
Garnish: Physalis fruit on rim
Method: Cut passion fruit in half and scoop out flesh into shaker. Add vodka, passion fruit syrup, pear and lemon juice, shake with ice and strain into ice-filled glass. Top up with Champagne.

1	fresh	Passion fruit
2	shot(s)	Zubrówka (Bison grass) vodka
¼	shot(s)	Passion fruit syrup
1	shot(s)	Freshly extracted pear juice
½	shot(s)	Freshly squeezed lemon juice
Top up with		Piper-Heidsieck Brut Champagne

Origin: Created in 2001 by Max Warner at Baltic Bar, London, England.
Comment: Autumnal in colour with a wonderful meld of complementary flavours.

BLING! BLING!

Glass: Shot
Method: Muddle raspberries in base of shaker. Add vodka, lime and sugar, shake with ice and fine strain into glass. Top up with Champagne.

8	fresh	Raspberries
½	shot(s)	Absolut vodka
½	shot(s)	Freshly squeezed lime juice
½	shot(s)	Sugar (gomme) syrup
Top up with		Piper-Heidsieck Brut Champagne

Origin: Created in 2001 by Phillip Jeffrey at the GE Club, London, England.
Comment: An ostentatious little number.

CHAMPAGNE COCKTAIL

Glass: Flute
Garnish: Orange peel twist
Method: Rub sugar cube with orange peel, then place in base of glass and soak with Angostura. Cover soaked cube with Cognac, then top up with Champagne.

1	cube	Brown sugar
3	dashes	Angostura aromatic bitters
1	shot(s)	Rémy Martin Cognac
Top up with		Piper-Heidsieck Brut Champagne

Origin: Said to have originated from a winning recipe by John Dougherty named Business Brace at the 1899 New York Cocktail competition.
Comment: A classic cocktail that gets sweeter as you reach the dissolving cube at the bottom.

EARL GREY FIZZ

Glass: Flute
Garnish: Lemon knot
Method: Shake first three ingredients with ice and strain into chilled glass. Top up with Champagne.

1	shot(s)	Zubrowka bison vodka
½	shot(s)	Strong cold Earl Grey tea
¼	shot(s)	Sugar (gomme) syrup
Top up with		Piper-Heidsieck Brut Champagne

Origin: Created in 2002 by Henry Besant at Lonsdale House, London, England.
Comment: Looks like a glass of Champagne but has a well judged little extra something.

ELDERBUBBLE

Glass: Flute
Garnish: Stick of cucumber
Method: Shake first three ingredients with ice and strain into chilled glass. Top up with Champagne.

1	shot(s)	Pölstar cucumber vodka
3/4	shot(s)	Elderflower cordial
1/8	shot(s)	Freshly squeezed lemon juice
Top up with		Piper-Heidsieck Brut Champagne

Origin: Created in 2002 by Michael Mahe and popularised at Hush, London, England.
Comment: A refreshing, summery Champagne cocktail.

FRENCH 75

Glass: Flute
Garnish: Maraschino cherry in drink
Method: Shake first three ingredients with ice and strain into glass, top up with Champagne.

3/4	shot(s)	Plymouth gin
1/2	shot(s)	Freshly squeezed lemon juice
1/2	shot(s)	Sugar (gomme) syrup
Top up with		Piper-Heidsieck Brut Champagne

Origin: Legend has it that the drink was created by Harry MacElhone at his Harry's Bar, Paris in 1925 and was named after the 75 field gun used by the French army during the First World War. However, like other drinks in the forst edition of Harry's own book, The ABC of mixing drinks, he credits the drink to Macgarry of Buck's Club, London, England.
Comment: Fresh, clean, sophisticated - very drinkable and hasn't dated.

FRESCA NOVA UPDATED

Glass: Flute
Method: Shake first four ingredients with ice and fine strain into chilled glass. Top up with Champagne.

1 1/2	shot(s)	Grand Marnier liqueur
3/4	shot(s)	Freshly squeezed orange juice
1/2	shot(s)	Sugar (gomme) syrup
1	shot(s)	Double (heavy) cream
Top up with		Piper-Heidsieck Brut Champagne

Origin: Created by Jamie Terrell for Philip Holzberg at Vinexpo 1999.
Comment: Cream, orange and Champagne work surprisingly well. Be sure to add the Champagne slowly.

JA-MORA

Glass: Flute
Garnish: Float single raspberry.
Method: Shake first four ingredients with ice and strain into glass. Top up with Champagne.

1	shot(s)	Freshly squeezed orange juice
1	shot(s)	Pressed apple juice
1	shot(s)	Absolut vodka
1	shot(s)	Chambord black raspberry liqueur
Top up with		Piper-Heidsieck Brut Champagne

Origin: Created by Jamie Terrell and Andres Masso in 1998. Named after 'mora', the Spanish for raspberry. The 'j' and 'a' stand for the names of its two creators.
Comment: Very moreish with loads of flavour.

PIMM'S COCKTAIL NEW

Glass: Martini
Garnish: Lemon & orange zest twist
Method: Shake first four ingredients with ice and strain into chilled glass. Top up with Champagne.

2	shot(s)	Pimm's No.1 Cup
1/2	shot(s)	Plymouth gin
1/4	shot(s)	Freshly squeezed lemon juice
1/4	shot(s)	Sugar (gomme) syrup
Top up with		Piper-Heidsieck Brut Champagne

Origin: Created by yours truly in 2004.
Comment: Luxuriate in this quintessentially English tipple.

ROYAL COSMOPOLITAN NEW

Glass: Martini
Garnish: Flamed orange zest twist
Method: Shake first four ingredients with ice and fine strain into chilled glass. Top up with Champagne.

1	shot(s)	Absolut Citron vodka
1/2	shot(s)	Cointreau / triple sec
1	shot(s)	Cranberry juice
1/4	shot(s)	Freshly squeezed lime juice
Top up with		Piper-Heidsieck Brut Champagne

Origin: Created in 2003 by Wayne Collins for Maxxium UK.
Comment: The classic Cosmopolitan with a layer of fizz on top adding a biscuity complexity. Sex And The City meets Ab Fab.

RUSSIAN SPRING PUNCH UPDATED

Glass: Sling
Garnish: Lemon slice & berries
Method: Shake first four ingredients with ice and strain into glass filled with crushed ice. Top up with Champagne, stir and serve with straws.

1	shot(s)	Absolut vodka
1/4	shot(s)	Sisca crème de cassis
1	shot(s)	Freshly squeezed lemon juice
1/4	shot(s)	Sugar (gomme) syrup
Top up with		Champagne

Origin: My version of a drink created by Dick Bradsell, London, England.
Comment: Well balanced, complex and refreshing – one of the best drinks to emerge during the 1990s.

VALENCIA

Glass: Flute
Garnish: 1/4 orange wheel on rim
Method: Pour first three ingredients into chilled glass and top up with Champagne.

1/2	shot(s)	Bols Apricot brandy liqueur
1/4	shot(s)	Freshly squeezed orange juice
4	dashes	Fee Brother's Orange bitters (optional)
Top up with		Piper-Heidsieck Brut Champagne

Origin: Adapted from the Valencia Cocktail No.2 in The Savoy Cocktail Book. Sometimes also served as a Martini with gin in place of Champagne.
Comment: Floral and fruity – makes Bucks Fizz look a tad sad.

PLYMOUTH GIN®

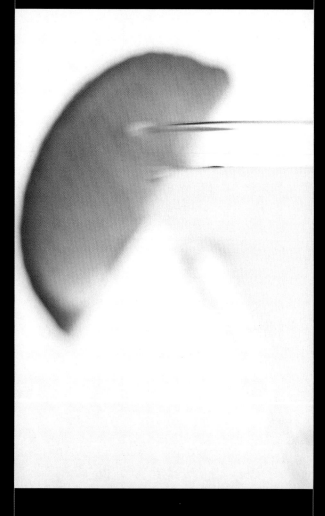

Since 1793, Plymouth Gin has been handcrafted in England's oldest working gin distillery - Black Friars in Plymouth. It is still bottled at the unique strength of 41.2% ABV, and is based on a recipe that is over 200 years old. Plymouth Gin, which can only be produced in Plymouth, differs from London gins due to the use of only sweet botanicals. This unique blend of botanicals combine with soft Dartmoor water to result in a wonderfully aromatic and smooth gin. Plymouth has been used by bartenders in cocktails since 1896, when it was first mixed in the original Dry Martini, and is favoured by many top bartenders due to its fresh juniper, lemony bite with deeper liquorice notes.

41.2% alc./vol. (82.4° proof)

Web: www.plymouthgin.com
Producer: Coates & Co Ltd, Plymouth.
UK distributor: Maxxium UK Ltd, Stirling, Scotland.
Tel: 01786 430 500
Email: enquiries@maxxium.com

ANGEL FACE MARTINI

Glass: Martini
Garnish: Peach or apricot slice on rim
Method: Shake all ingredients with ice and fine strain into chilled glass.

1	shot(s)	Plymouth gin
1	shot(s)	Calvados or applejack brandy
1	shot(s)	Bols apricot brandy liqueur
1/8	shot(s)	Sugar (gomme) syrup
1	shot(s)	Chilled water

Origin: Adapted from a recipe first published in The Savoy Cocktail Book in the 1950s.
Comment: A golden combination of gin, apple and apricot.

APRICOT MANGO MARTINI

Glass: Martini
Garnish: Mango slice
Method: Muddle mango in the base of a shaker. Add other ingredients, shake with ice and fine strain into glass.

1	handful	Fresh chopped mango
2	shot(s)	Plymouth gin
1/2	shot(s)	Bols apricot brandy liqueur
3/4	shot(s)	Freshly squeezed lemon juice
1/2	shot(s)	Sugar (gomme) syrup

Comment: A simple, great tasting variation on the fresh fruit Martini.

ARNAUD MARTINI

Glass: Martini
Garnish: Blackberry on rim
Method: Stir all ingredients with ice and strain into chilled glass.

1 1/2	shot(s)	Plymouth gin
1 1/2	shot(s)	Cinzano Extra Dry vermouth
1 1/2	shot(s)	Sisca crème de cassis

Origin: A classic (retro) cocktail named after the stage actress Yvonne Arnaud.
Comment: An interesting balance of blackcurrant, vermouth and gin. Sweet palate and dry finish.

BEE'S KNEES MARTINI # 2

Glass: Martini
Garnish: Orange wedge
Method: In base of shaker stir honey with gin until honey dissolves. Add lemon and orange juice, shake with ice and fine strain into chilled glass.

2	shot(s)	Plymouth gin
4	spoons	Runny honey
1	shot(s)	Freshly squeezed lemon juice
1	shot(s)	Freshly squeezed orange juice

Variation: Made with light rum in place of gin this drink becomes a 'Honeysuckle Martini'.
Origin: Adapted from a recipe in David Embury's 'The Fine Art Of Mixing Drinks'.
Comment: This honeyed citrus concoction really is the bee's knees.

BRADFORD

Glass: Martini
Garnish: Olive on stick or lemon zest twist
Method: Shake all ingredients with ice and fine strain into chilled glass.

2¹/₂	shot(s)	Plymouth gin
¹/₂	shot(s)	Cinzano Extra Dry vermouth
3	dashes	Fee Brothers orange bitters (optional)

Origin: A Bradford is a Martini which is shaken rather than stirred. Like the Martini itself the origin of the Bradford is lost in time.
Comment: More approachable than a stirred Traditional Dry Martini and downright soft compared to a Naked Martini.

BRAMBLE

Glass: Old-fashioned
Garnish: Blackberry & lemon slice
Method: Fill glass with crushed ice, add gin, lemon juice and sugar syrup and stir. Top up with more crushed ice. Then lace drink with blackberry liqueur by slowly pouring over fresh ice. It should make a pleasing 'bleeding' effect in the glass. Serve immediately with two short straws.

2	shot(s)	Plymouth gin
1¹/₂	shot(s)	Freshly squeezed lemon juice
¹/₂	shot(s)	Sugar (gomme) syrup
¹/₂	shot(s)	Bols Blackberry liqueur

Origin: Created in the mid-80s by Dick Bradsell at Fred's Club, Soho, London, England.
Comment: One of the best and most popular drinks created in the 1980s.

BREAKFAST MARTINI

Glass: Martini
Garnish: Slice of toast on rim
Method: Stir marmalade with gin in base of shaker until it dissolves. Add other ingredients, shake with ice and fine strain into chilled glass.

1	spoon	Orange marmalade (rindless)
1³/₄	shot(s)	Plymouth gin
³/₄	shot(s)	Cointreau / triple sec
³/₄	shot(s)	Freshly squeezed lemon juice
³/₄	shot(s)	Sugar (gomme) syrup

Origin: Created in the late 1990s by Salvatore Calabrese at the Library Bar, London, England, this is very similar to the Marmalade Cocktail created in the 1920s by Harry Craddock and published in The Savoy Cocktail Book.
Comment: The success or failure of this tangy drink is partly reliant on the quality of marmalade used.

CLOVER LEAF MARTINI

Glass: Martini
Garnish: Clover/mint leaf
Method: Muddle raspberries in base of shaker. Add other ingredients, shake with ice and fine strain into chilled glass.

10	fresh	Raspberries
2¹/₂	shot(s)	Plymouth gin
³/₄	shot(s)	Freshly squeezed lemon juice
¹/₄	shot(s)	Grenadine syrup
¹/₄	shot(s)	Sugar (gomme) syrup
¹/₂	fresh	Egg white

Variant: Traditionally made with raspberry syrup with no grenadine or fresh raspberries.
AKA: Without the mint leaf garnish this drink is called a 'Clover Club'.
Origin: A classic cocktail that's thought to have been created at the Bellevue-Stratford Hotel in Philadelphia.
Comment: Carpet scaring red, this drink is fruity, strong and recommended. Muddle some mint with the raspberries to add interest.

CURDISH MARTINI

Glass: Martini
Garnish: Lemon zest twist
Method: Shake all ingredients with ice and strain into glass.

2	shot(s)	Plymouth gin
¹/₂	shot(s)	Sourz Sour Apple liqueur
²/₃	shot(s)	Freshly squeezed lime juice
2	spoons	Lemon curd

Origin: Created in 2001 by Tadgh Ryan at West Street, London, England.
Comment: Beautifully balanced with the tang of lemon curd.

DIRTY MARTINI UPDATED

Glass: Martini
Garnish: Olive on stick
Method: Stir all ingredients with ice and strain into a chilled glass.

2¹/₂	shot(s)	Plymouth gin
¹/₄	shot(s)	Brine from cocktail olives
¹/₄	shot(s)	Cinzano Extra Dry vermouth

Variant: Substitute vodka for gin.
Comment: This drink varies from delicious to disgusting, depending on the liquid in your jar of olives. Oil will produce a revolting emulsion: make sure that your olives are packed in brine.

NEW	A DRINK NEW TO DIFFORDS GUIDE.
UPDATED	ENTRY CHANGED SINCE LAST VOLUME.

DRY MARTINI TRADITIONAL

Glass: Martini
Garnish: Olive on stick or lemon zest twist
Method: Stir vermouth with ice in a mixing glass and strain to discard excess vermouth, leaving only a coating on the ice. Pour gin into mixing glass containing coated ice, stir and strain into a chilled glass.

³/₄	shot(s)	Cinzano Extra Dry vermouth
2¹/₂	shot(s)	Plymouth gin
3	dashes	Fee Brothers orange bitters (optional)

Variant: The proportion of gin to vermouth is a matter of taste, some say 7 to 1, others that one drop is sufficient. We recommend you ask the drinker how they would like their Martini, in the same manner you might ask how they have their steak. If the drinker orders a 'Sweet Martini' use sweet red vermouth rather than dry and use a cherry as garnish instead of an olive. A 'Wet Martini' is a Martini with extra vermouth - don't strain the vermouth out.
Variant: A 'Dickens' is a Martini without a twist, a 'Gibson' is a Martini with onions instead of an olive or a twist and a 'Franklin Martini' is named after Franklin Roosevelt and has two olives.
Origin: Although Martini vermouth is commonly used to make this recipe, the name is coincidental. It is said that this cocktail was invented in 1911 by a New York bartender called Martini di Arma di Taggia who was the head bartender at the fashionable Knickerbocker Hotel and that a French vermouth (Noilly Prat) was originally used with orange bitters.
Comment: If a Martini is shaken it becomes a 'Bradford'. Shaken Martinis taste very different due to further dilution and the air bubbles shaking introduces to the drink.

EARL GREY MAR-TEA-NI

Glass: Martini
Garnish: Lemon zest twist
Method: Shake all ingredients with ice and fine strain into chilled glass.

2	shot(s)	Plymouth gin
1¹/₄	shot(s)	Strong cold Earl Grey tea
³/₄	shot(s)	Freshly squeezed lemon juice
¹/₂	shot(s)	Sugar (gomme) syrup
¹/₂	fresh	Egg white

Origin: Created by Audrey Saunders at Bemelmans Bar at The Carlyle, New York City.
Comment: A fantastic and very English drink created by a New Yorker. The botanicals of gin combine wonderfully with the flavours and tannins of Earl Grey.

ELDERFLOWER COLLINS

Glass: Collins
Garnish: Physalis on rim
Method: Shake first four ingredients with ice and strain into ice-filled glass. Top up with soda water (club soda).

2	shot(s)	Plymouth gin
¹/₂	shot(s)	Elderflower cordial
1	shot(s)	Freshly squeezed lemon juice
¹/₈	shot(s)	Sugar (gomme) syrup
Top up with		Soda water (club soda)

Comment: Just as it says on the lid – a Collins with a hint of elderflower.

ENGLISH MARTINI

Glass: Martini
Garnish: Rosemary
Method: Muddle rosemary in base of shaker. Add other ingredients, stir with ice and strain into chilled glass.

1	sprig	Rosemary
2¹/₂	shot(s)	Plymouth gin
³/₄	shot(s)	Elderflower cordial
¹/₂	shot(s)	Sugar (gomme) syrup

Origin: Adapted from a drink created in 2003 at MJU, Millennium Hotel, London, England.
Comment: Would be great served with roast lamb.

FORBIDDEN FRUITS

Glass: Collins
Garnish: Berries on stick
Method: Muddle berries in base of shaker can. Add other ingredients, shake with ice and strain into glass filled with crushed ice.

4	fresh	Blackberries
4	fresh	Blueberries
4	fresh	Strawberries
4	fresh	Raspberries
2	shot(s)	Plymouth gin
1	shot(s)	Fresh lime juice
¹/₂	shot(s)	Sugar (gomme) syrup
Top up with		Ginger Beer

Origin: Created in 2001 by Andres Masso at Lab Bar, London, England.
Comment: Long and fruity with something of a bite.

GIBSON MARTINI

Glass: Martini
Garnish: Two cocktail onions
Method: Stir vermouth with ice in a mixing glass. Strain, discarding vermouth, to leave only a coating on the ice. Pour gin into mixing glass containing coated ice and stir. Finally strain contents of mixing glass into glass.

¹/₂	shot(s)	Cinzano Extra Dry vermouth
2¹/₂	shot(s)	Plymouth gin

Origin: There are several stories as to this drink's origin. 1/ That it was named after the well-endowed Gibson Girls - hence the two onions.
2/ That it was invented in the 1940s for the American illustrator Charles Dana Gibson at The Player's Club in New York City and the onions represent the milky white breasts of the women he drew.
Variant: With vodka in place of gin.
Comment: A must-try for gin martini fans.

NEW	A DRINK NEW TO DIFFORDS GUIDE.
UPDATED	ENTRY CHANGED SINCE LAST VOLUME.

GIMLET

Glass: Martini
Garnish: Split lime wedge or cherry
Method: Stir all ingredients with ice and fine strain into chilled glass.

2½	shot(s)	Plymouth gin
1¼	shot(s)	Rose's lime cordial

Variant: Other spirits, particularly vodka may be substituted for gin.
Origin: In 1747, James Lind, a Scottish surgeon, discovered that consumption of citrus fruits helped prevent scurvy, one of the most common illnesses on board ship. (It is now understood that scurvy is caused by a Vitamin C deficiency and that it is the vitamins in citrus fruit which help ward off the condition.) Later, Lachlan Rose, the owner of a shipyard in Leith, solved the problem of how to keep citrus juice fresh for months on board ship. In 1867 he patented a process for preserving fruit using salts of sulphur. To give his new product wider appeal he sweetened the mixture, packaged it in an attractive bottle and named it 'Rose's Lime Cordial'.

A 'gimlet' was originally the name of a small tool used to tap the barrels of spirits which were carried on British Navy ships: this could be the origin of the drink's name. Another story cites a naval doctor, Rear-Admiral Sir Thomas Desmond Gimlette (1857-1943), who is said to have mixed gin with lime 'to help the medicine go down'.
Comment: Classically this drink is shaken rather than stirred. However you choose to mix this, it is a simple blend of gin and sweet lime.

GIN FIZZ UPDATED

Glass: 8oz Collins
Garnish: Slice of lemon & mint
Method: Shake first three ingredients vigorously with crushed ice and fine strain into empty chilled glass. Top up with charged water from siphon while stirring.

2¼	shot(s)	Plymouth gin
1½	shot(s)	Freshly squeezed lemon juice
¾	shot(s)	Sugar (gomme) syrup
Top up with		Charged water from siphon

Variant: With the addition of egg white this drink becomes a 'Silver Fizz', with egg yolk it becomes a 'Golden Fizz'. A Royal Fizz is with one whole egg. A Diamond Fizz uses Champagne instead of charged water. A Green Fizz is with a dash of green crème de menthe. A Purple Fizz is with equal parts sloe gin and grapefruit juice in place of gin and lemon juice.
Origin: This mid-19th century classic is basically a sour lengthened with charged water. At first glance there is little difference between a Gin Fizz and a Tom Collins. However, there are several distinguishing features. A Collins should be served in a 12oz or larger tall glass while that used for a Fizz should be no bigger than eight ounces. A Fizz should also be made using charged water from a siphon and not soda from a bottle or can as the fizzing produced by the burst of pressure from the siphon bulb is key to the drink. Carbonic acid gas is given off slowly in tiny bubbles so cans or bottles of soda water (club soda) do not suit a Fizz. Lastly a Fizz should be served in a pre-chilled glass without ice.
Comment: Everyone has heard of this clean, refreshing, long drink but few have actually tried it.

GIN GARDEN MARTINI

Glass: Martini
Garnish: Float cucumber slice
Method: Muddle cucumber in base of shaker. Add other ingredients, shake with ice and fine strain into chilled glass.

1	inch	Chopped peeled cucumber
2	shot(s)	Plymouth gin
1	shot(s)	Pressed apple juice
½	shot(s)	Elderflower cordial

Origin: Created in 2001 through a collaboration between Daniel Warner at Zander and Tobias Blazquez Garcia at Steam, London, England.
Comment: The archetypal English spirit, fruit and vegetable combo.

GIN GENIE

Glass: Collins
Garnish: Mint sprig
Method: Muddle mint in base of shaker. Add other ingredients, shake with ice and strain into glass filled with crushed ice.

8	fresh	Mint leaves
1½	shot(s)	Plymouth gin
1	shot(s)	Freshly squeezed lemon juice
1	shot(s)	Plymouth sloe gin
½	shot(s)	Sugar (gomme) syrup

Origin: Created in 2002 by Wayne Collins for Maxxium UK.
Comment: A great, fruit-led long drink for gin-loving Bowie fans.

GIN SOUR

Glass: Old-fashioned
Garnish: Lemon wedge on rim
Method: Shake all ingredients with ice and strain into empty chilled glass.

2	shot(s)	Plymouth gin
2	shot(s)	Freshly squeezed orange juice
1	shot(s)	Freshly squeezed lemon juice
½	shot(s)	Sugar (gomme) syrup
½	fresh	Egg white

Comment: Smooth and sour with the obligatory gin kick.

GIN-GER TOM

Glass: Collins
Garnish: Lime squeeze and mint sprig
Method: Pour ingredients into ice-filled glass and stir.

2	shot(s)	Plymouth gin
1	shot(s)	Ginger syrup
1	shot(s)	Freshly squeezed lime juice
¼	shot(s)	Sugar (gomme) syrup
Top up with		Sparkling mineral water

Origin: Created by Jamie Terrell.
Comment: A Tom Collins with lime and ginger – very refreshing.

GRAPE DELIGHT

Glass: Martini
Garnish: Grapes in drink
Method: Muddle grapes in base of shaker. Add rest of ingredients, shake with ice and strain into glass.

10	fresh	Seedless red grapes
1½	shot(s)	Plymouth gin
½	shot(s)	Plymouth sloe gin
⅓	shot(s)	Sugar (gomme) syrup
½	shot(s)	Freshly squeezed lime juice
4	dashes	Angostura aromatic bitters

Comment: The rust colour of this drink comes from the Angostura bitters, sloe gin and the muddled skins of red grapes. These combine to provide its delicate balanced flavour.

GYPSY MARTINI

Glass: Martini
Garnish: Rosemary
Method: Muddle rosemary and raisins in base of shaker. Add gin, sugar and water, shake with ice and strain into glass.

1	sprig	Fresh rosemary (remove stalk)
10		Raisins
2	shot(s)	Plymouth gin
½	shot(s)	Sugar (gomme) syrup
1	shot(s)	Chilled water

Origin: Adapted from a recipe created by Jason Fendick in 2002 for Steam, London, England.
Comment: Jason's original recipe called for raisin infused gin and we'd recommend you make this drink that way if time permits.

INK MARTINI

Glass: Martini
Garnish: Orange zest twist
Method: Shake all ingredients with ice and fine strain into chilled glass.

1¼	shot(s)	Plymouth gin
½	shot(s)	Bols Blue curaçao
½	shot(s)	Teichenné peach schnapps liqueur
2	shot(s)	Cranberry juice

Origin: Created in 2002 by Gentian Naci at Bar Epernay, Birmingham, England.
Comment: This simple, appropriately named drink is surprisingly quaffable.

JASMINE **UPDATED**

Glass: Martini
Garnish: Lemon zest twist
Method: Shake all ingredients with ice and fine strain into chilled glass.

1	shot(s)	Plymouth gin
½	shot(s)	Campari
½	shot(s)	Cointreau / triple sec
1	shot(s)	Freshly squeezed lemon juice
½	shot(s)	Sugar (gomme) syrup
¾	shot(s)	Chilled mineral water

Origin: Created by Alex Turner in 2001.
Comment: The distinctive flavour of Campari is enhanced by lemon and orange.

KEE-WEE MARTINI **UPDATED**

Glass: Martini
Garnish: Kiwi slice on rim
Method: Cut kiwi fruit in half, scoop out flesh into base of shaker and muddle. Add other ingredients, shake with ice and fine strain into chilled glass.

1	fresh	Kiwi fruit
2	shot(s)	Plymouth gin
¼	shot(s)	Freshly squeezed lemon juice
½	shot(s)	Sugar (gomme) syrup

Origin: My version of this ubiquitous drink.
Comment: The citrus hints in the kiwi combine brilliantly with those in the gin and fresh lemon juice.

MAIDEN'S PRAYER MARTINI

Glass: Martini
Garnish: Flamed orange zest twist
Method: Shake all ingredients with ice and fine strain into chilled glass.

1½	shot(s)	Plymouth gin
½	shot(s)	Cointreau / triple sec
1½	shot(s)	Freshly squeezed orange juice
¾	shot(s)	Freshly squeezed lemon juice

Origin: My adaptation of a classic recipe.
Comment: A Gin Sour with triple sec in place of sugar and without the smoothing properties of egg white. Some like it rough!

MAINBRACE

Glass: Martini
Garnish: Orange zest twist
Method: Shake all ingredients with ice and fine strain into chilled glass.

1½	shot(s)	Plymouth gin
1½	shot(s)	Cointreau / triple sec
1½	shot(s)	Freshly squeezed grapefruit juice

Comment: Full-on grapefruit laced with gin and a hint of orange. Tart finish.

MARTINEZ

Glass: Martini
Garnish: Orange twist
Method: Stir all ingredients with ice and strain into chilled glass.

2	shot(s)	Plymouth gin
½	shot(s)	Cinzano Rosso (sweet) vermouth
¼	shot(s)	Cointreau / triple sec
¼	shot(s)	Sugar (gomme) syrup
3	dashes	Fee Brothers orange bitters (optional)

Origin: A variation on a nineteenth century drink, supposed to be a forerunner of the Martini. Originally this would have been made with a sweet style of gin known as 'Old Tom'.
Comment: The ingredients combine well and the flavours are well balanced. This medium dry Martini is somewhat more approachable than a modern Dry Martini.

THE MAYFLOWER MARTINI

Glass: Martini
Garnish: Edible flower petal
Method: Shake all ingredients with ice and fine strain into chilled glass.

1¹/₂	shot(s)	Plymouth gin
¹/₂	shot(s)	Bols apricot brandy liqueur
1	shot(s)	Pressed apple juice
¹/₄	shot(s)	Elderflower cordial
¹/₂	shot(s)	Freshly squeezed lemon juice

Origin: Created in 2002 by Wayne Collins for Maxxium UK.
Comment: Fragrant balance of English fruits and flowers.

MILLION DOLLAR

Glass: Martini
Garnish: Physalis on rim (cape gooseberry)
Method: Shake all ingredients with ice and fine strain into chilled glass.

2	shot(s)	Plymouth gin
³/₄	shot(s)	Pressed pineapple juice
³/₄	shot(s)	Cinzano Rosso (sweet) vermouth
¹/₈	shot(s)	Grenadine syrup
¹/₂	fresh	Egg white

Origin: A classic (retro) cocktail which can be found in all the old bar tomes. Thought to have been created around 1910 by Ngiam Tong Boon at Raffles Hotel, Singapore. (He is more famous for creating the Singapore Sling.)
Comment: Smooth, almost rosewater flavour.

MONARCH MARTINI

Glass: Martini
Garnish: Lemon zest twist
Method: Lightly muddle mint in base of shaker. Add other ingredients, shake with ice and fine strain into chilled glass.

7	fresh	Mint leaves
1¹/₂	shot(s)	Plymouth gin
¹/₂	shot(s)	Freshly squeezed lemon juice
³/₄	shot(s)	Elderflower cordial
¹/₂	shot(s)	Sugar (gomme) syrup
¹/₂	shot(s)	Chilled mineral water

Origin: Created in 2003 by Douglas Ankrah at Townhouse, London, England. Doug's original recipe omitted water and included a dash of peach bitters.
Comment: Wonderfully floral and minty – worthy of a right royal drinker.

OPAL MARTINI UPDATED

Glass: Martini
Garnish: Flamed orange zest twist
Method: Shake all ingredients with ice and fine strain into chilled glass.

1¹/₂	shot(s)	Plymouth gin
³/₄	shot(s)	Cointreau / triple sec
1¹/₂	shot(s)	Freshly squeezed orange juice

Origin: The combination of gin and orange dates back at least as far as 1906, when the Bronx was created. The mixture made a surprising comeback in the wonderful world of rap, when Snoop Doggy Dogg hymned 'Gin 'n' Juice'.
Comment: Simple but effective.

PARADISE MARTINI

Glass: Martini
Garnish: Flamed orange zest twist
Method: Shake all ingredients with ice and fine strain into chilled glass.

2	shot(s)	Plymouth gin
³/₄	shot(s)	Bols Apricot brandy liqueur
1³/₄	shot(s)	Freshly squeezed orange juice
3	dashes	Fee Brothers Orange bitters (optional)

Origin: An old, old recipe that in recent times has been revitalized by Dale DeGroff.
Comment: Wonderfully fruity cocktail that when well made beautifully harnesses and balances its ingredients.

PINK GIN NEW

Glass: Martini
Garnish: Lemon zest twist
Method: Stir all ingredients with ice and strain into chilled glass.

2	shot(s)	Plymouth gin (from freezer)
2	shot(s)	Chilled mineral water
1	dash	Angostura aromatic bitters

Origin: Gin was a favourite of the Royal Navy – along with rum, which was served as a daily ration right up until the 70s. It was often mixed with healthy ingredients to make them more palatable, such as lime juice, which was drunk to prevent scurvy.

Pink gin was originally used against stomach upsets, as Angostura aromatic bitters were considered medicinal.
Comment: Normally I'd advocate liberal use of Angostura bitters but this refined and subtle drink benefits from frugality.

RAMOS GIN FIZZ (SIMPLE FORMULA)

Glass: Collins
Garnish: Lemon wedge
Method: Shake all but soda with ice and strain into ice-filled glass. Top up with soda.

2	shot(s)	Plymouth gin
³/₄	shot(s)	Freshly squeezed lemon juice
1¹/₂	shot(s)	Sugar (gomme) syrup
¹/₂	fresh	Egg white
Top up with		Soda water (from siphon)

Comment: Sweetened and smoothed gin with a hint of lemon.

THOSE DRINKS I'VE SAMPLED RECENTLY ARE GRADED AS FOLLOWS:

● DISGUSTING   ●◐ PRETTY AWFUL   ●● BEST AVOIDED
●●◐ DISAPPOINTING   ●●● ACCEPTABLE   ●●●○ GOOD
●●●● RECOMMENDED   ●●●●◐ HIGHLY RECOMMENDED
●●●●● OUTSTANDING / EXCEPTIONAL

RASPBERRY COLLINS

Glass: Collins
Garnish: Three raspberries & lemon slice
Method: Muddle raspberries in base of shaker. Add next five ingredients, shake with ice and strain into an ice-filled glass. Top up with soda, stir and serve with straws.

10	fresh	Raspberries
2	shot(s)	Plymouth gin
1¹/₂	shot(s)	Freshly squeezed lemon juice
¹/₂	shot(s)	Bols Raspberry (framboise) liqueur
¹/₂	shot(s)	Sugar (gomme) syrup
3	dashes	Fee Brothers Orange bitters (optional)
Top up with		Soda water (club soda)

Variant: Raspberry Debonnaire
Origin: Created in 1999 by Cairbry Hill, London, England.
Comment: This fruity drink is the most popular modern adaptation of the classic Collins.

RICKEY (GIN RICKEY) NEW

Glass: Collins (small 8oz)
Garnish: Immerse length of lime peel in drink.
Method: Shake first three ingredients with ice and strain into ice-filled glass. Top up with soda water.

2	shot(s)	Plymouth gin
¹/₂	shot(s)	Freshly squeezed lime juice
¹/₄	shot(s)	Sugar (gomme) syrup
Top up with		Soda water

Variant: Can also be based on any other spirituous liquor: e.g. vodka. Also try substituting apricot brandy for the gin to make an Apricot Rickey.
Origin: Created at the Shoemaker's restaurant in Washington, circa 1900, and named after Colonel Joe Rickey, for whom it was invented. Many confuse the Rickey and the Collins. For the record, a Rickey is made with lime juice and a Collins with lemon juice. A Rickey is usually served in a shorter glass than a Collins but this difference is secondary.
Comment: Clean, sharp and refreshing.

SAIGON COOLER

Glass: Collins
Garnish: Three raspberries
Method: Muddle raspberries in base of shaker. Add other ingredients, shake with ice and fine strain into ice-filled glass.

6	fresh	Raspberries
2	shot(s)	Plymouth gin
¹/₂	shot(s)	Chambord black raspberry liqueur
3¹/₂	shot(s)	Cranberry juice
³/₄	shot(s)	Freshly squeezed lime juice

Origin: Created at Bam-Bou, London, England.
Comment: Well balanced sweet 'n' sour with a rich fruity flavour.

SAKE-TINI

Glass: Martini
Garnish: Three thin slices of cucumber
Method: Stir all ingredients with ice and strain into chilled glass.

1	shot(s)	Plymouth gin
2¹/₂	shot(s)	Sake
¹/₂	shot(s)	Grand Marnier liqueur

Comment: Sake adds the perfect aromatic edge to a vodka-tini.

SINGAPORE SLING #2

Glass: Sling
Garnish: Split lemon wheel
Method: Shake first four ingredients with ice and strain into ice-filled glass, then top up with soda.

1	shot(s)	Plymouth gin
1	shot(s)	Bols cherry brandy liqueur
1	shot(s)	Bénédictine D.O.M. liqueur
4	dashes	Angostura aromatic bitters
Top up with		Soda water (club soda)

Comment: Said to be the original Singapore Sling recipe.

SUMMER MARTINI

Glass: Martini
Garnish: Berries on a cocktail stick
Method: Muddle berries in base of shaker. Add other ingredients; shake with ice and fine strain into chilled glass.

3	fresh	Blackberries
3	fresh	Raspberries
3	fresh	Strawberries
¹/₂	shot(s)	Bols Blackberry liqueur
¹/₂	shot	Bols Raspberry (framboise) liqueur
¹/₂	shot	Bols Strawberry (fraise) liqueur
2	shot(s)	Plymouth gin
³/₄	shot(s)	Cinzano Extra Dry vermouth
2	dashes	Fee Brothers Orange bitters

Origin: Created in 2003 by Wayne Collins for Maxxium UK.
Comment: A drink which combines a trio of summer berries with the classic aromatic Martini.

TANGO MARTINI # 1

Glass: Martini
Method: Shake ingredients with ice and strain into glass.

1¹/₂	shot(s)	Plymouth gin
1	shot(s)	Cinzano Rosso vermouth
1	shot(s)	Cinzano Extra Dry vermouth
¹/₂	shot(s)	Cointreau/triple sec
¹/₂	shot(s)	Freshly squeezed orange juice

Comment: A dry, bitter orange and gin cocktail.

TOM COLLINS

Glass: Collins
Garnish: Lemon slice
Method: Shake first three ingredients with ice and strain into ice-filled glass, then top up with soda.

2	shot(s)	Plymouth gin
1	shot(s)	Freshly squeezed lemon juice
1/2	shot(s)	Sugar (gomme) syrup
Top up with		Soda water (club soda)

Variant: This cocktail is traditionally made using Old Tom gin which is now very difficult to source.
Comment: Clean, refreshing, ancient classic. As good in microfibres as it was in crinolines.

VENUS MARTINI

Glass: Martini
Garnish: Raspberry in drink
Method: Muddle raspberries in base of shaker. Add other ingredients, shake with ice and fine strain into a chilled glass.

7	fresh	Raspberries
2	shot(s)	Plymouth Gin
1	shot(s)	Cointreau / triple sec
1/4	shot(s)	Sugar (gomme) syrup
4	dashes	Peychaud's aromatic bitters (optional)

Comment: Raspberry with hints of bitter orange and gin – surprisingly dry.

VESPER MARTINI

Glass: Martini
Garnish: Lemon zest twist
Method: Vigorously shake ingredients with ice and fine strain into glass.

3	shot(s)	Plymouth gin
1	shot(s)	Absolut vodka
1/2	shot(s)	Cinzano Extra dry vermouth

Origin: This is the real James Bond 'shaken' Dry Martini from Fleming's book Casino Royale. In chapter seven, 007 explains to a Casino bartender exactly how he likes his Dry Martini mixed and served. When made, he compliments the bartender, but tells him it would be better made with a grain-based vodka. Bond also explains his Martini to Felix Leiter, the CIA man, saying, "This drink's my own invention. I'm going to patent it when I can think of a good name." In chapter eight, Bond meets the beautiful double agent Vesper Lynd. She explains why her parents named her Vesper and Bond asks if she'd mind if he named his favourite Martini after her.

Comment: Most bartenders advocate that a Martini should be stirred and not shaken, some citing the ridiculous argument that shaking will bruise the gin. The Vesper is always shaken, an action that aerates the drink, makes it colder and more dilute than simply stirring. It also gives the drink a slightly clouded appearance and can leave small shards of ice on the surface of the drink, but the use of a fine strainer removes these.

WATERMELON & BASIL MARTINI

Glass: Martini
Garnish: Watermelon wedge on rim
Method: Muddle melon in base of shaker. Add other ingredients; shake with ice and fine strain into chilled glass.

1 1/2	cup(s)	Diced ripe watermelon
7	fresh	Torn basil leaves
2	shot(s)	Plymouth gin
1/2	shot(s)	Sugar (gomme) syrup

Comment: Refreshing watermelon with interesting herbal hints from the basil and gin.

WET MARTINI

Glass: Martini
Garnish: Olive or twist?
Method: Stir all ingredients with ice and strain into chilled glass.

3	shot(s)	Plymouth gin
1 1/2	shot(s)	Cinzano Extra Dry vermouth

Origin: A generous measure of vermouth to three of gin, hence the name 'Wet' Martini.
Comment: Reputed to be a favourite of HRH Prince Charles.

WHITE LADY

Glass: Martini
Garnish: Lemon zest twist
Method: Shake all ingredients with ice and fine strain into chilled glass.

2	shot(s)	Plymouth gin
1	shot(s)	Cointreau / triple sec
1	shot(s)	Freshly squeezed lemon juice
1/4	shot(s)	Sugar (gomme) syrup
1/2	fresh	Egg white

Origin: Created in 1919 by Harry MacElhone at Ciro's Club, London, England.
Comment: A simple but lovely classic drink with a sour edge.

WIBBLE UPDATED

Glass: Martini
Garnish: Sprayed lemon zest twist
Method: Shake all ingredients with ice and fine strain into chilled glass.

1	shot(s)	Plymouth gin
1	shot(s)	Plymouth sloe gin liqueur
1	shot(s)	Freshly squeezed grapefruit juice
1/4	shot(s)	Freshly squeezed lemon juice
1/8	shot(s)	Sugar (gomme) syrup
1/8	shot(s)	Bols blackberry liqueur

Origin: Created in 1999 by Dick Bradsell at The Player, London, England, for Nick Blacknell, a director of Plymouth Gin.
Comment: As Dick says, 'It may make you wobble, but it won't make you fall down.' Complex and balanced.

PLYMOUTH SLOE® GIN LIQUEUR

The making of fruit liqueurs is a long tradition in the British countryside and Plymouth Gin keeps true to a unique 1883 recipe. The sloe berries are slowly and gently steeped in Plymouth Gin, soft Darmoor water and a further secret ingredient. It is an unhurried process and is bottled only when the Head Distiller decides the perfect flavour has been reached. The result is an entirely natural product with no added flavourings or colourings.

This richly flavoured liqueur is initially dry but opens with smooth sweet juicy cherry, raspberry, lightly jammy notes and a complimentary mixture of figs, cloves, set honey and stewed fruits. 26% alc./vol. (52°proof)

Producer: Coates & Co (Plymouth) Ltd, Black Friars Distillery, Plymouth, England. **UK distributor:** Maxxium UK, Stirling. **Tel:** 01786 430 500.
Email:enquiries@maxxium.com

BLACKTHORN ENGLISH

Glass: Martini
Garnish: Flamed orange zest twist
Method: Shake all ingredients with ice and fine strain into chilled glass.

1¹/₂	shot(s)	Plymouth sloe gin
³/₄	shot(s)	Plymouth gin
³/₄	shot(s)	Cinzano Rosso (sweet) vermouth
3	dashes	Fee Brothers orange bitters
1	shot(s)	Chilled water

Origin: Classic (retro) cocktail whose origins are unknown.
Comment: A dry, subtle rust-coloured Martini.

CARPANO MARTINI

Glass: Martini
Garnish: Orange zest twist
Method: Shake ingredients with ice and strain into glass.

1 ¹/₄	shot(s)	Plymouth sloe gin
1	shot(s)	Punt E Mes
¹/₄	shot(s)	Freshly squeezed lime juice
¹/₄	shot(s)	Sugar (gomme) syrup

Origin: Created by David Myers at Titanic, London, England.
Comment: A strong tasting but well balanced and refreshing drink.

CHARLIE CHAPLIN

Glass: Martini
Method: Shake ingredients with ice and strain into glass.

1¹/₂	shot(s)	Plymouth sloe gin
1¹/₂	shot(s)	Bols apricot brandy liqueur
1¹/₂	shot(s)	Freshly squeezed lemon juice

Comment: Old school, fruity cocktail.

GIN GENIE

Glass: Collins
Garnish: Mint sprig
Method: Muddle mint in base of shaker. Add other ingredients, shake with ice and strain into glass filled with crushed ice.

8	fresh	Mint leaves
1¹/₂	shot(s)	Plymouth gin
1	shot(s)	Freshly squeezed lemon juice
1	shot(s)	Plymouth sloe gin
¹/₂	shot(s)	Sugar (gomme) syrup

Origin: Created in 2002 by Wayne Collins for Maxxium UK.
Comment: A great, fruit-led long drink for gin-loving Bowie fans.

GRAPE DELIGHT

Glass: Martini
Garnish: Grapes in drink
Method: Muddle grapes in base of shaker. Add rest of ingredients, shake with ice and strain into glass.

10	fresh	Seedless red grapes
1¹/₂	shot(s)	Plymouth gin
¹/₂	shot(s)	Plymouth sloe gin
¹/₃	shot(s)	Sugar (gomme) syrup
¹/₂	shot(s)	Freshly squeezed lime juice
4	dashes	Angostura aromatic bitters

Comment: The rust colour of this drink comes from the Angostura bitters, sloe gin and the muddled skins of red grapes. These combine to provide its delicate balanced flavour.

HEDGEROW SLING

Glass: Sling
Garnish: Seasonal berries & lemon slice
Method: Shake first three ingredients with ice and strain into ice-filled glass, then top up with soda and pour crème de mûre on top.

2	shot(s)	Plymouth sloe gin
1	shot(s)	Freshly squeezed lemon juice
¹/₄	shot(s)	Sugar (gomme) syrup
¹/₂	shot(s)	Bols blackberry liqueur
Top up with		Soda water

Origin: Created by Brian Duell at Detroit, London, England.
Comment: Citrus and berries with fizz and an alcoholic float.

RED RUM MARTINI

Glass: Martini
Garnish: Redcurrants draped over rim
Method: Muddle redcurrants in base of shaker. Add other ingredients, shake with ice and fine strain into chilled glass.

2	dozen	Fresh redcurrants
2	shot(s)	Appleton Estate V/X aged rum
¹/₂	shot(s)	Plymouth Sloe Gin
¹/₂	shot(s)	Freshly squeezed lemon juice
¹/₂	shot(s)	Vanilla sugar syrup

Origin: Created by Jason Scott in 2002 at Oloroso, Edinburgh, Scotland. This cocktail, which is red and contains rum, is named after 'Red Rum', the only horse in the history of the Grand National to win the race three times (on the other two occasions he ran he came second). His last Grand National win was in 1977 at the age of 12 by a remarkable 25 lengths. He became a British hero, made an appearance on the BBC Sports Personality of the Year show and paraded right up until his death in 1995 at the age of 30.
Comment: A beautifully fruity, adult balance of bitter-sweet flavours.

SAILOR'S COMFORT

Glass: Old-fashioned
Garnish: Lime wedge
Method: Shake first four ingredients with ice and strain into ice-filled glass. Top up with soda water (club soda).

1	shot(s)	Plymouth sloe gin
1	shot(s)	Southern Comfort liqueur
1	shot(s)	Rose's lime cordial
4	dashes	Angostura aromatic bitters
Top up with		Soda water (club soda)

Origin: Discovered in 2002 at Lightship Ten, London, England.
Comment: Lime, peach and hints of berry make a light easy drink.

SLOW SCREW

Glass: Collins
Garnish: Orange slice
Method: Shake first two ingredients with ice and strain into ice-filled glass, then top up with orange juice.

1	shot(s)	Plymouth sloe gin
1	shot(s)	Absolut vodka
Top up with		Freshly squeezed orange juice

Comment: A Screwdriver with sloe gin.

SMOKEY MARTINI UPDATED

Glass: Martini
Garnish: Strips of orange zest in drink
Method: Stir all ingredients with ice and strain into chilled glass.

2	shot(s)	Plymouth gin
1	shot(s)	Plymouth sloe gin
¹/₄	shot(s)	Cinzano Extra Dry vermouth
4	dashes	Fee Brothers orange bitters

Origin: Created in 1997 by Giovanni Burdi at Match EC1, London, England.
Comment: Dry and sophisticated with a distinctive 'smoke'. The basic Martini formula (gin plus vermouth) is enhanced with sloe gin and the traditional orange bitters variation.

WIBBLE UPDATED

Glass: Martini
Garnish: Sprayed lemon zest twist
Method: Shake all ingredients with ice and fine strain into chilled glass.

1	shot(s)	Plymouth gin
1	shot(s)	Plymouth sloe gin
1	shot(s)	Freshly squeezed grapefruit juice
¹/₄	shot(s)	Freshly squeezed lemon juice
¹/₈	shot(s)	Sugar (gomme) syrup
¹/₈	shot(s)	Bols blackberry liqueur

Origin: Created in 1999 by Dick Bradsell at The Player, London, England, for Nick Blacknell, a director of Plymouth Gin.
Comment: As Dick says, 'It may make you wobble, but it won't make you fall down.' Complex and balanced.

RÉMY MARTIN GRAND CRU® COGNAC

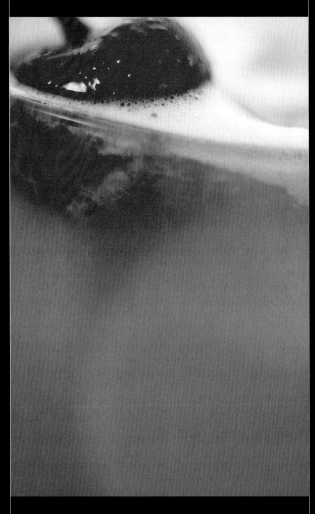

When Rémy Martin founded his company in 1724 he was already an experienced producer of Cognac. He set out to make the Cognacs that carried his name amongst the finest. This tradition is still pursued at Rémy Martin with all the company's blends being made exclusively using grapes from only the two premier crus, Grande and Petite Champagne. The wine is double distilled on the lees in small stills and aged in small oak casks from the nearby Limousin forest.

Rémy Martin V.S.O.P., a blend of 45% Petite Champagne and 55% Grande Champagne, is also the world's best selling V.S.O.P. while Rémy Martin V.S. Grand Cru is one of the few to be made solely using grapes from the Petite Champagne region.

Rémy Martin is the ideal Cognac to use in cocktails whether you choose the V.S. or V.S.O.P. Both feature lots of rich, ripe, fruit and vanilla with tasting notes including fruitcake and stewed fruit. 40% alc./vol. (80°proof)

Web: www.remy.com Distiller: Rémy Martin & Co SA, Cognac, France. UK distributor: Maxxium UK Ltd, Stirling, Scotland. Tel: 01786 430 500 Email: enquiries@maxxium.com

APPLE OF ONE'S EYE

Glass: Collins
Garnish: Apple wedge on rim
Method: Shake first three ingredients with ice and strain into ice-filled glass. Top up with ginger beer.

2	shot(s)	Rémy Martin Cognac
1/2	shot(s)	Freshly squeezed lime juice
3	shot(s)	Pressed apple juice
Top up with		Jamaican ginger beer

Comment: This spicy concoction is definitely something to cherish.

APRIL SHOWER UPDATED

Glass: Martini
Garnish: Orange zest twist
Method: Shake all ingredients with ice and fine strain into chilled glass.

2	shot(s)	Rémy Martin Cognac
1/2	shot(s)	Bénédictine D.O.M. liqueur
2	shot(s)	Freshly squeezed orange juice

Comment: This mustard coloured, medium dry, Cognac-based drink harnesses the uniquely herbal edge of Bénédictine.

BETWEEN THE SHEETS

Glass: Martini
Garnish: Flamed orange zest twist
Method: Shake all ingredients with ice and fine strain into chilled glass.

1	shot(s)	Havana Club light rum
1	shot(s)	Rémy Martin Cognac
1/2	shot(s)	Cointreau / triple sec
3/4	shot(s)	Freshly squeezed lemon juice
1/2	shot(s)	Sugar (gomme) syrup
1/2	shot(s)	Chilled water

Origin: Created in the 1930s by Harry MacElhone, of Harry's New York Bar in Paris, and derived from the Sidecar.
Comment: When made correctly this is a beautifully balanced drink to rival even a Daiquiri.

BRANDY SOUR UPDATED

Glass: Old-fashioned
Garnish: Maraschino cherry
Method: Shake all ingredients with ice and strain into ice-filled glass.

2	shot(s)	Rémy Martin Cognac
1	shot(s)	Freshly squeezed lemon juice
1/2	shot(s)	Sugar (gomme) syrup
1/2	fresh	Egg white
3	dashes	Angostura aromatic bitters

Comment: After the Whiskey Sour, this is the most requested sour. Try it and you'll see why – but don't omit the egg white.

CALL ME OLD-FASHIONED

Glass: Old-fashioned
Garnish: Orange peel twist
Method: Stir sugar syrup and Angostura with two ice cubes in a glass. Add one shot of Cognac and two more ice cubes. Stir some more and add another two ice cubes and another shot of Cognac. Stir lots more and add more ice if required.

2	shot(s)	Rémy Martin Cognac
¹⁄₄	shot(s)	Sugar (gomme) syrup
2	dash	Angostura aromatic bitters

Origin: Named by me in 2001.
Comment: An Old-Fashioned made with Cognac instead of whiskey – works well.

CLOCKWORK ORANGE

Glass: Collins
Garnish: Orange wheel in glass
Method: Shake all ingredients with ice and strain into ice-filled glass.

1¹⁄₂	shot(s)	Rémy Martin Cognac
1¹⁄₂	shot(s)	Grand Marnier liqueur
4	shot(s)	Freshly squeezed orange juice

Comment: Not as memorable as the film but a pleasant orange drink all the same.

EAST INDIA COCKTAIL

Glass: Martini
Garnish: Flamed orange zest twist and dust with freshly grated nutmeg
Method: Shake all ingredients with ice and fine strain into chilled glass.

1¹⁄₂	shot(s)	Rémy Martin Cognac
1	shot(s)	Grand Marnier liqueur
2	shot(s)	Pressed pineapple juice
2	dashes	Angostura aromatic bitters

Origin: An old classic created by Frank Meier at the Ritz Bar, Paris. Dale DeGroff rightly claims creation of a very similar drink called a 'Millennium Cocktail'.
Comment: A rich but quite bitter short drink based on Cognac.

FRENCH MULE

Glass: Collins
Garnish: Sprig of mint
Method: Shake first four ingredients with ice and strain into an ice-filled glass. Top up with ginger beer, stir and serve with straws.

2	shot(s)	Rémy Martin Cognac
1	shot(s)	Freshly squeezed lime juice
1	shot(s)	Sugar (gomme) syrup
4	dashes	Angostura aromatic bitters
Top up with		Ginger beer

Comment: This French answer to the vodka based Moscow Mule uses Cognac to make a spicy, long, refreshing drink.

GRAPE ESCAPE

Glass: Collins
Garnish: Mint sprig
Method: Muddle grapes and mint in base of shaker. Add Cognac and sugar, shake with ice and strain into glass filled with crushed ice. Top up with Champagne and stir. Serve with straws.

8	fresh	Seedless white grapes
5	fresh	Mint leaves
2	shot(s)	Rémy Martin Cognac
¹⁄₂	shot(s)	Sugar (gomme) syrup
Top up with		Piper-Heidsieck Brut Champagne

Origin: Created in 2000 by Brian Lucas and Max Warner at Long Bar @ Sanderson, London, England.
Comment: A cracking drink – subtle and refreshing.

PIERRE COLLINS

Glass: Collins
Method: Shake first three ingredients with ice and strain into ice-filled glass, then top up with soda.

2	shot(s)	Rémy Martin Cognac
1	shot(s)	Freshly squeezed lemon juice
¹⁄₂	shot(s)	Sugar (gomme) syrup
Top up with		Soda water (club soda)

Comment: Distinctive and tasty.

RANDY

Glass: Old-fashioned
Garnish: Orange zest twist
Method: Stir ingredients with ice and strain into ice-filled glass.

1¹⁄₂	shot(s)	Rémy Martin Cognac
1¹⁄₂	shot(s)	Warre's Otima Tawny Port
¹⁄₂	shot(s)	Grand Marnier liqueur
¹⁄₄	shot(s)	Vanilla syrup

Origin: Created in 2003 by yours truly.
Comment: Named after the rhyming slang for port and brandy, the two base ingredients of this cocktail. Love interest comes courtesy of orange and vanilla.

ZOOM

Glass: Martini
Method: Shake ingredients with ice and strain into glass.

2¹⁄₂	shot(s)	Rémy Martin Cognac
3	spoon	Runny honey
1	shot(s)	Double (heavy) cream
1	shot(s)	Milk

Variant: Base on other spirits such as gin, rum or whiskey.
Variant: Add ¹⁄₄ shot of crème de cacao for a chocolate finish.
Origin: A classics (retro) drink, the origins of which are lost in time.
Comment: Cognac smoothed with honey and cream. Softened with milk & cream.

SAGATIBA PURA CACHAÇA

Cachaça is the national spirit of Brazil and dates back to the sixteenth century. Until recently it was rarely seen outside its home country but today, thanks to the Caipirinha, Cachaça is enjoyed in bars, restaurants and nightclubs from Tokyo to Rome.

There are thousands of Cachaça distillers in Brazil, producing a huge volume of Cachaça. Sadly, much of it is aimed at the lower end of the home market. However, the recent growth in exports has enabled a select group of producers to create elite, top quality Cachaças.

Sagatiba is one of these producers. Utilising a revolutionary multi-distillation process, the company produces an extremely pure, clean spirit which none the less maintains its distinctive Cachaça flavour. Because of this smoothness it is much more versatile than traditional Cachaças.

Web: www.sagatiba.com **Producer:** Sagatiba S.A. Brazil
UK distributor: Coe Vintners, Ilford, Essex. **Tel:** 020 8551 4966 **Email:** enquiries@coevintners.com

---

AZURE MARTINI UPDATED

●●●●○

Glass: Martini
Garnish: Apple slice on rim
Method: Shake all ingredients with ice and fine strain into chilled glass.

2	shot(s)	Sagatiba cachaça
1/4	shot(s)	Goldschläger cinnamon schnapps
1	shot(s)	Pressed apple juice
1/2	shot(s)	Freshly squeezed lime juice
1/4	shot(s)	Sugar (gomme) syrup

Origin: Created by Ben Reed at the Met Bar, London, England, and originally made with muddled fresh apple.
Comment: A twangy cocktail – reminiscent of a cinnamon laced apple pie.

BATIDA ABACI UPDATED

●●●●◑

Glass: Collins
Garnish: Pineapple wedge on rim
Method: Shake all ingredients with ice and strain into ice-filled glass.

2¹/4	shot(s)	Sagatiba cachaça
3	shot(s)	Freshly extracted pineapple juice
1/2	shot(s)	Sugar (gomme) syrup
1/2	shot(s)	Freshly squeezed lemon juice

Variant: This drink is great made with just about any fruit. When made with strawberries it's called a 'Batida Morango', with passion fruit it becomes a 'Batida Maracuja' and with guava a 'Batida Goiaba'. It can also be served frozen: simply blend all ingredients with a 12oz scoop of crushed ice and an extra 1/4 shot of sugar syrup.
Origin: This is a traditional Brazilian working-man's drink.
Comment: Unfortunately, this excellent drink has not transferred as quickly from its native Brazil as the Caipirinha.

BATIDA MARACUJA NEW

●●●●○

Glass: Collins
Garnish: Lemon wheel in drink
Method: Cut passion fruit in half and scoop out flesh into shaker. Add other ingredients, shake with ice and fine strain into ice-filled glass.

2	fresh	Passion fruit
2¹/2	shot(s)	Sagatiba cachaça
³/4	shot(s)	Freshly squeezed lemon juice
³/4	shot(s)	Sugar (gomme) syrup

Origin: The Batida is a traditional Brazilian drink and 'maracuja' means passion fruit in Portuguese.
Comment: The flavour of cachaça combines wonderfully with passion fruit. Adjust sugar syrup to taste.

BEJA FLOR UPDATED

●●●●○

Glass: Martini
Garnish: Banana chunk on rim
Method: Shake all ingredients with ice and fine strain into chilled glass.

2	shot(s)	Sagatiba cachaça
1	shot(s)	Cointreau / triple sec
1	shot(s)	Bols crème de banane
1/2	shot(s)	Freshly squeezed lemon juice

Comment: Sharp and quite dry but with a sweet banana twang.

BERRY CAIPIRINHA

Glass: Rocks
Method: Muddle lime and berries in base of glass. Add other ingredients and fill glass with crushed ice. Churn drink with barspoon and serve with short straws.

3/4	fresh	Lime cut into wedges
3	fresh	Raspberries
3	fresh	Blackberries
2	shot(s)	Sagatiba cachaça
3/4	shot(s)	Sugar (gomme) syrup

Variant: Black 'N' Blue Caipirovska
Comment: A fruity version of the popular Brazilian drink.

CACHAÇA DAIQUIRI

Glass: Martini
Method: Shake ingredients with ice and strain into glass.

2	shot(s)	Sagatiba cachaça
1/2	shot(s)	Freshly squeezed lime juice
1/4	shot(s)	Sugar (gomme) syrup
3/4	shot(s)	Chilled water

Comment: Might be in a Martini glass but it tastes like a Caipirinha.

CAIPIRINHA

Pronounced: Ki-Pee-Ree-Nya
Glass: Rocks
Method: Muddle lime in base of glass to release the juices and oils in its skin. Pour cachaça and sugar into glass, add crushed ice and churn with barspoon. Serve with straws.

3/4	fresh	Lime cut into wedges
2	shot(s)	Sagatiba cachaça
3/4	shot(s)	Sugar (gomme) syrup

Variant: Caipiruva, Caipirissima, Berry Caipirinha, Caipirovska and Black 'N' Blue Caipirovska.
Origin: Cachaça, a spirit distilled from sugar cane juice, is the national spirit of Brazil - and Brazilians consume an astonishing 2,000,000,000 litres of it a year. The Caipirinha is a traditional Brazilian cocktail, using sugar and green lemons known as 'limon subtil', which grow in the country. (Limes are the best substitute when these are not available.) The name means 'little countryside drink'. Caipirinhas and variations on the theme are staples in cachaçerias, Brazilian bars which specialise in cachaça.
Comment: When made well this is a wonderfully refreshing drink.

CAIPIRUVA

Glass: Old-fashioned
Method: Muddle grapes in base of shaker. Add other ingredients, shake with ice and strain into glass filled with crushed ice.

10	fresh	Seedless grapes
2	shot(s)	Sagatiba cachaça
3/4	shot(s)	Freshly squeezed lime juice
3/4	shot(s)	Sugar (gomme) syrup

Comment: A grape juice laced twist on the Caipirinha.

MANGO BATIDA NEW

●●●●○

Glass: Collins
Garnish: Dried mango
Method: Shake all ingredients with ice and strain into ice-filled glass.

2½	shot(s)	Sagatiba Cachaça
2	shot(s)	Sweetened mango purée
1	shot(s)	Freshly squeezed lemon juice

Origin: Formula by yours truly in 2004.
Comment: Depending on the sweetness of the mango purée, this drink may benefit from the addition of a dash of sugar syrup.

PASSION FRUIT CAIPIRINHA NEW

●●●●◐

Glass: Old-fashioned
Method: Muddle the lime wedges in the base of a sturdy glass to release the juices and oils from the skin. (Be careful not to break the glass.) Cut the passion fruit in half and scoop out the flesh into the glass. Pour Cachaça and sugar syrup into the glass, add crushed ice and churn with a barspoon. Serve with straws.

1	fresh	Passion fruit
3/4	fresh	Lime cut into wedges
2	shot(s)	Sagatiba Cachaça
3/4	shot(s)	Sugar (gomme) syrup

Comment: A tasty fruit Caipirinha. You may end up sipping this from the glass as the passion fruit pips tend to clog straws.

RASPBERRY CAIPIRINHA

●●●●○

Glass: Rocks
Method: Muddle lime and raspberries in base of glass. Add other ingredients and fill glass with crushed ice. Churn drink with barspoon and serve with short straws.

3/4	fresh	Lime cut into wedges
8	fresh	Raspberries
2	shot(s)	Sagatiba Cachaça
3/4	shot(s)	Sugar (gomme) syrup

Variant: Substitute other berries and fruits. Add raspberry liqueur in place of sugar. Base on rum in place of Cachaça to make a Raspberry Caiprissima.
Comment: A fruity twist on the popular Caipirinha.

TROPICAL CAIPIRINHA

●●●●◐

Glass: Rocks
Garnish: Two squeezed lime wedges in drink
Method: Shake all ingredients with ice and strain into glass filled with crushed ice.

1	shot(s)	Sagatiba cachaça
1	shot(s)	Malibu coconut rum liqueur
1	shot(s)	Pressed pineapple juice
1	shot(s)	Freshly squeezed lime juice
1/4	shot(s)	Sugar (gomme) syrup

Origin: Created by yours truly in 2003.
Comment: In drink circles, tropical usually spells sweet. This drink may have a 'tropical' flavour but it also boasts an adult sourness.

SAUZA® HORNITOS® TEQUILA

Sauza Hornitos Tequila is produced by a company founded by Don Cenobio Sauza in 1873 and built by three successive generations of the Sauza family. Sauza was the first Tequila to be internationally exported and remains a dominant brand in Tequila, Mexico. Unlike many of its competitors, Sauza Hornitos is made using 100% agave spirit, evidenced in the rich agave flavours found on its palate. It is classified as a 'Reposado Tequila', indicating that it has benefited from a period of resting in oak. Unusually, the production process involves baking the agave rather than steaming, giving this Tequila a slightly smoky flavour. Fittingly, the name 'Hornitos' means 'little ovens'.

The elegant and subtle but animated flavour of Sauza Hornitos is well suited to cocktails. Careful tasting reveals muscovado and marzipan, balanced by light, dry earthy, herby, grassy agave, cinnamon, ripe citrus and gingerbread. 38% alc./vol. (76°proof)

Web: www.sauzatequila.com **Producer:** Tequila Sauza, S.A. de C.V., Guadalajara, Jalisco, Mexico. **UK distributor:** Allied Domecq, Spirits & Wine (UK) Ltd, Horsham, West Sussex, RH12 1ST
Tel: 01403 222 600
Email: mailbox@balance-spirits.com

ACAPULCO UPDATED

Glass: Collins
Garnish: Pineapple wedge on rim
Method: Shake all ingredients with ice and strain into ice-filled glass.

1	shot(s)	Sauza Hornitos Tequila
1	shot(s)	Mount Gay Eclipse golden rum
1	shot(s)	Freshly squeezed grapefruit juice
2¹/₂	shot(s)	Pressed pineapple juice
¹/₂	shot(s)	Sugar (gomme) syrup

Comment: An innocuous, fruity mixture laced with Tequila and rum.

BIRD OF PARADISE UPDATED

Glass: Martini
Garnish: Nutmeg dust
Method: Shake all ingredients with ice and fine strain into chilled glass.

1¹/₄	shot(s)	Sauza Hornitos Tequila
³/₄	shot(s)	Bols white crème de cacao
¹/₂	shot(s)	Disaronno Originale amaretto
1	shot(s)	Double (heavy) cream
³/₄	shot(s)	Milk

Comment: If you like Tequila and creamy drinks, the two don't mix much better than this.

BLUE MARGARITA

Glass: Coupette
Garnish: Salt rim & lime wedge on rim
Method: Shake all ingredients with ice and fine strain into chilled glass.

2	shot(s)	Sauza Hornitos Tequila
1	shot(s)	Bols Blue Curaçao
1	shot(s)	Freshly squeezed lime juice
¹/₄	shot(s)	Sugar (gomme) syrup

Variation: Blend with crushed ice.
Comment: As the name suggests, a Margarita only blue.

BUENA VIDA

Glass: Old-fashioned
Garnish: Pineapple wedge on rim
Method: Shake all ingredients with ice and strain into glass filled with crushed ice.

2	shot(s)	Sauza Hornitos Tequila
1³/₄	shot(s)	Squeezed pink grapefruit juice
³/₄	shot(s)	Pressed pineapple juice
¹/₂	shot(s)	Vanilla syrup
3	dash	Angostura aromatic bitters

Comment: The fruits combine brilliantly with the Tequila and spice comes courtesy of Angostura.

CACTUS JACK

Glass: Martini
Garnish: Pineapple leaf
Method: Shake all ingredients with ice and fine strain into chilled glass.

1	shot(s)	Sauza Hornitos Tequila
³/₄	shot(s)	Bols Blue curaçao
1¹/₄	shot(s)	Freshly squeezed orange juice
1	shot(s)	Pressed pineapple juice
¹/₂	shot(s)	Freshly squeezed lemon juice

Comment: Vivid in colour, this orange led, Tequila based drink has a balanced sweet and sourness.

CHIMAYO

Glass: Martini
Method: Shake ingredients with ice and strain into glass.

2	shot(s)	Sauza Hornitos Tequila
1	shot(s)	Sisca crème de cassis
2	shot(s)	Pressed apple juice

Origin: Created by Adewale at the Arts Café, Leeds, England.
Comment: Simple and effective – apple juice and cassis take the 'bite' off the Tequila.

COOL MARTINI

Glass: Martini
Method: Shake ingredients with ice and strain into glass.

2	shot(s)	Midori melon liqueur
1	shot(s)	Sauza Hornitos Tequila
2	shot(s)	Cranberry juice

Comment: Tastes nothing like the ingredients - which include melon, Tequila and cranberry juice. Try it and see if you taste toffee. Whatever, it's enjoyable and complex.

EL DIABLO

Glass: Collins
Garnish: Squeeze lime wedge and drop into drink
Method: Shake first four ingredients with ice and strain into ice-filled glass. Top up with ginger beer.

2	shot(s)	Sauza Hornitos Tequila
1	shot(s)	Sisca crème de cassis
1	shot(s)	Freshly squeezed lime juice
1/2	shot(s)	Sugar (gomme) syrup
Top up with		Ginger ale

Origin: Thought to have originated in California during the 1940s.
Comment: The name of this drink translates as 'The Devil' and it's devilishly good.

DIRTY SANCHEZ

Glass: Collins
Garnish: Lime wheel on rim
Method: Shake all but ginger beer with ice. Strain into ice-filled glass and top up with ginger beer.

2	shot(s)	Sauza Hornitos Tequila
3/4	shot(s)	Agavero Tequila liqueur
1/2	shot(s)	Chambord black raspberry liqueur
1/2	shot(s)	Freshly squeezed lime juice
Top up with		Jamaican ginger beer

Origin: Created in 2001 by Phillip Jeffrey and Ian Baldwin at the GE Club, London, England.
Comment: A wonderfully refreshing and complex long summer drink.

EASY TIGER

Glass: Martini
Garnish: Orange zest twist
Comment: Muddle ginger in base of shaker. Add honey and Tequila and stir so as to dissolve honey. Add other ingredients, shake with ice and fine strain into chilled glass.

2	slices	Fresh ginger (thumb nail sized)
2	spoons	Runny honey
2	shot(s)	Sauza Hornitos Tequila
1	shot(s)	Freshly squeezed lime juice
3/4	shot(s)	Chilled water

Created by: Alex Kammerling in 1999.
Comment: Tangy, zesty with rich honey and ginger.

ELEGANTE MARGARITA

Glass: Coupette
Garnish: Lime wedge & salted rim (optional)
Method: Shake all ingredients with ice and strain into glass.

1 1/2	shot(s)	Sauza Hornitos Tequila
1/2	shot(s)	Cointreau / triple sec
1/2	shot(s)	Rose's lime cordial
3/4	shot(s)	Freshly squeezed lime juice
1/2	shot(s)	Sugar (gomme) syrup

Origin: Created in 1999 by Robert Plotkin and Raymon Flores of BarMedia, USA.
Comment: One of the best Margarita recipes around. Richly endowed with flavour.

THE FLIRT

Glass: Martini
Garnish: Lipstick on half of rim
Method: Shake all ingredients with ice and fine strain into chilled glass.

2	shot(s)	Sauza Hornitos Tequila
3/4	shot(s)	Bols apricot brandy liqueur
1	shot(s)	Freshly squeezed lime juice
1	shot(s)	Cranberry juice

Origin: Created in 2002 by Dick Bradsell at Lonsdale House, London, England.
Comment: A fruity drink to upset glass washers throughout the land.

FLORIDITA MARGARITA

Glass: Coupette
Garnish: Lime wedge & salted rim (optional)
Method: Shake all ingredients with ice and strain into glass.

1 1/2	shot(s)	Sauza Hornitos Tequila
1/2	shot(s)	Cointreau / triple sec
1/2	shot(s)	Cranberry juice
1/4	shot(s)	Rose's lime cordial
1 1/2	shot(s)	Freshly squeezed grapefruit juice
3/4	shot(s)	Freshly squeezed lime juice
1/2	shot(s)	Sugar (gomme) syrup

Origin: Created in 1999 by Robert Plotkin and Raymon Flores of BarMedia, USA.
Comment: A blush coloured Margarita-style drink with a well-matched amalgamation of flavours.

FLUTTER

Glass: Martini
Garnish: Orange zest twist
Method: Shake all ingredients with ice and fine strain into chilled glass.

2	shot(s)	Sauza Hornitos Tequila
1	shot(s)	Kahlúa coffee liqueur
1¼	shot(s)	Pressed pineapple juice

Origin: Created in 2003 by Tony Conigliaro at Lonsdale House, London, England.
Comment: The three ingredients combine brilliantly.

FREDDY FUDPUCKER

Glass: Collins
Garnish: Orange slice in glass
Method: Pour Tequila and orange juice into ice-filled glass and stir. Float Galliano.

2	shot(s)	Sauza Hornitos Tequila
4½	shot(s)	Freshly squeezed orange juice
½	shot(s)	Galliano liqueur

Variant: Harvey Wallbanger
Comment: A Harvey Wallbanger for those that prefer to Tequila to vodka.

MANGO MARGARITA NEW

Glass: Coupette
Garnish: Lime wedge on rim
Method: Shake all ingredients with ice and fine strain into chilled glass.

2	shot(s)	Sauza Hornitos Tequila
1	shot(s)	Sweetened mango purée
1	shot(s)	Cointreau / triple sec
1	shot(s)	Freshly squeezed lime juice

Origin: Formula by yours truly in 2004.
Comment: The character of the Tequila is not overwhelmed by the fruit.

MARGARITA STRAIGHT UP

Glass: Coupette
Garnish: Salt rim & lime wedge
Method: Shake ingredients with ice and strain into chilled glass.

2	shot(s)	Sauza Hornitos Tequila
1	shot(s)	Cointreau / triple sec
1	shot(s)	Freshly squeezed lime juice

Variant: Margaritas made with premium Tequilas are sometimes referred to as 'Deluxe' or 'Cadillac' Margaritas.
Tip: For the perfect salt rim, liquidise sea salt to make it finer, then run a lime wedge around the outside edge of the glass before dipping the rim in salt.
Origin: There are countless versions of how the Margarita was invented - as so often, nobody really knows. It's not impossible that several people came up with the same drink at the same time and gave it the same name independently.
Comment: A refreshing, sour classic, with a perfect balance of citrus and agave. Rimming only half the glass with salt gives the drinker the option of enjoying the cocktail with or without salt.

MARGARITA FROZEN UPDATED

Glass: Hurricane
Garnish: Salt rim & split lime wedge
Method: Blend ingredients with a 12oz scoop of crushed ice and serve.

1½	shot(s)	Sauza Hornitos Tequila
¾	shot(s)	Cointreau / triple sec
¾	shot(s)	Freshly squeezed lime juice
¾	shot(s)	Sugar (gomme) syrup

Comment: A true classic - citrus freshness with the subtle agave of Tequila, served frozen with a biting salt rim.

MARGARITA ON THE ROCKS

Glass: Rocks
Garnish: Salt rim & split lime wedge.
Method: Shake ingredients with ice and strain into ice-filled glass.

2	shot(s)	Sauza Hornitos Tequila
1	shot(s)	Cointreau / triple sec
1	shot(s)	Freshly squeezed lime juice

Comment: Tangy citrus, Tequila and salt. This drink is better served straight-up or frozen.

MAYAN

Glass: Old-fashioned
Garnish: Coffee beans
Method: Shake all ingredients with ice and strain into ice-filled glass.

1½	shot(s)	Sauza Hornitos Tequila
½	shot(s)	Kahlúa coffee liqueur
2½	shot(s)	Pressed pineapple juice

Comment: Tequila, coffee and pineapple juice combine in this medium dry short drink.

MELON MARGARITA

Glass: Coupette
Garnish: Melon balls on stick
Method: Muddle melon in base of shaker. Add other ingredients, shake with ice and fine strain into chilled glass.

1	cup	Diced honeydew melon
2	shot(s)	Sauza Hornitos Tequila
1	shot(s)	Midori melon liqueur
1	shot(s)	Freshly squeezed lime juice

Comment: Looks like stagnant pond water but tastes fantastic.

MEXICAN MARTINI NEW

Glass: Martini
Garnish: Pineapple leaf on rim
Method: Shake all ingredients with ice and fine strain into chilled glass.

2	shot(s)	Sauza Hornitos Tequila
¼	shot(s)	Sisca crème de cassis
2	shot(s)	Pressed pineapple juice

Origin: Discovered in 2004 at Indigo Yard, Edinburgh, Scotland.
Comment: Tequila, pineapple and blackcurrant combine in this medium dry cocktail.

MEXICAN MULE

Glass: Collins
Garnish: Lime wedge
Method: Shake ingredients with ice and strain into ice-filled glass.

1¹/₂	shot(s)	Sauza Hornitos Tequila
³/₄	shot(s)	Freshly squeezed lime juice
¹/₄	shot(s)	Sugar (gomme) syrup
Top up with		Ginger ale

Comment: A Tequila version of a Moscow Mule.

PINEAPPLE MARGARITA

●●●●○

Glass: Coupette
Garnish: Split pineapple wedge
Method: Shake all ingredients with ice and fine strain into chilled glass.

2	shot(s)	Sauza Hornitos Tequila
³/₄	shot(s)	Cointreau / triple sec
1¹/₂	shot(s)	Pressed pineapple juice

Variant: Add half shot pineapple syrup, blend with crushed ice and serve frozen.
Comment: A Tequila Margarita with a pineapple fruit kick.

PLAYA DEL MAR

●●●●◐

Glass: Martini
Garnish: Pineapple wedge on rim
Method: Shake all ingredients with ice and fine strain into chilled glass.

1	shot(s)	Sauza Hornitos Tequila
¹/₂	shot(s)	Cointreau / triple sec
1¹/₂	shot(s)	Cranberry juice
1	shot(s)	Pressed pineapple juice
¹/₄	shot(s)	Sugar (gomme) syrup
¹/₂	shot(s)	Freshly squeezed lime juice

Origin: Created in 1997 by Wayne Collins at Navajo Joe, London, England.
Comment: A complex taste with a hint of Tequila.

RASPBERRY MARGARITA

●●●●○

Glass: Coupette
Garnish: Lime wedge on rim
Method: Muddle raspberries in base of shaker. Add other ingredients, shake with ice and fine strain into chilled glass.

10	fresh	Raspberries
2	shot(s)	Sauza Hornitos Tequila
1	shot(s)	Cointreau / triple sec
1	shot(s)	Freshly squeezed lime juice
¹/₂	shot(s)	Sugar (gomme) syrup

Comment: Just that – a raspberry flavoured Margarita.

RUDE COSMOPOLITAN UPDATED

●●●●◐

Glass: Martini
Garnish: Orange zest twist
Method: Shake all ingredients with ice and fine strain into chilled glass.

1¹/₂	shot(s)	Sauza Hornitos Tequila
1	shot(s)	Cointreau / triple sec
1	shot(s)	Cranberry juice
¹/₂	shot(s)	Freshly squeezed lime juice
¹/₄	shot(s)	Rose's lime cordial
3 dashes		Fee Brothers orange bitters (optional)

AKA: Mexico City
Comment: Don't let the pink appearance of this Cosmopolitan (made with Tequila in place of vodka) fool you into thinking that this is a fluffy cocktail. It's both serious and superb.

RUDE GINGER COSMOPOLITAN NEW

●●●●○

Glass: Martini
Garnish: Orange zest twist
Method: Muddle ginger in base of shaker. Add other ingredients, shake with ice and fine strain into chilled glass.

2	slices	Fresh root ginger (thumbnail sized)
1¹/₂	shot(s)	Sauza Hornitos Tequila
1	shot(s)	Cointreau / triple sec
1	shot(s)	Cranberry juice
¹/₂	shot(s)	Freshly squeezed lime juice
¹/₄	shot(s)	Rose's lime cordial

Origin: Created in 2003 by Jeremy Adderley at Halo, Edinburgh, Scotland.
Comment: To quote Halo's list, "Looks like a Cosmo, goes like a Mexican!"

STRAWBERRY MARGARITA NEW

●●●●○

Glass: Martini
Garnish: Strawberry on rim
Method: Muddle strawberries in base of shaker. Add other ingredients, shake with ice and fine strain into chilled glass.

5	fresh	Hulled strawberries
2	shot(s)	Sauza Hornitos Tequila
1	shot(s)	Freshly squeezed lime juice
1	shot(s)	Sugar (gomme) syrup

Origin: Formula by yours truly in 2004.
Comment: Fresh strawberries combine well with Tequila in this fruit margarita.

TEQUILA'TINI

●●●◐○

Glass: Martini
Garnish: Lime zest twist
Method: Shake all ingredients with ice and fine strain into chilled glass.

2¹/₂	shot(s)	Sauza Hornitos Tequila
1	shot(s)	Cinzano Extra Dry vermouth
3	dashes	Angostura aromatic bitters
¹/₂	shot(s)	Sugar (gomme) syrup

Comment: If you like Tequila and strong drinks – this is for you.

SOURZ SOUR APPLE ® LIQUEUR

The combination of sweet and sour is one of the most popular in cooking and is key to many of the best and most classic cocktails. In these citrus fruit is balanced by sugar, whether as syrup or in a liqueur. However, it was only in the late nineties when the innovative Sourz Sour Apple liqueur was launched that this classic balance of flavours could be found on the bar shelf. Sourz Sour Apple has a refreshing, mouth puckering sweet and sour rich apple flavour. Its bright lime green colour and modern bell-shaped bottle are as audacious as its flavour. Sourz is also available in pineapple and Tropical Blue flavours.

Sourz Sour Apple tastes of fresh, rich, ripe cooking apples with a clean citrus acidity and hints of marzipan, cinnamon, baked apples and a touch of honey.
15% alc./vol. (30°proof)

Producer: Munson Shaw Co, Deerfield, Illinois, USA. UK distributor: Maxxium UK Ltd, Stirling, Scotland.
Tel: 01786 430 500 Email: enquiries@maxxium.com

APPLE PIE

Glass: Shot
Method: Layer by carefully pouring ingredients in the following order.

³/₄	shot(s)	After Shock Red
³/₄	shot(s)	Sourz Sour Apple liqueur
¹/₂	shot(s)	Baileys Irish Cream liqueur

Origin: Created in 2002 by Wayne Collins for Maxxium UK.
Comment: Looks innocent but packs a real flavour punch.

BIG APPLE MARTINI

Glass: Martini
Garnish: Apple wedge on rim
Method: Shake all ingredients with ice and fine strain into chilled glass.

2¹/₂	shot(s)	Absolut vodka
1	shot(s)	Sourz Sour Apple liqueur
1	shot(s)	Apple schnapps liqueur

Origin: One of the most popular cocktails in New York City shortly after the Millennium.
Comment: There's no apple juice in this Martini, but it has an appealing light minty green hue.

THE GAME BIRD

Glass: Flute
Garnish: Lemon zest twist
Method: Shake all ingredients but ginger ale with ice and strain into glass. Top up with ginger ale.

2	shot(s)	The Famous Grouse Scotch whisky
1	shot(s)	Sourz Sour Apple liqueur
¹/₂	shot(s)	Elderflower cordial
¹/₂	shot(s)	Freshly squeezed lemon juice
¹/₄	shot(s)	Sugar (gomme) syrup
Top up with		Ginger ale

Origin: Created by Wayne Collins in 2002.
Comment: Wayne created this cocktail to be made using Famous Grouse, hence the name. Like most of his creations this is delicious: fruity, spicy and well-balanced.

PINK FLAMINGO

Glass: Collins
Garnish: Apple wheel
Method: Shake all ingredients with ice and fine strain into chilled glass.

2	shot(s)	Absolut Mandrin vodka
1	shot(s)	Sourz Sour Apple liqueur
¹/₂	shot(s)	Freshly squeezed lime juice
1	shot(s)	Cranberry juice

Origin: Created in 2002 by Wayne Collins for Maxxium UK.
Comment: Soapy and citrus flavoured – but in a nice way.

RED APPLE MARTINI NEW

Glass: Martini
Garnish: Stemmed maraschino cherry
Method: Shake all ingredients with ice and fine strain into chilled glass.

1½	shot(s)	Buffalo Trace Bourbon
½	shot(s)	Sourz Sour Apple liqueur
2	shot(s)	Cranberry juice

Variant: Sour Apple Martini
Comment: As Apple Martinis go this one is rather good.

SIDECAR NAMED DESIRE

Glass: Martini
Garnish: Sugar rim
Method: Vigorously shake all ingredients with ice and fine strain into chilled glass.

2	shot(s)	Rémy Martin Cognac
1	shot(s)	Sourz Sour Apple liqueur
1½	shot(s)	Freshly squeezed lemon juice
¼	shot(s)	Sugar (gomme) syrup

Comment: Take a classic Sidecar and add some love interest – apple!

SOUR APPLE MARTINI #2 (DELUXE US VERSION) NEW

Glass: Martini
Garnish: Float thin apple slice
Method: Shake all ingredients with ice and fine strain into chilled glass.

2	shot(s)	Absolut vodka
1	shot(s)	Sourz Sour Apple liqueur
½	shot(s)	Freshly squeezed lime juice
¼	shot(s)	Sugar (gomme) syrup
½	fresh	Egg white

Comment: Apple fortified with vodka and sexed up with a hint of orange and a sour edge.

SOURPUSS MARTINI

Glass: Martini
Garnish: Physalis (Cape gooseberry) on rim
Method: Shake all ingredients with ice and fine strain into chilled glass.

1	shot(s)	Absolut Citron vodka
½	shot(s)	Midori melon liqueur
½	shot(s)	Sourz Sour Apple liqueur
2	shot(s)	Pressed apple juice

Origin: Created in 2001 by Colin 'Big Col' Crowden at Time, Leicester, England.
Comment: A lime-green, flavourful cocktail balancing sweet and sour.

VANILIA SENSATION

Glass: Martini
Garnish: Float apple slice
Method: Shake all ingredients with ice and fine strain into chilled glass.

2	shot(s)	Absolut Vanilia vodka
1	shot(s)	Sourz Sour Apple liqueur
½	shot(s)	Cinzano Extra Dry vermouth

Origin: A drink created in 2003 and promoted by Absolut.
Comment: A pleasing vanilla twist on an apple Martini.

VIAGRA FALLS

Glass: Martini
Garnish: Flamed orange zest twist
Method: Shake all ingredients with ice and fine strain into chilled glass.

1	shot(s)	La Fée absinthe
1¾	shot(s)	Sourz Sour Apple liqueur
1¾	shot(s)	Chilled mineral water
½	spoon	Fee Brothers Orange bitters

Origin: Created by Jack Leuwens, London, England.
Comment: Aniseed and apple – sure to get your pecker up.

WINTER MARTINI

Glass: Martini
Garnish: Apple slice
Method: Vigorously shake all ingredients with ice and fine strain into chilled glass.

2½	shot(s)	Rémy Martin Cognac
1	shot(s)	Sourz Sour Apple liqueur
½	shot(s)	Sugar (gomme) syrup

Origin: Merc Bar, New York City.
Comment: A simple and Calvados-like drink.

ZHIVAGO MARTINI

Glass: Martini
Garnish: Apple slice in rim
Method: Shake all ingredients with ice and fine strain into chilled glass.

1½	shot(s)	Absolut Vanilia vodka
½	shot(s)	Buffalo Trace Bourbon
½	shot(s)	Sourz Sour Apple liqueur
1	shot(s)	Freshly squeezed lime juice
¾	shot(s)	Sugar (gomme) syrup

Origin: Created in 2002 by Alex Kammerling.
Comment: Perfectly balanced sweet and sour – sweet apple, vanilla and Bourbon balanced by lime juice.

| NEW | A DRINK NEW TO DIFFORDS GUIDE. |
| UPDATED | ENTRY CHANGED SINCE LAST VOLUME. |

SOUTHERN COMFORT®

Southern Comfort is over a hundred years old. In the 1860s New Orleans saloons commonly served harsh tasting American whiskey straight from the barrel. M.W. Heron, a local bar owner on Bourbon Street, experimented to soften his, producing the famous Southern Comfort recipe, which is said to consist of more than 100 secret ingredients and was originally served straight from the barrel. The scene on every bottle of Southern Comfort is entitled 'Home on the Mississippi' and was created in 1874 by Nathaniel Currier and James Ives. It depicts the Woodland Plantation, which was originally built as a sugar cane plantation and mill in 1834 and remains the last of the great plantation houses on the West Bank of the Mississippi River.

Southern Comfort's unique flavour includes hints of crème caramel, crème brûlée, banana milkshake, orange marmalade, lemon zest and honey. 35% alc./vol. (70°proof)

Web: www.southerncomfort.com **Producer:** Brown-Forman Beverages UK, St Louis, Missouri, USA. **UK distributor:** Bacardi-Martini, Southampton. **Tel:** 02380 318 084
Email: trade_enquiries@bacardi.com

ALABAMA SLAMMER #1 UPDATED

Glass: Martini
Garnish: Sprayed orange zest twist
Method: Shake all ingredients with ice and fine strain into chilled glass.

1	shot(s)	Absolut vodka
1	shot(s)	Southern Comfort liqueur
2	shot(s)	Freshly squeezed orange juice
1/4	shot(s)	Grenadine syrup

Comment: Medium sweet, fruity and scarlet.

THE BIG EASY

Glass: Collins
Garnish: Half orange wheel
Method: Shake first three ingredients with ice and strain into ice-filled glass. Top up with ginger ale.

1³/₄	shot(s)	Southern Comfort liqueur
³/₄	shot(s)	Cointreau / triple sec
2	shot(s)	Freshly squeezed orange juice
Top up with		Ginger ale

Comment: Fruity and refreshing with a hint of spice.

CANTEEN MARTINI NEW

Glass: Martini
Garnish: Cherry in drink
Method: Shake all ingredients with ice and fine strain into chilled glass.

1¹/₂	shot(s)	Havana Club light rum
1¹/₂	shot(s)	Southern Comfort liqueur
¹/₂	shot(s)	Disaronno Originale amaretto
¹/₂	shot(s)	Freshly squeezed lime juice

Origin: Originally created by Joey Guerra at Canteen, New York City, and adapted by author and columnist Gary Regan.
Comment: Tangy, sweet and sour – Southern Comfort drinkers will love this.

DEVIL'S MANHATTAN UPDATED

Glass: Martini
Garnish: Lemon zest twist
Method: Stir all ingredients with ice and strain into chilled glass.

2	shot(s)	Buffalo Trace Bourbon
1	shot(s)	Southern Comfort liqueur
1	shot(s)	Cinzano Rosso (sweet) vermouth
4	dashes	Angostura aromatic bitters

Comment: A Manhattan with a shot of Comfort.

NEW	A DRINK NEW TO DIFFORDS GUIDE.
UPDATED	ENTRY CHANGED SINCE LAST VOLUME.

HAWAIIAN COCKTAIL NEW

●●●●◖○

Glass: Martini
Garnish: Pineapple wedge & cherry on rim
Method: Shake all ingredients with ice and fine strain into chilled glass.

1	shot(s)	Havana Club light rum
1	shot(s)	Southern Comfort liqueur
3/4	shot(s)	Disaronno Originale amaretto
1	shot(s)	Freshly squeezed orange juice
1	shot(s)	Pressed pineapple juice

Origin: Discovered in Las Vegas in 2004.
Comment: Sweet, tangy and fruity. One to chase a meal.

SAILOR'S COMFORT

●●●●◖○

Glass: Old-fashioned
Garnish: Lime wedge
Method: Shake first four ingredients with ice and strain into ice-filled glass. Top up with soda water (club soda).

1	shot(s)	Plymouth sloe gin liqueur
1	shot(s)	Southern Comfort liqueur
1	shot(s)	Rose's lime cordial
4	dashes	Angostura aromatic bitters
Top up with		Soda water (club soda)

Origin: Discovered in 2002 at Lightship Ten, London, England.
Comment: Lime, peach and hints of berry make a light easy drink.

LOUISIANA TRADE

●●●●●○

Glass: Rocks
Garnish: Lime wedge squeezed and dropped into drink.
Method: Shake all ingredients with ice and strain into glass filled with crushed ice.

2	shots	Southern Comfort liqueur
1/2	shot(s)	Maple syrup
1/4	shot(s)	Sugar (gomme) syrup
1	shot(s)	Freshly squeezed lime juice

Origin: Created in 2001 by Mehdi Otmann at Zeta, London, England.
Comment: Peach and apricot with a lime freshness and a rich sweetness courtesy of maple syrup.

SCARLETT O'HARA

Glass: Martini
Garnish: Cranberries
Method: Shake ingredients with ice and strain into glass.

2	shot(s)	Southern Comfort liqueur
1	shot(s)	Freshly squeezed lime juice
2	shot(s)	Cranberry juice

Origin: Created in 1939 and named after the heroine of Gone With The Wind, the Scarlett O'Hara is said by many to have put Southern Comfort on the proverbial drink map.
Comment: The tang of lime and the dryness of cranberry works perfectly with the apricot sweetness of Southern Comfort.

RED OR DEAD NEW

●●●○○

Glass: Collins
Garnish: Lime wedge in glass
Method: Shake all ingredients with ice and strain into ice-filled glass.

1 1/2	shot(s)	Southern Comfort liqueur
3/4	shot(s)	Campari
3/4	shot(s)	Freshly squeezed lime juice
3	shot(s)	Cranberry juice

Comment: This long ruby drink balances sweetness, sourness and bitterness.

SOUTHERN TEA-KNEE

●●●●●

Glass: Martini
Garnish: Apricot slice on rim
Method: Shake all ingredients with ice and fine strain into chilled glass.

1	shot(s)	Southern Comfort liqueur
1/2	shot(s)	Plymouth gin
1/2	shot(s)	Bols apricot brandy liqueur
1/2	shot(s)	Bols crème de banane
2	shot(s)	Strong cold Earl Grey tea

Origin: I created this in December 2002 while experimenting with Southern Comfort.
Comment: Sweet fruity flavours balanced by tannin bitterness in the tea.

RHETT BUTLER

●●●●●○

Glass: Old-fashioned
Garnish: Lime wedge
Method: Shake all ingredients with ice and fine strain into chilled glass.

1	shot(s)	Grand Marnier liqueur
1	shot(s)	Southern Comfort liqueur
2	shot(s)	Cranberry juice
1	shot(s)	Freshly squeezed lime juice

Comment: A simple and well-balanced classic drink.

WAGON WHEEL NEW

●●●○○

Glass: Old-fashioned
Garnish: Lemon wheel in drink
Method: Shake all ingredients and fine strain into glass filled with crushed ice.

1 1/2	shot(s)	Southern Comfort liqueur
1 1/2	shot(s)	Rémy Martin Cognac
3/4	shot(s)	Freshly squeezed lemon juice
1/4	shot(s)	Grenadine syrup

Comment: This classic cocktail will be best appreciated by lovers of southern Comfort.

111

TEICHENNÉ® BUTTERSCOTCH SCHNAPPS

A family owned distiller and liqueur producer, the Teichenné firm was founded in 1956 when Juan Teichenné Senaux launched his distillery in the small town of L'Arboç (40 miles south of Barcelona). Born in France, Mr. Teichenné had moved to Spain as part of the French wine industry's search for new production sources. In those early days, production was very small, concentrating on 'handmade' brandies and liqueurs for sale locally in the Penedès Region.

Expansion did not start until the 70s, when Joan Teichenné Canals took over the business after his father's death. In the 80s Teichenné led the Spanish boom in liqueur schnapps.

These fruit liqueurs also opened doors to international markets which have grown significantly ever since. In the UK, Teichenné is most noted for its distinctive butterscotch schnapps, as well as peach and numerous other flavours.

Since its arrival in the UK in 1996, bartenders have raved over this flavoursome schnapps liqueur. Rich butterscotch and fudge with a hint of cinnamon, baked apple and nutmeg. 20% alc./vol. (40°proof)

Web: www.teichenne.com **Producer:** Teichenné S.A., Tarragona, Spain. **UK distributor:** Inspirit Brands, London. **Tel:** 020 7377 9457 **Email:** info@inspiritbrands.com

---

BANOFFEE MARTINI

Glass: Martini
Garnish: Dust with chocolate powder
Method: Muddle banana in base of shaker. Add other ingredients, shake with ice and fine strain into chilled glass.

¼	fresh	Banana
1½	shot(s)	Absolut Vanilia
¾	shot(s)	Teichenné butterscotch schnapps
¾	shot(s)	Bols crème de banane
1	spoon	Maple syrup
½	shot(s)	Double (heavy) cream
½	shot(s)	Milk

Origin: Adapted from a recipe created in 2002 by Barry Wilson, Zinc Bar & Grill, Edinburgh, Scotland.
Comment: Thick and rich, one for after the cheese course.

BON BON MARTINI

Glass: Martini
Garnish: Lemon zest (or a Bon Bon)
Method: Shake all ingredients with cubed ice and strain into glass.

1	shot(s)	Absolut Vanilia vodka
½	shot(s)	Teichenné butterscotch schnapps
¾	shot(s)	Limoncello liqueur
¾	shot(s)	Freshly squeezed lemon juice
¼	shot(s)	Vanilla syrup
1	shot(s)	Chilled water

Origin: Discovered in 2001 at Lab Bar, London, England.
Comment: Relive your youth and the taste of those big round sweets in this Martini.

BOURBON COOKIE

Glass: Old-fashioned
Garnish: Cinnamon dust
Method: Shake all ingredients with ice and fine strain into ice-filled glass.

2	shot(s)	Buffalo Trace Bourbon
½	shot(s)	Double (heavy) cream
½	shot(s)	Milk
½	shot(s)	Mango or passion fruit syrup
½	shot(s)	Teichenné butterscotch schnapps

Origin: Created in 2002 by Andres Masso, London, England.
Comment: Looks tame but packs a flavoursome punch.

BUTTERSCOTCH DAIQUIRI

Glass: Martini
Method: Shake ingredients with ice and strain into glass.

2	shot(s)	Havana Club light rum
1	shot(s)	Teichenné butterscotch schnapps
1	shot(s)	Freshly squeezed lime juice
½	shot(s)	Sugar (gomme) syrup

Comment: Tastes like butterscotch cut with lime.

BUTTERSCOTCH MARTINI

●●●●●○

Glass: Martini
Garnish: Butterscotch sweet
Method: Shake all ingredients with ice and fine strain into chilled glass.

2	shot(s)	Mount Gay Eclipse gold rum
3/4	shot(s)	Teichenné butterscotch schnapps
3/4	shot(s)	Bols white crème de cacao
1/8	shot(s)	Sugar (gomme) syrup
1/2	shot(s)	Chilled water

Comment: Sweet and suckable.

GINGERBREAD MARTINI NEW

●●●●○

Glass: Martini
Garnish: Slice of ginger
Method: Shake all ingredients with ice and fine strain into chilled glass.

1 1/2	shot(s)	Buffalo Trace Bourbon
3/4	shot(s)	Teichenné butterscotch schnapps
3/4	shot(s)	Stone's green ginger wine
2	shot(s)	Pressed apple juice

Origin: Created by yours truly in 2004.
Comment: Sticky, warming and spicy.

GIVE ME A DIME

●●●●●

Glass: Martini
Garnish: Crumbled Cadbury's Flake bar
Method: Shake all ingredients with ice and fine strain into chilled glass.

1 1/2	shot(s)	Bols white crème de cacao
1 1/2	shot(s)	Teichenné Butterscotch schnapps
1 1/2	shot(s)	Double (heavy) cream

Comment: Creamy, sweet and tasty.

GOLD MEMBER

●●●●●

Glass: Martini
Garnish: Apple wedge on rim
Method: Shake all ingredients with ice and fine strain into chilled glass.

3/4	shot(s)	Goldschläger cinnamon schnapps
3/4	shot(s)	Teichenné butterscotch schnapps
3/4	shot(s)	Apple schnapps liqueur
2 1/4	shot(s)	Pressed apple juice

Origin: I can't remember whose menu I ripped this off from: the proportions listed here are my own. If this is your drink, drop me a line and I'll credit you.
Comment: Hints of cinnamon and apple – an interesting tipple, if a tad sweet.

MET MANHATTAN

Glass: Martini
Garnish: Orange zest twist
Method: Shake ingredients with ice and strain into glass.

2	shot(s)	Buffalo Trace Bourbon
1	shot(s)	Grand Marnier liqueur
3/4	shot(s)	Teichenné butterscotch schnapps
1	dash	Fee Brothers orange bitters

Origin: The Met Bar, Metropolitan Hotel, London, England
Comment: A Manhattan with extra interest.

MONK'S CANDY BAR

Glass: Martini
Garnish: Sprinkle with nutmeg
Method: Shake ingredients with ice and strain into glass.

1 1/2	shot(s)	Frangelico hazelnut liqueur
1	shot(s)	Teichenné butterscotch schnapps
3/4	shot(s)	Kahlúa coffee liqueur
1	shot(s)	Double (heavy) cream
1	shot(s)	Milk

Comment: Hazelnut, butterscotch and coffee mixed with milk and cream makes a cocktail reminiscent of a candy bar.

SHAMROCK EXPRESS

Glass: Old-fashioned
Method: Shake ingredients with ice and strain into ice-filled glass.

1 1/2	shot(s)	Espresso coffee (cold)
3/4	shot(s)	Teichenné Butterscotch schnapps
1/2	shot(s)	Absolut vodka
1	shot(s)	Baileys Irish cream liqueur
1/4	shot(s)	Sugar (gomme) syrup

Origin: Created in 1999 by Greg Pearson at Mystique, Manchester, England.
Comment: Strong coffee with the sweetness of butterscotch.

TRIBBBLE

●●●●○

Glass: Shot
Method: Layer ingredients by carefully pouring in the following order.

1/2	shot(s)	Teichenné Butterscotch schnapps
1/2	shot(s)	Bols Crème de banane
1/2	shot(s)	Baileys Irish Cream liqueur

Origin: A new drink created by the bartenders at TGI Friday's UK in 2002.
Comment: Named 'Tribbble' with three 'Bs' due to its three layers: butterscotch, banana and Baileys.

THOSE DRINKS I'VE SAMPLED RECENTLY ARE GRADED AS FOLLOWS:

● DISGUSTING	●● PRETTY AWFUL	●● BEST AVOIDED
●●○ DISAPPOINTING	●●● ACCEPTABLE	●●●○ GOOD
●●●● RECOMMENDED	●●●●○ HIGHLY RECOMMENDED	
●●●●● OUTSTANDING / EXCEPTIONAL		

NEW	A DRINK NEW TO SAUCE GUIDES.
UPDATED	ENTRY CHANGED SINCE LAST VOLUME.

TEICHENNÉ® PEACH SCHNAPPS

In the eighties, when schnapps were just beginning to emerge as a new category of liqueur, Juan Teichenné led the way and Teichenné Peach Schnapps was one of the Spanish producer's original flavours. This fresh and approachable liqueur was quickly picked up by the world's bartenders and peach schnapps became a key ingredient in many contemporary classic cocktails.

While Teichenné have since developed their schnapps range to include a plethora of excellent new flavours, Teichenné Peach Schnapps remains one of the bestselling, illustrating its quality and mixability.

Teichenné Peach Schnapps has a rich nose of ripe peach skin and peach kernel, giving it a soft, succulent flavour which lightens on the palate.
20% alc./vol. (40°proof)

Web: www.teichenne.com **Producer:** Teichenné S.A., Tarragona, Spain. **UK distributor:** InSpirit Brands, London. **Tel:** 020 7377 9457
Email: info@inspiritbrands.com

BELLINI (DIFFORD'S FORMULA) NEW

●●●●○

Glass: Flute
Garnish: Peach slice on rim
Method: Shake first four ingredients with ice and fine strain into chilled glass. Add Prosecco and gently stir. (Alternatively, blend all ingredients quickly without ice and serve.)

2	shot(s)	Puréed white peaches
¼	shot(s)	Teichenné peach schnapps liqueur
¼	shot(s)	Peach eau de vie (de pêche)
1/8	shot(s)	Freshly squeezed lemon juice
Top up with		Prosecco sparkling wine

Comment: My version is more alcoholic and drier that the classic Bellini. It may seem counter-intuitive to put sparkling wine in a blender, but try this drink after a quick whizz with no ice. (Use well chilled ingredients and glass.)

BELLINI-TINI

Glass: Martini
Garnish: Peach wedge
Method: Shake ingredients with ice and strain into glass.

2	shot(s)	Absolut vodka
½	shot(s)	Teichenné peach schnapps liqueur
½	shot(s)	Fresh white peach purée
4	dashes	Peach bitters (optional)

Comment: Peachy, peachy, peachy! Based on the Bellini, funnily enough.

BIKINI MARTINI UPDATED

●●●●○

Glass: Martini
Garnish: Orange zest
Method: Shake all ingredients with ice and fine strain into chilled glass.

2	shot(s)	Plymouth gin
¾	shot(s)	Bols blue curaçao
¼	shot(s)	Teichenné peach schnapps liqueur
¼	shot(s)	Freshly squeezed lemon juice
¾	shot(s)	Chilled water

Origin: Adapted from a cocktail created in 1999 by Dick Bradsell for an Agent Provocateur swimwear launch.
Comment: A vivid blue combination of lemon, orange and peach laced with gin.

JACUZZI

Glass: Flute
Garnish: Peach slice
Method: Shake first three ingredients with ice and strain into glass, then top up with Champagne.

1	shot(s)	Teichenné peach schnapps liqueur
½	shot(s)	Plymouth gin
1	shot(s)	Freshly squeezed orange juice
Top up with		Piper-Heidsieck Brut Champagne

Comment: Gin balances the sweetness of peach schnapps in this fruity Champagne cocktail.

JEREZ

Glass: Old-fashioned
Method: Stir all ingredients with ice and strain into ice-filled glass.

1/2	shot(s)	Tio Pepe Fino Sherry
1/2	shot(s)	Pedro Ximénez Sherry
1	shot(s)	Teichenné peach schnapps liqueur
1	shot(s)	Sauvignon Blanc wine
1	shot(s)	La Vieille Prune (prunelle)
1	dash	Angostura aromatic bitters

Origin: This drink heralds from one of the noble houses of Spain – well that's what the Sherry PR told me, anyway. I've changed the recipe slightly.
Comment: Sherry depth and stoned fruit flavours.

MISSISSIPPI SCHNAPPER

Glass: Martini
Garnish: Flamed orange twist
Method: Shake all ingredients with ice and fine strain into chilled glass.

2	shot(s)	Jack Daniel's Tennessee whiskey
3/4	shot(s)	Teichenné peach schnapps liqueur
1/2	shot(s)	Cointreau / triple sec
1/4	shot(s)	Freshly squeezed lime juice
1/4	shot(s)	Sugar (gomme) syrup

Origin: Created in 1999 by Dan Cottle at Velvet, Manchester, England.
Comment: Orange predominates with peach sweetness balanced by whiskey and lime.

PALE RIDER

Glass: Collins
Method: Shake ingredients with ice and strain into ice-filled glass.

2	shot(s)	Absolut Kurant vodka
1/2	shot(s)	Teichenné peach schnapps liqueur
2	shot(s)	Cranberry juice
1	shot(s)	Pressed pineapple juice
1	shot(s)	Freshly squeezed lime juice
3/4	shot(s)	Sugar (gomme) syrup

Origin: Created in 1997 by Wayne Collins at Navajo Joe, London, England.
Comment: A rollercoaster of flavours with a sweet fruity finish.

PEACH DAIQUIRI

Glass: Martini
Garnish: Peach wedge on rim
Method: Shake all ingredients with ice and fine strain into chilled glass.

2	shot(s)	Havana Club light rum
1	shot(s)	Teichenné peach schnapps liqueur
1/2	shot(s)	Freshly squeezed lime juice
1/8	shot(s)	Sugar (gomme) syrup
1/2	shot(s)	Chilled mineral water

Origin: My take on the Cuban Daiquiri de Melocoton.
Comment: Harder and drier than you'd expect.

SEX ON THE BEACH # 1

Glass: Rocks
Method: Shake ingredients with ice and strain into ice-filled glass.

1	shot(s)	Absolut vodka
1	shot(s)	Chambord black raspberry liqueur
1	shot(s)	Teichenné Peach schnapps liqueur
2 1/2	shot(s)	Pressed pineapple juice

Variant: With melon liqueur in place of peach schnapps.
Comment: Deliciously fun without sand in your privates. This drink is fruity flavoured with black raspberries, pineapple, peach and a vodka edge.

TROPICAL CREAM

Glass: Martini
Garnish: Kiwi fruit on rim
Method: Shake all ingredients with ice and fine strain into chilled glass.

1/2	shot(s)	Havana Club light rum
1	shot(s)	Midori melon liqueur
1/2	shot(s)	Frangelico hazelnut liqueur
1/2	shot(s)	Teichenné peach schnapps liqueur
1/2	shot(s)	Malibu coconut rum liqueur
1	shot(s)	Freshly squeezed orange juice
1	shot(s)	Double (heavy) cream

Comment: A velvety, smooth, fruity cocktail.

WOO WOO

Glass: Rocks
Garnish: Split lime wedge
Method: Shake ingredients with ice and strain into ice-filled glass.

1	shot(s)	Teichenné Peach schnapps liqueur
1	shot(s)	Absolut vodka
3 1/2	shot(s)	Cranberry juice

Comment: Fruity, dry cranberry laced with vodka and peach.

YUM

Glass: Collins
Method: Shake ingredients with ice and strain into ice-filled glass

1 1/2	shot(s)	Mandarine Napoléon liqueur
1/2	shot(s)	Teichenné Peach schnapps liqueur
1	shot(s)	Freshly squeezed lemon juice
1/4	shot(s)	Sugar (gomme) syrup
1/4	shot(s)	Chambord black raspberry liqueur
3	shot(s)	Pressed apple juice

Comment: Apt name – yummy!

NEW	A DRINK NEW TO SAUCE GUIDES.
UPDATED	ENTRY CHANGED SINCE LAST VOLUME.

THE FAMOUS GROUSE® SCOTCH

Matthew Gloag, a retailer in Perth, developed his blend of Scotch to appeal to the growing numbers of sporting gentlemen travelling to the North East Highlands to participate in hunting, shooting and fishing. During 1896, he chose the fitting name 'Grouse Brand' and his daughter sketched the Red Grouse label that became its trademark. The popularity the new whisky enjoyed meant that people soon referred it as The Famous Grouse.

The Famous Grouse is based on malts such as The Macallan and Highland Park which are married with grain whiskies in oak casks for six months prior to bottling. Because Grouse is married at a lower strength than most other whiskies it does not require heavy filtration prior to bottling. This helps retain flavour and give a smooth mouthfeel to the whisky.

The Famous Grouse is Scotland's best selling whisky. It is malty, peaty, yet light with flavours of bitter chocolate, cocoa, toffee apple, fruit cake and subtle Sherry. 40% alc./vol. (80°proof)

Web: www.famousgrouse.com **Producer:** Highland Distillers Plc, West Kinfauns, Perth, Scotland. **UK distributor:** Maxxium Brands, Stirling. **Tel:** 01786 430 500. **Email:** enquiries@maxxium.com

BLOOD & SAND

Glass: Martini
Method: Shake ingredients with ice and strain into glass.

1	shot(s)	The Famous Grouse Scotch whisky
1	shot(s)	Bols Cherry brandy liqueur
1	shot(s)	Cinzano Rosso (sweet) vermouth
1	shot(s)	Freshly squeezed orange juice

Origin: Made for the premiere of the Rudolph Valentino film, Blood and Sand.
Comment: One of the best Scotch cocktails.

BOBBY BURNS

●●●●○

Glass: Martini
Garnish: Stemmed maraschino cherry in drink
Method: Shake all ingredients with ice and fine strain into chilled glass.

1½	shot(s)	The Famous Grouse Scotch whisky
1½	shot(s)	Cinzano Rosso (sweet) vermouth
¼	shot(s)	Bénédictine D.O.M. liqueur

Comment: Strictly speaking this drink should be stirred, but I prefer mine shaken so that's how it appears here.

BRUBAKER OLD-FASHIONED

●●●●○

Glass: Old-fashioned
Garnish: Two lemon zest twists.
Method: Stir malt extract in glass with Scotch so as to dissolve malt extract. Add ice and one shot of Scotch and stir. Add rest of Scotch, sugar and Angostura and stir some more. Add more ice and keep stirring so that ice dilutes the drink.

2	spoons	Malt Extract (available in health-food shops)
2	shot(s)	The Famous Grouse Scotch whisky
¼	shot(s)	Sugar (gomme) syrup
3	dashes	Angostura aromatic bitters

Origin: Created in 2003 by Shelim Islam at the GE Club, London, England. Shelim named this drink after a horse in the sports section of a paper (which is also a film made in the seventies starring Robert Redford).
Comment: If you like Scotch you should try this extra malty dram. After all that stirring you'll deserve one.

FLYING SCOTSMAN UPDATED

●●●●○

Glass: Old-fashioned
Method: Stir all ingredients with ice and strain into ice-filled glass.

2	shot(s)	The Famous Grouse Scotch whisky
2	shot(s)	Cinzano Rosso (sweet) vermouth
¼	shot(s)	Sugar (gomme) syrup
4	dashes	Angostura aromatic bitters

Comment: Sweetened Scotch with plenty of spice: like a homemade whisky liqueur.

THE GAME BIRD

Glass: Flute
Garnish: Lemon zest twist
Method: Shake all ingredients but ginger ale with ice and strain into glass. Top up with ginger ale.

2	shot(s)	The Famous Grouse Scotch whisky
1	shot(s)	Sourz Sour Apple liqueur
½	shot(s)	Elderflower cordial
½	shot(s)	Freshly squeezed lemon juice
¼	shot(s)	Sugar (gomme) syrup
Top up with		Ginger ale

Origin: Created by Wayne Collins in 2002.
Comment: Wayne created this cocktail to be made using Famous Grouse, hence the name. Like most of his creations this is delicious: fruity, spicy and well-balanced.

GE BLONDE

Glass: Martini
Garnish: Apple wedge
Method: Shake all ingredients with ice and strain into glass.

1¾	shot(s)	The Famous Grouse Scotch whisky
1¼	shot(s)	Sauvignon Blanc wine
1	shot(s)	Pressed apple juice
⅓	shot(s)	Sugar (gomme) syrup
¼	shot(s)	Freshly squeezed lemon juice

Origin: A combined effort by the staff of London's GE Club in January 2002, this was named by Linda, a waitress at the club who happens to be blonde. She claimed the name was inspired by the cocktail's straw colour.
Comment: The type of 'fresh' apple juice used and the brand of Scotch greatly affect the balance of this delicate drink.

HAIR OF THE DOG

Glass: Martini
Garnish: Grate fresh nutmeg
Method: Stir honey with Scotch so as to dissolve honey. Add other ingredients, shake with ice and fine strain into chilled glass.

3	spoons	Runny honey
2	shot(s)	The Famous Grouse Scotch whisky
1	shot(s)	Double (heavy) cream
1	shot(s)	Milk

Origin: Traditionally drunk as a pick-me-up hangover cure.
Comment: This drink's name and reputation as a hangover cure may lead you to wrongly assume it tastes unpleasant. Honey, whisky and cream combine wonderfully.

HEATHER JULEP

Glass: Collins
Garnish: Mint sprig
Method: Lightly muddle mint with Scotch in base of shaker. (Only the leaves should be used, as the stems are bitter. The leaves should be bruised, not crushed, as crushing releases bitter juices.) Place shaker and its contents in refrigerator with serving glass for at least two hours. Remove glass from refrigerator and half fill with crushed ice. Place Drambuie and sugar into shaker base with Scotch and mint. Shake with ice and strain into glass. Churn the drink with the crushed ice using a bar spoon. Top up the glass with more crushed ice so as to fill it and churn again. Serve with two long straws.

12	fresh	Mint leaves
2½	shot(s)	The Famous Grouse Scotch whisky
½	shot	Drambuie liqueur
¾	shot(s)	Sugar (gomme) syrup

Origin: Adapted from a drink discovered in 2001 at Teatro, London, England.
Comment: This Scottish twist on the Bourbon based Mint Julep is well worth the time it takes to make.

HIGHLAND SLING

Glass: Sling
Garnish: Apple wedge on rim
Method: Shake all ingredients with ice and strain into ice-filled glass.

1½	shot(s)	The Famous Grouse Scotch whisky
½	shot(s)	Galliano liqueur
1	shot(s)	Cranberry juice
½	shot(s)	Bols apricot brandy liqueur
2	shot(s)	Pressed apple juice

Comment: A surprisingly good combination of diverse flavours.

HONEY & MARMALADE DRAM'TINI

Glass: Martini
Garnish: Strips of orange peel **Method:** Stir honey with Scotch in base of shaker until honey dissolves. Add lemon and orange juice, shake with ice and fine strain into chilled glass.

2	shot(s)	The Famous Grouse Scotch whisky
4	spoons	Runny honey
1	shot(s)	Freshly squeezed lemon juice
1	shot(s)	Freshly squeezed orange juice

Origin: I adapted this recipe from the Honeysuckle-Tini, which is also in this guide.
Comment: This citrussy drink seems to enrich and enhance the flavour of Scotch.

HOT TODDY

Glass: Toddy
Garnish: Cinnamon stick
Method: Place bar spoon in glass, add ingredients and stir.

2	shot(s)	The Famous Grouse Scotch whisky
1	shot(s)	Sugar (gomme) syrup
3		Cloves
1/2	shot(s)	Freshly squeezed lemon juice
1	spoon	Runny honey
Top up with		Boiling water

Comment: Spicy, warming and great for when you're feeling down with a cold or flu.

MYSTIQUE

Glass: Old-fashioned
Garnish: Orange twist & cherry
Method: Stir ingredients with ice and strain into ice-filled glass.

3/4	shot(s)	Drambuie liqueur
3/4	shot(s)	Teichenné peach schnapps liqueur
1/2	shot(s)	The Famous Grouse Scotch whisky
4	dashes	Fee Brothers orange bitters
1/4	shot(s)	Maraschino syrup

Origin: Created by Greg Pearson at Mystique, Manchester, England in 1999. Joint winner of the Manchester Food & Drink Festival cocktail competition.
Comment: Peach combines brilliantly with the Drambuie and Scotch.

LINSTEAD UPDATED ●●●●●◐

Glass: Martini
Garnish: Float lemon zest twist
Method: Shake all ingredients with ice and fine strain into chilled glass.

2	shot(s)	The Famous Grouse Scotch whisky
2	shot(s)	Pressed pineapple juice
1/4	shot(s)	Sugar (gomme) syrup
1/8	shot(s)	La Fée absinthe

Comment: The absinthe comes through first with the pineapple, leaving the Scotch till the end. Great combo.

PEAR SHAPED (POPULAR VERSION) ●●●●●○

Glass: Collins
Glass: Pear wedge on rim
Method: Shake all ingredients with ice and strain into ice-filled glass.

2	shot(s)	The Famous Grouse Scotch whisky
1	shot(s)	Xanté pear & cognac liqueur
3	shot(s)	Pressed apple juice
1/2	shot(s)	Freshly squeezed lime juice
1/4	shot(s)	Vanilla sugar syrup

Origin: Adapted from a drink created in 2003 by Jamie Terrell at Dick's Bar, Atlantic, London, England.
Comment: Scotch, pear and apple combine wonderfully in this medium sweet long drink.

MAC ORANGE'TINI ●●●●●○

Glass: Martini
Garnish: Flamed orange zest twist
Method: Shake all ingredients with ice and fine strain into chilled glass.

2	shot(s)	The Famous Grouse Scotch whisky
3/4	shot(s)	Stone's ginger wine
2	shot(s)	Freshly squeezed orange juice
4	dashes	Fee Brothers orange bitters
1/2	spoon	Sugar (gomme) syrup

Comment: A Whisky Mac with orange topping off the ginger.

POLLY'S SPECIAL ●●●●●○

Glass: Martini
Garnish: Grapefruit wedge on rim
Method: Shake all ingredients with ice and fine strain into chilled glass.

1 3/4	shot(s)	The Famous Grouse Scotch whisky
1	shot(s)	Freshly squeezed grapefruit juice
1	shot(s)	Grand Marnier liqueur
1/4	shot(s)	Sugar (gomme) syrup

Origin: I adapted this recipe from a 1947 edition of Trader Vic's Bartender's Guide.
Comment: Sweet, sour, flavoursome and balanced – for grown-ups who like the taste of alcohol.

MILK & HONEY MARTINI ●●●●●◐

Glass: Martini
Garnish: Grate fresh nutmeg over drink
Method: Stir Scotch with honey in base of shaker until honey dissolves. Add other ingredients, shake with ice and fine strain into chilled glass.

2	shot(s)	The Famous Grouse Scotch whisky
3	spoons	Runny honey
1/2	shot(s)	Honey liqueur
3/4	shot(s)	Double (heavy) cream
3/4	shot(s)	Milk

Origin: I created this in December 2002.
Comment: The rich flavour of Scotch is tamed by honey and cream.

R U BOBBY MOORE?

Glass: Martini
Garnish: Apple wedge on rim
Method: Shake all ingredients with ice and fine strain into chilled glass.

1½	shot(s)	Zubrowka bison vodka
1	shot(s)	Sauvignon Blanc wine
1	shot(s)	The Famous Grouse Scotch whisky
1	shot(s)	Pressed apple juice
¼	shot(s)	Sugar (gomme) syrup

Origin: I created this drink in 2002 and named it after the rhyming slang for 'are you bloody sure?'.
Comment: Scotch goes brilliantly with apple which also mixes well with Zubrówka. The addition of wine makes the whole combination interestingly different.

RED NECK MARTINI

Glass: Martini
Garnish: Orange zest twist
Method: Shake all ingredients with ice and fine strain into chilled glass.

2	shot(s)	The Famous Grouse Scotch whisky
1	shot(s)	Dubonnet Red
1	shot(s)	Bols Cherry brandy liqueur

Origin: Created by Sylvain Solignac in 2002 at Circus Bar, London, England.
Comment: Nicely balanced, aromatic and not too sweet – the flavour of the Scotch shines through.

ROB ROY

Glass: Martini
Garnish: Cherry & orange zest twist (discard orange)
Method: Stir all ingredients with ice and strain into chilled glass.

2	shot(s)	Famous Grouse Scotch whisky
1	shot(s)	Cinzano Rosso (sweet) vermouth
2	dashes	Angostura aromatic bitters
⅛	shot(s)	Maraschino syrup (optional)

Variant: Affinity
Origin: A classic (retro) cocktail of unknown origins, but thought to have been created circa 1940 and named after a Broadway show.
Comment: A Sweet Manhattan made with Scotch in place of Bourbon. The dry, peaty whisky and bitters ensure it's not too sweet.

RUSTY NAIL

Glass: Old-fashioned
Garnish: Lemon zest twist
Method: Stir ingredients with ice and strain into ice-filled glass.

2	shot(s)	The Famous Grouse Scotch whisky
1	shot(s)	Drambuie liqueur

Comment: The classic drink combining Scotch and the heather-honey smoothness of Drambuie – simple but great.

SCOTCH BOUNTY MARTINI

Glass: Martini
Method: Shake ingredients with ice and strain into glass.

1	shot(s)	The Famous Grouse Scotch whisky
1	shot(s)	Bols White crème de cacao
½	shot(s)	Malibu Coconut rum liqueur
2	shot(s)	Freshly squeezed orange juice
⅛	shot(s)	Grenadine syrup

Comment: A medium-sweet combination of Scotch, coconut and orange.

SMOKIE MARTINI UPDATED

Glass: Martini
Garnish: Lemon zest twist
Method: Stir all ingredients with ice and strain into a chilled glass.

2½	shot(s)	Plymouth gin
½	shot(s)	Cinzano Extra Dry vermouth
¼	shot(s)	The Famous Grouse Scotch whisky

Variant: Substitute vodka for gin.
Comment: A pleasant variation on the classic Dry Martini.

THRILLER MARTINI

Glass: Martini
Garnish: Orange zest
Method: Shake all ingredients with ice and fine strain into chilled glass.

2½	shot(s)	The Famous Grouse Scotch whisky
¾	shot(s)	Stone's Green ginger wine
¾	shot(s)	Freshly squeezed orange juice
⅛	shot(s)	Sugar (gomme) syrup

Comment: Spiced Scotch with a hint of orange.

WHISKEY COBBLER UPDATED

Glass: Old-fashioned
Garnish: Lemon slice & mint sprig
Method: Stir ingredients with ice and strain into glass filled with crushed ice.

2	shot(s)	The Famous Grouse Scotch whisky
½	shot(s)	Rémy Martin Cognac
½	shot(s)	Grand Marnier liqueur

Comment: A hardcore yet sophisticated drink.

WHISKY MAC

Glass: Rocks
Method: Pour ingredients into ice-filled glass and stir.

2	shot(s)	The Famous Grouse Scotch whisky
1½	shot(s)	Stone's green ginger wine

Comment: An old classic, but it still works.

TUACA ITALIAN LIQUEUR

Pronounced 'Too-Wa-Ka' this golden amber, brandy based spirit liqueur is flavoured with vanilla and orange essence. Tuaca comes from Italy's Tuscany region and is said to have been created at the height of the 16th century Renaissance for Lorenzo di Medici, a ruler of Florence and patron to Michelangelo and Botticelli.

During World War II, American servicemen stationed in Livorno, Italy (a seaside resort on Tuscany's Mediterranean Coast) discovered Tuaca's smooth flavour. On their return home they searched for the brand but were unable to find it – finally in the late 1950s an astute importer brought Tuaca across the ocean. Tuaca is now well established in the States and has more recently been introduced to Britain.

Taste: Smooth yet powerful liqueur with dark chocolate, espresso coffee and vanilla flavours predominating - reminiscent of tiramisu with more subtle hints of nutmeg and orange. 35% alc./vol. (70°proof)

Web. www.danesltd.co.uk **Producer:** Distillerie Tuoni & Canepa S.p.A, Livorno, Italy. **UK distributor:** Danes Ltd.
Tel: 01273 674 022
Email: poul@tuaca.co.uk

APPLE CRUMBLE MARTINI #2

Glass: Martini
Garnish: Dust with ground cinnamon
Method: Shake all ingredients with ice and fine strain into chilled glass.

2	shot(s)	Tuaca Italian liqueur
1/2	shot(s)	Freshly squeezed lemon juice
2	shot(s)	Pressed apple juice

Origin: Created in 2002 by Eion Richards at Bonds Bar, London, England.
Comment: Easy to make and equally easy to drink.

DRAMATIC MARTINI UPDATED

Glass: Martini
Garnish: Grate nutmeg over drink
Method: Shake all ingredients with ice and fine strain into chilled glass.

1	shot(s)	Tuaca liqueur
1	shot(s)	Grand Marnier liqueur
1	shot(s)	Baileys Irish Cream liqueur
1	shot(s)	Milk

Comment: Creamy and sweet with orangey herbal notes.

GALVANISED NAIL NEW

Glass: Martini
Garnish: Float apple slice
Method: Shake all ingredients with ice and fine strain into chilled glass.

1¹/2	shot(s)	Tuaca Italian liqueur
3/4	shot(s)	Drambuie liqueur
1/4	shot(s)	The Famous Grouse Scotch whisky
1/8	shot(s)	Freshly squeezed lemon juice
2	shot(s)	Pressed apple juice

Origin: Created in 2003 by yours truly, taking inspiration from the Rusty Nail.
Comment: Honey, vanilla, Scotch and apple with a hint of spice.

HONEY WALL

Glass: Martini
Garnish: Flamed orange zest twist
Method: Stir all ingredients with ice and fine strain into chilled glass.

1¹/2	shot(s)	Appleton Estate V/X aged rum
1¹/2	shot(s)	Tuaca Italian liqueur
1¹/2	shot(s)	Kikor chocolate liqueur

Origin: Created in 2002 by Dick Bradsell at Downstairs at Alfred, London, England.
Comment: Strong, rich and chocolatey.

IRISH MANHATTAN

Glass: Martini
Garnish: Shamrock
Method: Stir all ingredients with ice and strain into chilled glass.

1¹/₂	shot(s)	Buffalo Trace Bourbon
1	shot(s)	Tuaca Italian liqueur
¹/₂	shot(s)	Grand Marnier liqueur
¹/₄	shot(s)	Vanilla syrup

Origin: Adapted from a drink discovered in 2001 at Detroit, London, England.
Comment: There's nothing Irish about this drink, but it's good all the same.

THE ITALIAN JOB #2

Glass: Sling
Garnish: Orange peel twist
Method: Shake first three ingredients with ice and strain into glass filled with crushed ice. Top up with wine and serve with straws.

1	shot(s)	Tuaca Italian liqueur
1	shot(s)	Disaronno Originale amaretto
1	shot(s)	Cranberry juice
Top up with		Red wine (Shiraz)

Origin: Discovered in 2002 at Rapscallion, London, England.
Comment: Mix layers with straw prior to drinking for vanilla-ed, almond fruity wine.

MYSTIQUE MARTINI

Glass: Martini
Garnish: Raspberries on stick
Method: Stir all ingredients with ice and fine strain into chilled glass.

2	shot(s)	The Famous Grouse Scotch whisky
1	shot(s)	Tuaca Italian liqueur
³/₄	shot(s)	Chambord black raspberry liqueur

Origin: Created in 2002 by Tim Halilaj, Albania.
Comment: Rust coloured and fruit charged.

ORANGE CUSTARD MARTINI

Glass: Martini
Garnish: Orange zest twist
Method: Shake all ingredients with ice and strain into glass.

2	shot(s)	Warninks advocaat
1	shot(s)	Tuaca Italian liqueur
¹/₂	shot(s)	Grand Marnier liqueur
¹/₄	shot(s)	Vanilla syrup

Origin: I created this drink in 2002 after rediscovering Advocaat on a trip to Amsterdam.
Comment: Creamy and smooth with orange and vanilla and something of a kick.

SOPHISTICATED SAVAGE

Glass: Rocks
Garnish: Lime sugared rim
Method: Shake ingredients with ice and strain into ice-filled glass.

2	shot(s)	Tuaca liqueur
1	shot(s)	Sagatiba Cachaça
¹/₂	fresh	Egg white
¹/₂	shot(s)	Freshly squeezed lime juice

Created by: Poul Jensen.
Comment: A sour drink with a horse kick leading into a smooth subtle finish.

STEALTH SHOT

Glass: Shot
Method: Layer in glass by carefully pouring ingredients in the following order.

¹/₂	shot(s)	Kahlúa coffee liqueur
¹/₂	shot(s)	Tuaca Italian liqueur
¹/₂	shot(s)	Baileys Irish Cream liqueur

Origin: Created by Poul Jensen, at St. James', Brighton, England.
Comment: Yep, it's another of the B-52 family, named after Stealth bombers.

WALNUT MARTINI UPDATED

Glass: Martini
Garnish: Float walnut half
Method: Stir all ingredients with ice and strain into chilled glass.

2	shot(s)	Absolut vodka
³/₄	shot(s)	Tuaca Italian liqueur
³/₄	shot(s)	Toschi Nocello Walnut liqueur
³/₄	shot(s)	Cinzano Extra Dry vermouth

Origin: Created by yours truly.
Comment: Nutty but nice.

WONKY MARTINI

Glass: Martini
Garnish: Orange zest twist
Method: Stir all ingredients with ice and strain into chilled glass.

1¹/₂	shot(s)	Absolut Vanilia vodka
1¹/₂	shot(s)	Tuaca Italian liqueur
1¹/₂	shot(s)	Cinzano Rosso (sweet) vermouth
3	dashes	Fee Brothers Orange bitters

Origin: Created in 2003 by yours truly.
Comment: The strength of a traditional Martini invigorated with more than a hint of orange and vanilla.

WRAY & NEPHEW® WHITE OVERPROOF RUM

Wray & Nephew is the world's top selling, award winning, high strength rum. Any spirit equal to or over 57% alc./vol. is termed "overproof". This unaged white rum is one such example.

Made by J Wray & Nephew, the oldest distilling company in Jamaica, this brand is more than just a rum, it is an intrinsic part of Jamaica's culture, heritage and tradition. Wray & Nephew is a staple in every Jamaican household where it is used as part of medicine, ritual and everyday living and accounts for over 90% of all rum consumed on the island.

Wray & Nephew has a wonderful, fruity natural aroma with a rich molasses top note and hints of pineapple, banana, orange and coconut. Although the product is strong, when used correctly the brand's complex bouquet and delivery of unique flavour characteristics make it an excellent base for cocktails and a must in punches. 63% alc./vol. (126° proof)

Web: www.rum.co.uk **Producer:** J. Wray & Nephew Ltd, Kingston, Jamaica. **UK distributor:** J. Wray & Nephew (UK) Ltd, London, **Tel:** 020 7378 8858 **Email.** info@rum.co.uk

---

AFTERBURNER UPDATED

Glass: Snifter
Method: Pour ingredients into glass, swirl to mix, flambé and then extinguish flame. Please take care and beware of hot glass rim.

1	shot(s)	White crème de menthe
1	shot(s)	Kahlúa coffee liqueur
¹/₂	shot(s)	Wray & Nephew overproof rum

Comment: A surprisingly smooth and moreish peppermint-laced drink.

ARCHANGEL

Glass: Collins
Garnish: Strawberry slice and basil leaf
Method: Shake ingredients with ice and strain into ice-filled glass.

1	shot(s)	Strawberry purée
3	shot(s)	Pressed pineapple juice
¹/₂	shot(s)	Sagatiba Cachaça
¹/₂	shot(s)	Wray & Nephew overproof rum
1	shot(s)	Teichenné peach schnapps liqueur
4	fresh	Basil leaves

Origin: Made by Sean Finnegan at Mash & Air, Manchester in 1999. Joint winner of the Manchester Food & Drink Festival cocktail competition.
Comment: Fragrant, fruity, sweet, well-balanced – the basil adds an extra dimension to the Batida base.

BEACH BLONDE

Glass: Collins
Garnish: Banana slice on rim
Method: Blend all ingredients with a scoop of crushed ice and serve with straws.

¹/₂	fresh	Peeled banana
1	shot(s)	Wray & Nephew overproof white rum
3	shot(s)	Warninks advocaat
3	shot(s)	Freshly squeezed orange juice

Origin: Created in 2002 by Alex Kammerling for Warninks.
Comment: Fruity, creamy holiday drinking.

CARIBBEAN PUNCH

Glass: Collins
Method: Shake all ingredients with ice and strain into a glass filled with crushed ice.

2 ¹/₄	shot(s)	Wray & Nephew overproof rum
¹/₂	shot(s)	Disaronno Originale amaretto
¹/₂	shot(s)	Malibu coconut rum liqueur
¹/₄	shot(s)	Galliano liqueur
¹/₄	shot(s)	Grenadine syrup
³/₄	shot(s)	Freshly squeezed lemon juice
3	shot(s)	Pressed pineapple juice

Comment: Red in colour and innocent looking, this flavoursome drink sure packs a punch.

COCO NAUT

Glass: Rocks
Method: Blend all ingredients with crushed ice and serve.

2	shot(s)	Wray & Nephew overproof rum
2	shot(s)	Coco López cream of coconut
1	shot(s)	Freshly squeezed lime juice

Comment: This snow-white drink is hardly innocent with a double shot of overproof rum nicely masked by sweet coconut.

COLD COMFORT

Glass: Old-fashioned
Method: Shake all ingredients vigorously with ice and strain into ice filled glass.

2	shot(s)	Wray & Nephew overproof rum
6	spoons	Runny honey
1	shot(s)	Freshly squeezed lime juice

Origin: I discovered this while in Jamaica in 2001.
Comment: Take at the first sign of a cold, and then retreat under your bedcovers. Repeat dose regularly while symptoms persist. Warning – do not take if currently being prescribed another form of medication.

JAMAICAN SUNSET

Glass: Collins
Method: Shake all ingredients with ice and strain into ice-filled glass.

1¹/₂	shot(s)	Wray & Nephew overproof rum
2	shot(s)	Cranberry juice
4	shot(s)	Freshly squeezed orange juice

Comment: Made with vodka as a base this drink would be called a Madras. Rum adds both strength and flavour.

REGGAE RUM PUNCH

Glass: Collins
Garnish: Wedge of pineapple spiked with a maraschino cherry on rim
Method: Shake all ingredients with cubed ice and strain into a glass filled with crushed ice.

³/₄	shot(s)	Freshly squeezed lime juice
³/₄	shot(s)	Bols Strawberry (fraise) liqueur
1	shot(s)	Strawberry syrup
2	shot(s)	Wray & Nephew overproof rum
1¹/₂	shot(s)	Pressed pineapple juice
2¹/₂	shot(s)	Freshly squeezed orange juice

Origin: The most popular punch in Jamaica, where it is sold under different names with slightly varying ingredients. It always contains orange, pineapple and most importantly overproof rum.
Comment: A bright red drink with a frothy top. Jamaicans have a sweet tooth and they love their rum - this drink combines sweetness and strength with a generous amount of fruit. If you can't obtain strawberry syrup use grenadine as an alternative.

ROMAN PUNCH

Glass: Collins
Method: Shake all ingredients with cubed ice and strain into glass filled with crushed ice.

1¹/₂	shot(s)	Bénédictine D.O.M. liqueur
³/₄	shot(s)	Freshly squeezed lemon juice
1¹/₂	shot(s)	Rémy Martin Cognac
³/₄	shot(s)	Wray & Nephew overproof rum
3	shot(s)	Chilled mineral water

Comment: Spirited and refreshing with Bénédictine herbal notes.

RUM PUNCH

Glass: Collins
Garnish: Lime wheel and cherry
Method: Shake all ingredients with cubed ice and strain into glass filled with crushed ice.

³/₄	shot(s)	Freshly squeezed lime juice (sour)
1¹/₂	shot(s)	Sugar (gomme) syrup (sweet)
2¹/₄	shot(s)	Wray & Nephew overproof rum (strong)
3	shot(s)	Chilled mineral water (weak)
4	dashes	Angostura aromatic bitters

Comment: The classic proportions of this drink (followed above) are 'one of sour, two of sweet, three of strong and four of weak' – referring to lime juice, sugar syrup, rum and water respectively. In Jamaica, the spiritual home of the Rum Punch, they like their rum overproof (over 57% alc./vol.). Hence, the strength of this drink demands a good shake and then serving with crushed ice to dilute and tame it.

SORREL RUM PUNCH

Glass: Collins
Method: Shake all ingredients with cubed ice and strain into glass filled with crushed glass.

³/₄	shot(s)	Freshly squeezed lime juice
1¹/₂	shot(s)	Sugar (gomme) syrup
2¹/₄	shot(s)	Wray & Nephew overproof rum
3	shot(s)	Sorrel ade

Origin: Another classic Jamaican drink based on overproof rum using the classic rum punch proportions of 'one of sour, two of sweet, three of strong and four of weak'.
Recipe: Homemade sorrel ade is made by soaking 140g of dried sorrel into 2.5 litres of water with 60g fresh ginger, half bar spoon of ground cloves and a dash or two of honey or brown sugar to taste. Bring this mixture to the boil then leave to cool and soak overnight. Strain and then keep refrigerated.
Comment: Sorrel ade looks a little like cranberry juice, and like cranberry juice has a bittersweet taste. This drink harnesses the flavour of sorrel ade and combines it with the traditional strength, flavour and bittersweetness of rum punch. Jamaica in a glass.

STONE & GRAVEL

Glass: Old-fashioned
Method: Pour ingredients into glass filled with crushed ice and stir.

1	shot(s)	Wray & Nephew overproof rum
3	shot(s)	Stone's ginger wine

Origin: A very popular drink in Jamaica.
Comment: Simple, strong and surprisingly good.

XANTÉ® LIQUEUR

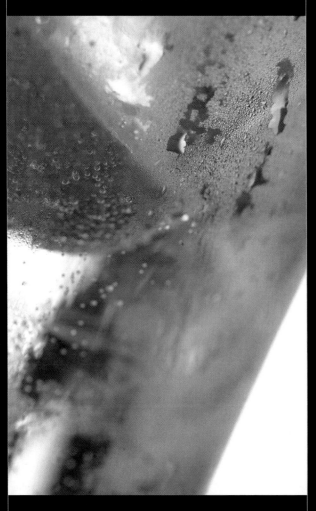

Pronounced 'zant-tay', this liqueur is based on Cognac and flavoured with natural pear essence. Launched at the end of 1995, Xanté is a modern liqueur not only in its presentation, but in its not being overly sweet, only containing 170 grams of sugar per litre. It was created by Richard Heinrich, the fourth generation of distillers and blenders at Maison Heinrich, a family firm established in 1894. Originally from Alsace, the Heinrich family moved to Belgium where they re-established their business and reputation for blending fine liqueurs. In 1997 the V&S Group (the owners of Absolut vodka) acquired rights to the brand and formula, allowing Xanté to be launched in other markets besides Scandinavia where it has already proved hugely successful.

Xanté is rich in flavour with hints of perfumed pear (almost pear marmalade) and spice, particularly cinnamon, fortified with Cognac. A beautiful balance of flavours with just enough sugar – not a sweetie. 38% alc./vol. (76°proof)

Web: www.xante.info **Producer:** The Xanté Company (V&S Group), Stockholm, Sweden. **UK distributor:** Fuel Brands Ltd, Stirling, Scotland. **Tel:** 01786 451 168. **Email:** g.shon@fuelbrands.co.uk

ASIAN PEAR MARTINI

Glass: Martini
Garnish: Pear slice on rim
Method: Shake all ingredients with ice and fine strain into glass.

2	shot(s)	Sake
1/4	shot(s)	Xanté pear liqueur
1/2	shot(s)	Poire William eau de vie
1 1/2	shot(s)	Freshly extracted pear juice
1/4	shot(s)	Freshly squeezed lemon juice

Origin: I created this drink in 2002.
Comment: Sake and pear juice with something of a kick.

INGA FROM SWEDEN NEW

Glass: Collins
Garnish: Strawberry
Method: Muddle strawberries in base of shaker. Add other ingredients, shake with ice and fine strain into ice-filled glass.

2	fresh	Strawberries
1 1/2	shot(s)	Xanté pear liqueur
1/2	shot(s)	Campari
2	shot(s)	Cranberry Juice
1/4	shot(s)	Sugar (gomme) syrup
1/4	shot(s)	Freshly squeezed lime juice

Comment: Inga must like a touch of bitter Italian with her fruit.

KENTUCKY PEAR

Glass: Martini
Garnish: Pear slice on rim
Method: Shake all ingredients with ice and fine strain into chilled glass.

1	shot(s)	Buffalo Trace Bourbon
1	shot(s)	Xanté pear liqueur
1	shot(s)	Freshly extracted pear juice
1	shot(s)	Pressed apple juice

Origin: Created in 2003 by Jes at The Cinnamon Club, London, England.
Comment: Pear, apple, vanilla and whiskey are partners in this richly flavoured drink.

NICE PEAR-TINI

Glass: Martini
Garnish: Pear slice on rim
Method: Shake all ingredients with ice and fine strain into chilled glass.

1	shot(s)	Rémy Martin Cognac
1/2	shot(s)	Xanté pear liqueur
1/2	shot(s)	Poire William eau de vie
2	shot(s)	Freshly extracted pear juice
1/4	shot(s)	Sugar (gomme) syrup

Origin: I created this in 2002.
Comment: Spirited, rich and fruity.

PEAR & CARDAMOM SIDECAR

Glass: Martini
Garnish: Pear slice on rim
Method: Break away outer shells of cardamom pods and muddle inner seeds in base of shaker. Add other ingredients, shake with ice and fine strain into glass.

7	pods	Green cardamom
1	shot(s)	Cointreau / triple sec
1	shot(s)	Xanté pear liqueur
1	shot(s)	Freshly squeezed lemon juice
1	shot(s)	Chilled mineral water

Origin: Created in 2002 by Jason Scott at Oloroso, Edinburgh, Scotland.
Comment: A wonderful meld of aromatic ingredients.

PEAR & VANILLA RICKEY NEW

●●●●◐○

Glass: Collins
Garnish: Lime wedge
Method: Shake first three ingredients with ice and strain into ice-filled glass. Top up with 7-Up.

1	shot(s)	Absolut Vanilia
1	shot(s)	Xanté pear liqueur
1	shot(s)	Freshly squeezed lime juice
Top-up with		7-Up or Sprite

Comment: Vanilla and pear with a creamy mouthfeel tamed by lime juice.

PEAR DROP NEW

●●●●◐○

Glass: Shot
Method: Shake all ingredients with ice and fine strain into chilled glass.

½	shot(s)	Absolut Citron vodka
½	shot(s)	Bols lychee liqueur
½	shot(s)	Xanté pear liqueur

Comment: Sweet, sticky and strong.

PEAR SHAPED (DELUXE VERSION)

●●●●●◔

Glass: Martini
Garnish: Pear slice on rim
Method: Cut passion fruit in half and scoop out flesh into base of shaker. Add other ingredients, shake with ice and fine strain into chilled glass.

1	fresh	Passion fruit
1½	shot(s)	The Famous Grouse Scotch whisky
1	shot(s)	Xanté pear liqueur
1	shot(s)	Freshly extracted pear juice
1	shot(s)	Pressed apple juice
¼	shot(s)	Freshly squeezed lime juice

Comment: Wonderful balance of flavours but pear predominates with a dry, yet floral finish.

SIDEKICK

●●●●○

Glass: Martini
Garnish: Quarter orange slice on rim
Method: Shake all ingredients with ice and fine strain into chilled glass.

2	shot(s)	Xanté pear liqueur
¾	shot(s)	Cointreau / triple sec
1	shot(s)	Freshly squeezed orange juice
½	shot(s)	Freshly squeezed lime juice

Origin: Adapted from a drink discovered in 2003 at the Temple Bar, New York City.
Comment: Rich pear and orange with a stabilising hint of sour lime.

SPARKLING PERRY

●●●●○

Glass: Flute
Garnish: Pear slice on rim
Method: Pour ingredients into glass and lightly stir.

¾	shot(s)	Poire William eau de vie
¾	shot(s)	Xanté pear liqueur
1	shot(s)	Freshly extracted pear juice
Top up with		Piper-Heidsieck Brut Champagne

Origin: Created in December 2002 by yours truly.
Comment: Tastes like perry (pear cider) with bells on.

SPICED PEAR

●●●●●

Glass: Old-fashioned
Garnish: Pear slice
Method: Shake all ingredients with ice and strain into ice-filled glass.

1	shot(s)	Xanté pear liqueur
1	shot(s)	Morgan's spiced rum
1	shot(s)	Freshly extracted pear juice
½	shot(s)	Freshly squeezed lime juice
½	shot(s)	Sugar (gomme) syrup

Origin: Created in 2002 by James Stewart, Edinburgh, Scotland.
Comment: Just as it says on the tin – spiced pear. Ooh yeah!

TEDDY BEAR'TINI

●●●●○

Glass: Martini
Garnish: Pear slice
Method: Shake all ingredients with ice and fine strain into chilled glass.

1½	shot(s)	Xanté pear liqueur
¾	shot(s)	Apple schnapps liqueur
1½	shot(s)	Pressed apple juice
1	pinch	Ground cinnamon

Origin: This drink was created in 2002 at The Borough, Edinburgh, Scotland. Originally named after a well-known cockney duo but renamed after the cockney rhyming slang for pear.
Comment: Beautifully balanced apple and pear with a hint of cinnamon spice.

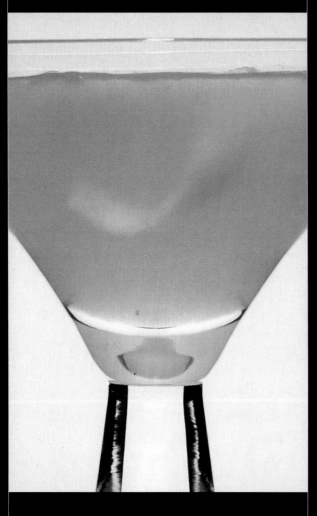

ZUBROWKA® BISON VODKA

Pronounced 'Zhu-bruff-ka', this Polish vodka is flavoured with Hierochloe Odorata grass, a blade of which is immersed in each bottle, giving the vodka a translucent greenish colour and a subtle flavour. The area where this grass grows in the Bialowieza Forest is the habitat of wild Polish Bison – so, although the bison don't eat this variety of grass, the vodka has the nickname 'Bison vodka'. The Hierochloe Odorata grass is harvested by hand in early summer when its flavour is best, then dried, cut to size and bound in bunches for delivery to the Bialystok distillery. The vodka is forced through the grass to impart the aromatic flavour to the vodka in a similar method to the way espresso coffee machines force water through coffee.

Herby, grassy with flavours of citrus, vanilla, lavender, tobacco, cold jasmine tea, caffè latte and hints of dry chocolate/vanilla. This subtle and delicately flavoured vodka is extremely mixable. 40% alc./vol. (80°proof)

Producer: Polmos Bialystok, Bialystok, Poland.
UK distributor: Marblehead Brand Development,
Glasgow, Scotland. Tel: 0141 955 9091
Email: information@marblehead.uk.com

AMBER

Glass: Collins
Garnish: Apple chevron & nutmeg dust
Method: Muddle ginger in base of shaker. Add other ingredients, shake with ice and strain into glass filled with crushed ice.

2	slices	Fresh root ginger (thumbnail sized)
1½	shot(s)	Zubrowka bison vodka
4	shot(s)	Pressed apple juice
½	shot(s)	Ginger syrup
½	shot(s)	Apple schnapps liqueur

Origin: Created in 2001 by Douglas Ankrah for Akbar at the Red Fort, Soho, London, England.
Comment: A great combination of adult flavours in a long, thirst-quenching drink. Also great served up.

AUTUMN PUNCH

Glass: Sling
Garnish: Physalis fruit on rim
Method: Cut passion fruit in half and scoop out flesh into shaker. Add vodka, passion fruit syrup, pear and lemon juice, shake with ice and strain into ice-filled glass. Top up with Champagne.

1	fresh	Passion fruit
2	shot(s)	Zubrówka bison vodka
¼	shot(s)	Passion fruit syrup
1	shot(s)	Freshly extracted pear juice
½	shot(s)	Freshly squeezed lemon juice
Top up with		Piper-Heidsieck Brut Champagne

Origin: Created in 2001 by Max Warner at Baltic Bar, London, England.
Comment: Autumnal in colour with a wonderful meld of complementary flavours.

CUCUMBER MARTINI

Glass: Martini
Garnish: Strip of cucumber
Method: Muddle cucumber in base of shaker. Add other ingredients, shake with ice and strain into glass.

2	inch	Peeled chopped cucumber
1	shot(s)	Zubrowka bison vodka
1	shot(s)	Absolut vodka
½	shot(s)	Sugar (gomme) syrup

Origin: There are many different Cucumber Martini recipes; this is mine.
Comment: Cucumber has never tasted so good.

ESCALATOR MARTINI

Glass: Martini
Garnish: Pear slice on rim
Method: Shake all ingredients with ice and fine strain into chilled glass.

1	shot(s)	Poire William eau de vie
½	shot(s)	Zubrowka bison vodka
2	shot(s)	Pressed apple juice
⅛	shot(s)	Sugar (gomme) syrup

Origin: Created in 2002 by Kevin Connelly, England. It's called an escalator because the 'apples and pears', rhyming slang for 'stairs', are shaken.
Comment: This orchard-fresh concoction was originally made with Korte Palinka (Hungarian pear schnapps) - if using that or Poire William liqueur, little or no sugar is necessary.

FRENCH BISON-TINI

Glass: Martini
Garnish: Raspberries
Method: Shake ingredients with ice and strain into glass.

2	shot(s)	Zubrowka bison vodka
2½	shot(s)	Pressed pineapple juice
½	shot(s)	Chambord black raspberry liqueur

Comment: A French Martini with the distinctive taste of Zubrowka.

FRISKY BISON UPDATED

●●●●◑

Glass: Martini
Method: Lightly bruise mint in base of shaker using a muddler. Add other ingredients, shake with ice and fine strain into chilled glass.

7	fresh	Mint leaves
2	shot(s)	Zubrowka bison vodka
1	shot(s)	Apple schnapps
1	shot(s)	Pressed apple juice
½	shot(s)	Freshly squeezed lime juice
¼	shot(s)	Sugar (gomme) syrup

Origin: Created by Tony Kerr in 1999 at Mash & Air in Manchester.
Comment: Sweet 'n' sour, fruity, minty and fresh.

MITCH MARTINI UPDATED

●●●●○

Glass: Martini
Garnish: Lemon zest twist
Method: Shake all ingredients with ice and fine strain into chilled glass.

2	shot(s)	Zubrowka bison vodka
2	shot(s)	Pressed apple juice
¼	shot(s)	Passion fruit syrup
½	shot(s)	Freshly squeezed lemon juice

Origin: Created in 1997 by Giovanni Burdi at Match EC1, London, England.
Comment: One of London's best contemporary classics.

PALOOKAVILLE NEW

●●●●○

Glass: Collins
Garnish: Lemon wedge
Method: Shake all ingredients with ice and strain into ice-filled glass.

2	shot(s)	Zubrowka bison vodka
¾	shot(s)	Apple schnapps liqueur
2	shot(s)	Pressed apple juice
¾	shot(s)	Freshly squeezed lemon juice
¾	shot(s)	Elderflower cordial

Origin: Adapted from a cocktail created in 2004 for Norman Cook, A.K.A. Fatboy Slim, by Chris Edwardes at Blanch House, his boutique hotel in the superstar DJ's home town of Brighton, England. The cocktail is named Palookaville after Cook's 2004 album, which is named in turn after a mythical, dead-end destination mentioned by Marlon Brando in On The Waterfront.
Comment: Polish combo of Zubrowka and apple with a distinctly English touch of elderflower.

POLISH MARTINI UPDATED

●●●●◑

Glass: Martini
Garnish: Lemon zest twist
Method: Shake all ingredients with ice and fine strain into chilled glass.

1½	shot(s)	Zubrowka bison vodka
1½	shot(s)	Krupnik honey liqueur
1½	shot(s)	Pressed apple juice

Origin: Created by Dick Bradsell, for his (Polish) father-in-law, Victor Sarge.
Comment: A round, smooth and extremely tasty Martini.

POOH'TINI

●●●●◑

Glass: Martini
Method: Stir spoons of honey into vodka in base of shaker can. Add other ingredients, shake with ice and fine strain into glass.

1¾	spoons	Runny honey
2	shot(s)	Zubrowka bison vodka
½	shot(s)	Krupnik honey liqueur
1½	shot(s)	Cold black camomile tea

Origin: Adapted from a drink discovered in 1999 at Lot 61, New York City.
Comment: Honey, tea and bison all meld well.

TATANKA

●●●●◑

Glass: Old-fashioned
Method: Shake all ingredients with ice and strain into ice-filled glass.

| 2 | shot(s) | Zubrowka bison vodka |
| 2½ | shot(s) | Pressed apple juice |

Origin: This drink hails from Poland and the name comes from the film 'Dances with Wolves'. Tatanka is a Native American word for buffalo and obviously refers to the Zubrowka this cocktail is based on.
Comment: The taste of this excellent drink (which is equally good served straight-up) is a little reminiscent of Earl Grey tea.

ZUB-WAY

●●●◐○

Glass: Collins
Garnish: Three raspberries
Method: Muddle raspberries and watermelon in base of shaker. Add other ingredients, shake with ice and strain into ice-filled glass.

12	fresh	Raspberries
2	cups	Diced ripe watermelon
2½	shot(s)	Zubrowka bison vodka
½	shot(s)	Sugar (gomme) syrup

Origin: Created by Jamie Terrell in 1999.
Comment: Few ingredients, but loads of flavour.

INDEX

A
Absolut Citron vodka 20
Absolut Kurant vodka 20
Absolut Mandrin vodka 24
Absolut Raspberri vodka 26
Absolut Vanilia vodka 28
Absolut vodka 12
Acapulco 104
Adam & Eve 72
Afterburner 122
Alabama Slammer #1 110
Alessandro 84
All White Frappé 82
Almond Martini 12
Amaro Dolce 26
Amber 126
Americano 58, 61
Angel Face 90
Angers Rose 58
Angostura aromatic bitters 30
Anis'tini 82
Apple & Cranberry Pie'tini 66
Apple Cart 64
Apple Crumble Martini #2 120
Apple Manhattan 54
Apple Martini #1 12
Apple of My Eire 86
Apple Pie 108
Apple Strudel Martini 44
Appleton Estate V/X Jamaica rum 32
Apricot Cosmo 12
Apricot Fizz 34
Apricot Mango Martini 90
Apricot Martini 34
April Shower 100
Aquarius 40
Archangel 122
Arnaud 61, 90
Asian Pear Martini 124
Autumn Punch 88, 126
Azure Martini 102

B
B-52 74
Baby Blue Martini 38
Balalaika 12, 64
Ballet Russe 13
Bamboo 61
Banana Banshee 42
Banana Bliss 42
Banana Colada 42
Bananas & Cream 42
Banoffee Martini 43, 112
Bartender's Root Beer 72
Bartenders Martini 61
Basil Beauty 20
Basil Grande 74
Batida Abaci 102
Batida Maracuja 102
Bay of Passion 86
Beach Blonde 122
Bee's Knees Martini #2 90
Beja Flor 43, 102
Bellini (Difford's Formula) 114
Bellini-tini 114
Berry Caipirinha 103
Berry Nice 22
Between The Sheets 100
Biarritz 74
Big Apple Martini 108
The Big Easy 110
Bikini Martini 38, 114
Bird of Paradise 52, 104
Bitter Sweet Symphony 13
Black & White Daiquiri 36
Black 'N' Blue Caipirovska 13
Black Dream 84
Black Jack 84
Black Martini 44
Black Nuts 84
Black Widow 50, 84
Blackthorn English 98
Blimey 68
Bling! Bling! 88
Blood & Sand 40, 61, 116
Bloodhound 58
Bloody Mary (modern recipe) 13
Blue Cosmo 38

Blue Lagoon 38
Blue Margarita 39, 104
Blue Monday 24
Blue Passion 39
Blue Raspberry Martini 26, 39
Blue Riband 39
Blue Star 39
Blueberry Tea 74
Bobby Burns 61, 116
BOLS Apricot Brandy liqueur 34
BOLS Blackberry liqueur 36
BOLS Blue Curaçao 38
BOLS Brown crème de cacao 44
BOLS Cherry Brandy liqueur 40
BOLS Crème de Banane 42
BOLS Lychee liqueur 46
BOLS Raspberry liqueur 34
BOLS Strawberry liqueur 50
BOLS White crème de cacao 52
Bombay 61, 75
Bon Bon Martini 112
Bossanova #1 72
Bossanova #2 32
Bourbon Blush 50, 54
Bourbon Cookie 54, 112
Bourbon Smash 54
Bradford 91
Bramble 36, 91
Brandy Alexander 44, 52
Brandy Sour 100
Brazilian Monk 44
Breakfast Martini 64, 91
Bronx 63
Brubaker Old Fashioned 116
Buena Vida 104
Buffalo Trace Bourbon 54
Bug Juice 24
Bumble Bee 82
Butterscotch Daiquiri 112
Butterscotch Martini 52, 113

C
Cachaça Daiquiri 103
Cactus Jack 104
Caipirinha 103
Caipirovska 13
Caipiruva 103
Call Me Old Fashioned 101
Campari 58
Canaries 40
Canteen Martini 110
Cape Codder 13
Caribbean Punch 122
Carol Channing 48
Carpano Martini 98
Cascade Martini 26
Cassanova 55
Castro 32
Champagne Cocktail 30, 88
Charlie Chaplin 98
Cherry Daiquiri 40
Cherry Mash Sour 40, 76
Chill Breeze 86
Chill-Out Martini 24
Chimayo 105
China Blue 46
China Blue Martini 46
Chinese Cosmopolitan 46
Chinese Passion 86
Chinese Whisper Martini 46
Chocolate 'N' Cranberry Martini 66
Chocolate Martini 52
Chocolate Mint Martini 53
Chocolate Puff 45
Cicada Cocktail 76
Cinzano Extra Dry vermouth 61
Cinzano Rosso vermouth 62
Claridge 34, 61
Clockwork Orange 101
Clover Leaf Martini 91
Club Cocktail 30, 88
Cobbled Raspberry Martini 13
Coco Naut 123
Cointreau 64
Cold Comfort 123
Collection Martini 20
Congo Blue 36

Cool Martini 78, 105
Coronation 61
Cosmopolitan #1 20, 64
Cosmopolitan #2 13
Cosmopolitan Delight 75
Cranberry & Mint Martini 66
Cranberry Sauce 66
Creamsicle 24
Crème de Café 82
Crime of Passion 87
Crimson Tide 22, 70
Cuban Master 80
Cucumber Martini 126
Cucumber Sake-tini 14
Cumbersome 58
Cuppa Joe 70
Curdish Martini 91

D
Daiquiri Natural 80
Dark Daiquiri 32
DC Martini 53
Death By Chocolate 45
Detroit Martini 14
Devil's Manhattan 63, 110
Dirty Banana 33
Dirty Martini 91
Dirty Sanchez 105
Dolce Amaro 59
Dolce Havana 59
Donna's Creamy'tini 45
Double Grape Martini 14
Double Vision 22
Dowa 14
Downhill Racer 33
Dramatic Martini 75, 120
Dry Martini (Traditional) 61, 92

E
E.T. 78
Earl Grey Fizz 88
Earl Grey Mar-Tea-Ni 92
East India Cocktail 101
East Indian 61
Easter Martini 28, 53
Easy Tiger 105
Eden 25
El Diablo 105
Elderbubble 89
Elderflower Collins 92
Elegante Margarita 65, 105
English Martini 92
Escalator Martini 126
Espresso Martini 14
Esquire Martini 26
Evita 78
Exotic Passion 87
The Famous Grouse 116

F
Finitaly 67
Finlandia Cranberry vodka 66
Finlandia Lime vodka 68
Finnberry Martini 67
Flaming Ferrari 85
Flatliner 83
The Flirt 105
Floridita Margarita 65, 105
Flutter 106
Flying Scotsman 63, 116
Forbidden Fruits 92
Forest Breeze 36
Forth Of July Martini 55
Four W Daiquiri 81
Frangelico Hazelnut liqueur 70
Freddy Fudpucker 106
French 75 89
French Bison-tini 127
French Martini #1 14
French Martini #2 27
French Mule 101
French Spring Punch 50
Fresca Nova 89
Friar Tuck 70
Frisky Bison 127
Frisky Lemonade 68
Fruit & Nut Chocolate Martini 22
Fruit & Nut Martini 70
Fruit Salad 43, 72

G
Galliano 72
Galvanised Nail 120

The Game Bird 108, 117
GE Blonde 117
Gibson Martini 92
Gimlet 93
Gin & It 63
Gin Fizz 93
Gin Garden Martini 93
Gin Genie 93, 98
Gin Sling 41
Gin Sour 93
Ginger Martini 14, 113
Ginger Nut 71
Gin-Ger Tom 93
Gingerbread Martini 55
Giuseppe's Habit 71
Give Me A Dime 113
Glass Tower 83
Godfrey 37
Gold Member 113
Golden Dream Martini 73
Golden Girl 33
Golden Screw 34
Grand Champagne Cosmo 75
Grand Cosmopolitan 75
Grand Marnier Cordon Rouge 74
Grand Mimosa 75
Grape Delight 94, 99
Grape Escape 101
Grape Martini 14
Grapefruit Daiquiri 33
Grapple Martini 15
Grassy Finnish 68
Great Mughal Martini 55
Green Eyes 39
Guyanan Raspberry Punch 48
Gypsy Martini 94

H
Hair Of The Dog 117
Hard Lemonade 15
Harvey Wallbanger 73
Hawaiian Cocktail 111
Hazel'ito 71
Hazelnut Martini 71
Heather Julep 117
Hedgerow Sling 37, 99
Highland Sling 117
Honey & Marmalade Dram'tini 117
Honey Wall 120
Honeysuckle'tini 81
Hop Toad 33
Hot Shot 73
Hot Toddy 118
Hot Tub Martini 15
Hunk Martini 28

I
Ice 'T' Knee 15
Inga From Sweden 124
Ink Martini 94
Irish Manhattan 55, 121
The Italian Job #2 121

J
Jack Daniel's Tennessee Whiskey 76
Jack Punch 76
Jacktini 76
Jacuzzi 114
Jaffa Martini 45
Jamaican Sunset 123
Ja-Mora 88
Japanese Slipper 78
Jasmine 59, 94
Jayne Mansfield 51
Jerez 115
Julep Martini 55
Jumping Jack Flash 43, 73, 77
The Juxtaposition 67

K
Katinka 35
Kee-Wee Martini 94
Kentucky Colonel 55
Kentucky Dream 55
Kentucky Muffin 56
Kentucky Pear 56, 124
Key Lime 68
Killer Punch 78
Kiwi Bellini 15
Kiwi Collins 15
Kiwi Martini (simple) 15
Koi Yellow 27
Koolaid 79